Perspectives on Sport and Exercise Psychology, Vol. 2

BORIS BLUMENSTEIN,
RONNIE LIDOR & GERSHON TENENBAUM (EDS.)

# PSYCHOLOGY OF SPORT TRAINING

Editors of the Series
Perspectives on Sport and Exercise Psychology:
Dieter Hackfort & Gershon Tenenbaum

British Library Cataloguing in Publication Data
A catalogue record for this book is available from the British Library

Blumenstein, Lidor & Tenenbaum (Eds.)
Psychology of Sport Training
Oxford: Meyer & Meyer Sport (UK) Ltd., 2007
ISBN: 978-1-84126-202-4

© 2007 by Meyer & Meyer Sport (UK) Ltd.
Aachen, Adelaide, Auckland, Budapest, Graz, Indianapolis, Johannesburg,
New York, Olten (CH), Oxford, Singapore, Toronto
Member of the World
Sport Publishers' Association (WSPA)
www.w-s-p-a.org
Printed and bound by: FINIDR, s. r. o., Český Těšín
ISBN: 978-1-84126-202-4
E-Mail: verlag@m-m-sports.com
www.m-m-sports.com

Perspectives on Sport and Exercise Psychology, vol. 2
Psychology of Sport Training

It
b
te
Fing
tick
are
in rea
borro

I

# CONTENTS

# ACKNOWLEDGEMENTS

Editing this book was a team effort, in which many individuals were involved and were willing to contribute. The editors would like to express their deepest appreciation to all the individuals who contributed chapters to this book; their cooperation and enthusiasm were key factors in its completion. We would like to acknowledge the work done by Dinah Olswang, from the Ribstein Center for Sport Medicine Sciences and Research at the Wingate Institute for Physical Education and Sport (Israel). Her assistance in preparing each chapter was instrumental in our goal of achieving uniformity throughout the book.

We would like to thank the members of the International Society of Sport Psychology (ISSP) Managing Council (2001-2005) for their support and guidance throughout the preparation of this book. Finally, we would like to extend our appreciation to Thomas Stengel and his staff at Meyer & Meyer Sport, our publisher, for providing us with the opportunity to produce this book.

# PREFACE

The second issue of the series on *Perspectives on Sport and Exercise Psychology* perfectly encompasses the idea and main objectives of the series: (a) to organize contributions on a topic of fundamental relevance to the field, and (b) to bring together leading experts in that particular area to provide the most updated knowledge for application through their research and insights. When Ronnie Lidor, Secretary General of ISSP and a researcher in the area of motor behavior, proposed this addition to the series, the need for and significance of such a volume immediately became evident. Boris Blumenstein, based on his extensive experience in applied sport psychology and cooperation with experts in the theory and methodology of sport training, undoubtedly selected the most essential issues for a sport psychology perspective on training and fundamental processes in training. Gershon Tenenbaum, former President of ISSP, is one of the most prominent researchers in sport psychology, and based on his international reputation and connections knew who could contribute best to the various issues in this second volume in the series.

The main purpose of the book is to provide insights from the examination of relationships among various aspects of athletic preparation. Preparation is considered with respect to its physical (such as endurance, strength, speed, and flexibility), technical, tactical, and psychological aspects. A link to the first volume in the series can be established by using an action theory perspective and categorizing the psychological aspects of preparation with respect to the person-task-environment system, and by differentiating preparations that are physical-oriented, skill-oriented, and competition-oriented. Motor control, motivation, will power, emotional stability, relaxation, and cognitive strategies such as imagery are discussed, and the reader will learn about their relevance in different phases of training and athletic preparation.

Certainly the book provides an interesting scope of issues relevant to the endeavour of integrating findings from different disciplines and approaches in sport sciences. We need such contributions in order to promote and enhance cooperation among sport scientists and to improve sport science-based training. I am convinced that this volume will induce a great deal of discussion in the sport science community, and will stimulate athletes and coaches to enlarge their utilization of the sport psychology methods provided here to enrich the training process.

*Prof. Dr. Dieter Hackfort, President ISSP*

# CHAPTER 1

## SPORT PSYCHOLOGY AND THE THEORY OF SPORT TRAINING: AN INTEGRATED APPROACH

BORIS BLUMENSTEIN, RONNIE LIDOR, AND GERSHON TENENBAUM

In the last four decades the field of sport and exercise psychology has changed dramatically, and has established itself as one of the most prominent sport sciences from both the research and applied perspectives (Dosil, 2006; Gill, 1997; Hackfort, Duda, & Lidor, 2005; Lidor, Morris, Bardaxoglou, & Becker, 2001). Recent handbooks on sport and exercise psychology (e.g., Dosil, 2006; Hackfort et al., 2005) reflect the academic and scientific progress that has been made in this field. A number of professional and applied textbooks (e.g., Andersen, 2000; Tenenbaum, 2001) are available for sport consultants and practitioners. In these sources useful guidelines and valuable advice can be found on ways to implement sport-enhancing psychological techniques when working with novice and top-level athletes, in both individual and team sports. Thus, it can be concluded that the field of sport and exercise psychology has become an integral part of training programs aiming to assist athletes in attaining a high level of achievement.

The contention made in this book is that although psychological preparation is now an essential fundamental of any sport training program, it cannot stand alone; that is to say, it should be appropriately and effectively linked with other types of athletic preparation. The literature on theory and methodology of sport training maintains that athletic preparation is composed of physical, technical, tactical, and psychological preparations (e.g., Bomba, 1999; Matveyev, 1981; Zatsiorsky, 1995). Each of these preparations is uniquely linked with the other, and the interaction among them defines the quality of the practice and its contribution to athletic goal attainment (Blumenstein, Lidor, & Tenenbaum, 2005; Bompa, 1999). The main assumption that is made in this chapter as well as in other chapters (e.g., chapters 2 and 7) is that the closer the interrelationships are among the physical, technical, tactical, and psychological preparations, the greater the contribution of

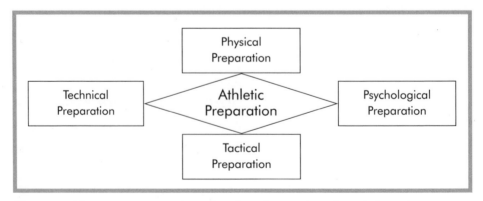

**Figure 1** Athletic preparations: Physical, technical, tactical, and psychological.

the training program to the success of the athlete. Figure 1 presents the four types of athletic preparation.

This chapter has two purposes: first, to provide the rationale for this book by examining the relationships among the different aspects of athletic preparation; second, to introduce the objectives and outline the structure of the book.

## PHASES AND PREPARATIONS IN TRAINING PROGRAMS FOR THE ELITE ATHLETE: A BRIEF OVERVIEW

According to leading sport theorists (e.g., Bompa, 1999; Matveyev, 1981; Zatsiorsky, 1995), a typical training program for elite athletes is composed of three main phases: preparation, competition, and transition. For both athletes and coaches the competition is considered the major phase, because the athlete is required to attain his or her highest level of performance while competing against others in challenging conditions. However, the preparation and the transition phases of the training program are essential for enabling the athlete to attain his or her top performance during the competition phase.

Each of the training phases has its own unique characteristics and objectives. During the preparation phase, the athlete develops a general framework of the physical, technical, tactical, and psychological preparations for the upcoming competition phase (Bompa, 1999). In general, the preparation phase is composed of two sub-phases: general preparation (GP) and specific preparation (SP). The emphasis made in GP is on improving general athletic and physical abilities, while the emphasis in SP is on advancing the abilities and skills required for specific sports.

In the competition phase the athlete attempts to achieve his or her best by utilizing the physical and psychological skills acquired during the preparation phase (Bompa, 1999). The competition is the "moment of truth" for individual athletes or teams; they have to perform better than others who have similar goals. They have to "pull it all together" in order to maximize their physical and psychological abilities and achieve their very best.

The transition phase enables the athlete to enhance physical and psychological rest and relaxation and maintain an acceptable level of GP (Bompa, 1999). This requires the athlete to stay active so that he or she will be prepared for the next preparation phase.

The four athletic preparations, namely the physical, technical, tactical, and psychological, are implemented in each phase of the training program (Bompa, 1999; Matveyev, 1981) (see Figure 2). Broadly speaking, the four preparations span across gender, age, and skill level. However, their length, intensity, and nature may vary according to the specific needs of the athlete, the team, or the situational circumstances.

The objectives of the physical preparation is to develop the relevant fitness components (e.g., endurance, strength, speed, and flexibility) required for the specific activity as well as for the particular sport event, and to refine the specific motor abilities required to attain a high level of achievement throughout the competition phase (Brown, 2001; Harre, 1982). During the preparation phase the physical preparation period can be characterized, for example, by (a) difficult and monotonous work, (b) weight-lifting training which is

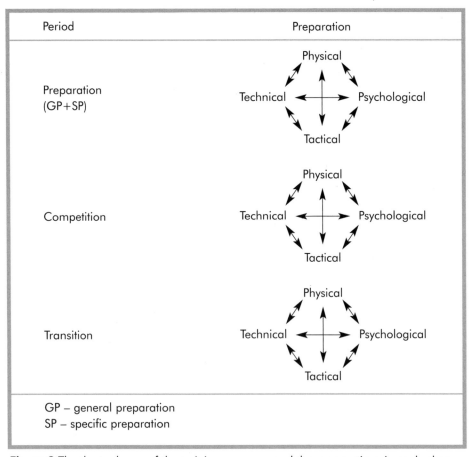

**Figure 2** The three phases of the training program and the preparations in each phase.

composed of a high number of repetitions, or (c) interval and distance running training. The physical preparation is very specific for the kind of sport in which the athlete is engaged, and it demands a high level of motivation, consistency, self-discipline, and patience.

The aim of the technical preparation is to enable the athlete to effectively acquire the skills required for optimal performance during the sport event (Bompa, 1999; Schmidt & Wrisberg, 2004). The athlete attempts to strengthen as well as to refine the arsenal of movements he or she is required to utilize during the sporting act, according to the requirements and characteristics of the specific sport. In addition, the athlete focuses on improving the accuracy and speed of his or her movements by practicing the skill in different performance environments in which competition or game situations are simulated.

The objective of the tactical preparation is to provide the athlete with the strategic knowledge required to effectively execute the skills he or she has acquired in the technical preparation (Bompa, 1999). During this preparation, both athletes and coaches are aiming toward the development of a competition strategy or a game plan. This preparation should allow the athlete to master the skills and techniques to a level that enables him or her to modify and execute them in real competition or game situations.

The objective of the psychological preparation is to provide the athlete with task-specific psychological techniques that can help him or her overcome emotional and mental barriers such as fear of failure, high anxiety, loss of "attention-focusing", and low self-confidence (Anshel, 2005; Bompa, 1999; Henschen, 2005). During the competition phase, for example, athletes should be able to handle pressure, to be mentally prepared for the specific game, and to cope with injuries.

## THE LINK OF PSYCHOLOGICAL PREPARATION TO PHYSICAL, TECHNICAL, AND TACTICAL PREPARATIONS

As was indicated earlier, psychological preparation has become an integral part of training programs in both individual and team sports (see Blumenstein, 2001; Blumenstein et al., 2005; Lidor, Blumenstein, & Tenenbaum, manuscript submitted for publication). Several review articles on the effectiveness of psychological interventions in sport (e.g., Greenspan & Feltz, 1989; Vealey, 1994; Weinberg & Comar, 1994) revealed positive effects for the intervention groups in comparison with the non-intervention groups. For example, Greenspan and Feltz (1989) reported that in 17 of the 20 studies reviewed, the intervention groups outperformed the non-intervention groups. Psychological interventions were administered in such sports as basketball, boxing, golf, karate, skiing, and volleyball. In another article, Vealey (1994) reviewed intervention studies that took place before 1992, and found that in 9 of the 11 studies performance was enhanced by the use of psychological interventions.

In addition to these reviews, a number of reports from sport psychologists who have worked with elite and Olympic athletes (e.g., Gould, Eklund, & Jackson, 1992; Gould, Murphy, Tammen, & May, 1991; May & Brown, 1989; Partington & Orlick, 1987) describe the positive impact of sport psychology services on athletes' preparation toward competitions and games in major sporting events, such as the Olympic games. Useful guidelines and valuable advice from leading sport psychologists can be obtained from these reports.

In this respect, Weinberg and Williams (2001) have argued that "psychological skills are learned and therefore need to be practiced systematically, just like physical skills" (p. 352). In order to achieve this objective, namely enabling athletes to practice psychological skills (e.g., interventional techniques) as well as physical ones, psychological preparation should be effectively and systematically linked with other preparations in the training program. The sport psychologist/sport consultant should work in cooperation not only with the coach and the athlete, but also with other individuals who are involved in the training process, such as the athletic trainer, the strength and conditioning coach, and the sports medicine physician. All those involved should be sensitive to the specific goals of the athlete or the team, as well

**Table 1** The Use of Psychological Techniques during Different Phases of the Training Program: Examples

| Psychological Techniques | Phases | Objectives | Duration | Applications |
|---|---|---|---|---|
| Relaxation | Preparation and transition | Mental recovery | 20-25 min | 1 time, end of the week |
| | Preparation and competition | Mental recovery | 10-15 min | 1-2 times during the weekly program; between practices and games |
| | Preparation and competition | Mental recovery and calming down | 5-10 min | 1-2 times during the weekly program; between practices and games |
| | Preparation and competition | Mental recovery, calming down, and focusing attention | 1-5 min | During the weekly program; between practices and games |
| | Preparation (SP) and competition | Mental recovery, calming down, focusing attention, and regulation of arousal | 5-10 sec | During the weekly program; between practices and games |
| Imagery | Preparation (SP) and competition | Mental recovery | 10-15 min (in natural/ simulated conditions) | During the weekly program; between competitions |
| | Preparation (SP) and competition | Mental readiness and focusing on technical aspects of performance | 1.30 min (e.g., competitive performance in rhythmic gymnastics) | During the weekly program; during warm-up sessions |
| | Preparation, transition, and competition | Mental readiness and focusing on technical aspects of performance | 2-5 min (e.g., competitive performance in combat sport) | Prior to the actual competition/ game/match |
| Combination – relaxation and imagery | Preparation and transition | Mental recovery | 20-25 min | End of the week |
| | Preparation and competition | Mental recovery and preparation to competition | 10-15 min | During the weekly program; during competitions |
| | Preparation and competition | Mental recovery and analysis of previous competitions; preparation for next competition/ game/match | 5-10 min | During simulated conditions in practices |

SP – specific preparation

as to the situational circumstances within the particular phase of the training program.
The entire professional staff involved in a training program should be aware of the different characteristics of the practice sessions in each phase of the training program, such as the length of the practice and its level of intensity. For example, the intensity required from the athlete during early-season practices in the preparation phase differs from that required during competition. In the preparation phase, particularly in GP, a combination of high volume of training and low-to-moderate intensity of training should prevail (Bompa, 1999). In addition, a large number of low-intensity exercises and repetitions are given to the athletes in this phase. It is important for the athlete to acquire the fundamentals of psychological techniques, such as relaxation and imagery, in order to recover rapidly and effectively from early-season exercises and be prepared for the next practice session.

In competition, another phase of the training program, the intensity of the performed technical elements increases and the repetitions decrease, while the total time of training decreases (Bompa, 1999). In addition, during practices in this phase the athlete is exposed to real environmental factors which are related to the actual competition or game. Therefore, the athlete should be prepared to use the psychological techniques that he or she has acquired during the preparation phase, both before and during the competition or the game. In this case, the duration of the practice of psychological techniques in the competition phase should be almost identical to the duration of the actual competition. If a match in judo lasts 5 min, then the length of the imagery technique, as an example, should be 5 min as well. If the length of the exercise in rhythmic gymnastics lasts 90 sec, then the imagery technique should take about the same time. Table 1 presents various uses of two popular psychological interventions, relaxation and imagery, during different phases of the training program. These techniques are examples of psychological interventions whose practical use is influenced by the specific objectives of each phase of the training program.

The various uses of psychological techniques such as relaxation and imagery during the different phases of the training program (as can be seen in Table 1) reflect our argument that a link should exist between psychological preparation and other types of preparations. In each phase of the season there are different objectives for the psychological preparation, which in turn reflect the objectives of other preparations.

## OBJECTIVES, EMPHASES, AND STRUCTURE OF THE BOOK

### THE OBJECTIVES OF THE BOOK

The next part of this chapter provides introductory information about the book, namely its main objectives, points of emphasis, and structure.

Based on our argument that an effective link among athletic preparations in each phase of the training program will assist coaches and athletes in benefiting from the training program, this book has six objectives:

(1) To describe the main components, phases, and preparations of a typical training program for the elite athlete (see chapters 2, 7, and 10 in this volume);

(2) To examine the use of sport psychology interventions in sport programs for the elite athlete (see chapters 3 and 6);

(3) To examine the relationship between the physical preparation and the psychological preparation (see chapter 3);

(4) To examine the relationship between the technical preparation and the psychological preparation (see chapter 4);

(5) To examine the relationship between the tactical preparation and the psychological preparation (see chapter 5);

(6) To examine the unique contribution of psychological preparation to recovery following training and competition (see chapter 8), and of psychological support for those who have incurred sport injuries (see chapter 9).

This book will emphasize that:

(a) Psychological preparation should play a major role in the athlete's preparation for the practice and the competition or game;

(b) Psychological preparation should be fully integrated with physical, technical, and tactical preparations;

(c) Systematic planning of psychological preparation is essential in each phase of the training program;

(d) Psychological preparation should be sensitive to the athlete's needs during the different phases of the training program;

(e) Psychological preparation should be carefully controlled by the sport psychologist/sport consultant in each phase of the training program.

This book consists of ten chapters. Chapter 1 (Boris Blumenstein, Ronnie Lidor, and Gershon Tenenbaum), *Sport Psychology and the Theory of Sport Training: An Integrated Approach*, is an introductory chapter which provides the rationale for the book as well as its main objectives. In addition, the background of each chapter included in the book (i.e., chapters 2 to 10) is provided.

Chapter 2 (Michael Carrera and Tudor Bompa), *Theory and Methodology of Training: General Perspectives*, focuses on basic concepts of theory and methodology of sport training that should be applied to both individual and team sports. The chapter defines terms such as "training" and "conditioning," and introduces objectives for effective training (e.g., multilateral physical development, sport-specific physical development, and technical factors) as well as principles for effective training (e.g., active participation, specialization, and individualization). Variables of training such as volume and intensity are discussed, and the term "periodization" is elaborated upon. Examples from individual and team sports are provided to illustrate different types of periodization.

Chapter 3 (Dave Collins and Alan MacPherson), *Psychological Factors of Physical Preparation*, discusses the importance of physical activity in sport and the psychological aspects of specific fitness components. More specifically, the chapter examines psychological aspects of endurance, strength and power, speed, agility, and flexibility. Among the psychological aspects discussed are effort perception, attentional focus, and control of emotions. Psychological techniques for training balance are presented for the coach and the athlete.

Chapter 4 (Thomas Schack and Michael Bar-Eli), *Psychological Factors of Technical Preparation*, focuses on technique training as a tool to stimulate processes in athletes that assist them in using their body, so that the desired outcome can be accomplished in the most effective manner. The chapter provides a theoretical background for technical preparation in sport. Among the issues discussed are definitions, the construction of movement techniques, and methods for measuring psychological factors in technical preparation. Technical preparation is examined in individual sports such as windsurfing and gymnastics, and in team sports such as volleyball and soccer. The chapter introduces computer-based methods which can be used in technical preparation.

Chapter 5 (Keith Henschen, Traci Statler, and Ronnie Lidor), *Psychological Factors of Tactical Preparation*, discusses the psychological support required by an athlete so that he or she can achieve and master the objectives of the tactical phase. The main argument made in this chapter is that the proficient performer should learn to appropriately "use his or her mind" while competing, and that "using" the mind during performance is just as crucial as the physical and technical aspects of performance. The chapter presents a theoretical background of tactical preparation in sport and introduces a philosophical approach to sport tactical preparation, as well as giving general thoughts on the subject. The use of five "Cardinal Mental Skills", namely (1) relaxation and activation, (2) concentration, (3) imagery, (4) self-talk, and (5) a pre-competition mental routine, is examined in tactical preparation of individual and team sports.

Chapter 6 (Daniel Gould and Sarah Carson), *Psychological Preparation in Sport*, summarizes the literature on psychological factors which have been found to influence athletic performance and ways to enhance athletes' mental preparation, and outlines implications for psychological training and preparation of athletes and teams. More specifically, the chapter discusses what the existing research has revealed about psychological preparation in sport and the various ways mental training can be used to enhance psychological preparation of individual athletes and teams. In addition, the chapter identifies psychological preparation and mental training principles that can be used as guides in professional practice. The principles of psychological preparation and mental training are presented for the individual and the team sport performer. Finally, the chapter provides case examples (e.g., helping athletes defeat performance-debilitating anxiety) of how these principles can be used to help athletes and teams facilitate their mental preparation for sport.

Chapter 7 (Ronnie Lidor, Boris Blumenstein, and Gershon Tenenbaum), *Periodization and Planning of Psychological Preparation in Individual and Team Sports*, provides a conceptualized framework for integrating the psychological preparation with the physical, technical, and tactical preparations. The contention that is made in the chapter is that the psychological preparation during the seasonal program must consider the physical, technical, and tactical preparations if maximal positive benefits are to be gained from the psychological preparation. The chapter demonstrates the interrelationships between the psychological preparation and the other three preparations during different phases of training programs in three individual sports – kayaking, judo, and rhythmic gymnastics, and in two team sports – soccer and basketball.

Chapter 8 (Anne-Marie Elbe and Michael Kellmann), *Recovery Following Training and Competition*, integrates knowledge about one of the key factors in preventing overtraining, namely recovery. The chapter defines and illustrates the foundations of the recovery process, and introduces different methods of measuring recovery. The chapter examines several highly intense phases in the training cycle of competitive athletes, such as training camps and during competitions. For each phase, the relevant recovery aspects are illustrated, and practical advice on how to integrate recovery activities into training is provided. It is demonstrated how athletes and coaches can apply these activities and integrate them into training and competitions. In addition, differentiations are made between recovery for individual athletes and for team athletes.

Chapter 9 (David Pargman), *Sport Injury: A Psychological Perspective*, discusses the negative effects of injury on athletes as well as the positive outcomes that occasionally accrue from sport injury. The chapter defines the term "sport injury" and outlines both the non-psychological and psychological factors related to injury. An attempt is made in this chapter to establish a connection between sport injury and selected psychological factors. Two dimensions of this connection are addressed: psychological factors with causal linkages to injury, and psychological implications in rehabilitation from sport injury. Several models and theories are presented for the first dimension, and factors such as social support, family support, and psychological interventions are discussed concerning the second dimension.

Chapter 10 (Vladimir Issurin), *A Modern Approach to High-Performance Training: The Block Composition Concept*, summarizes the most general positions of training periodization with respect to this classic approach which has been predominant for many years, particularly in regard to the block composition design that has become widely used during the last decade in high-performance athletes' preparation. The chapter presents the scope of training periodization and provides the rationale of why the traditional planning approach should be revised. In addition, the chapter introduces the block composition concept by summarizing the general principles of the renewed training system and providing guidelines for alternative training periodization and short-term planning.

*Psychology of Sport Training* represents the applied and scientific work of some of the leading experts in sport and exercise psychology and theory and methodology of sport training. The book's content is highly relevant, not only for sport psychology consultants, but also for individuals who are engaged in the training process, among them scientists, coaches, athletes, physical educators, and team managers. We hope that many of the sport psychology ideas and practices presented in this book will be implemented by both researchers and practitioners.

## REFERENCES

Andersen, M. B. (Ed.). (2000). *Doing sport psychology.* Champaign, IL: Human Kinetics.

Anshel, M. H. (2005). Strategies for preventing and managing stress and anxiety in sport. In D. Hackfort, J. L. Duda, & R. Lidor (Eds.), *Handbook of research in applied sport and exercise psychology: International perspectives* (pp. 199-215). Morgantown, WV: Fitness Information Technology.

Blumenstein, B. (2001). Sport psychology practice in two cultures: Similarities and differences. In G. Tenenbaum (Ed.), *The practice of sport psychology* (pp. 231-240). Morgantown, WV: Fitness Information Technology.

Blumenstein, B., Lidor, R., & Tenenbaum, G. (2005). Periodization and planning of psychological preparation in elite combat sport programs: *The case of judo. International Journal of Sport and Exercise Psychology*, 3, 7-25.

Bompa, T. (1999). *Periodization: The theory and methodology of training* (4th ed.). Champaign, IL: Human Kinetics.

Brown, J. (2001). *Sports talent: How to identify and develop outstanding athletes.* Champaign, IL: Human Kinetics.

Dosil, J. (2006). Applied sport psychology: A new perspective. In J. Dosil (Ed.), *The sport psychologist handbook – A guide for sport-specific performance enhancement* (pp. 3-17). West Sussex, UK: John Wiley & Sons.

Gill, D. (1997). Sport and exercise psychology. In J. D. Massengale & R. A. Swanson (Eds.), *The history of sport and exercise science* (pp. 293-320). Champaign, IL: Human Kinetics.

Gould, D., Eklund, R., & Jackson, S. (1992). 1988 U.S. Olympic wrestling excellence: I. Mental preparation, precompetition cognition, and affect. *The Sport Psychologist*, 6, 358-382.

Gould, D., Murphy, S., Tammen, V., & May, M. (1991). An evaluation of Olympic sport psychology consultant effectiveness. *The Sport Psychologist*, 5, 111-127.

Greenspan, M., & Feltz, D. (1989). Psychological interventions with athletes in competitive situations: A review. *The Sport Psychologist*, 3, 219-236.

Hackfort, D., Duda, J. L., & Lidor, R. (2005). Preface. In D. Hackfort, J. L. Duda, & R. Lidor (Eds.), *Handbook of research in applied sport and exercise psychology: International perspectives* (pp. ix-x). Morgantown, WV: Fitness Information Technology.

Harre, D. (Ed.). (1982). *Principles of sports training: Introduction to theory and methods of training.* Berlin: Sportverlag.

Henschen, K. (2005). Mental practice – Skill oriented. In D. Hackfort, J. L. Duda, & R. Lidor (Eds.), *Handbook of research in applied sport and exercise psychology: International perspectives* (pp. 19-34). Morgantown, WV: Fitness Information Technology.

Lidor, R., Blumenstein, B., & Tenenbaum, G. (manuscript submitted for publication). Psychological aspects of elite training programs in European basketball: Conceptualization, periodization and planning.

Lidor, R., Morris, T., Bardaxoglou, N., & Becker, B. (2001). *The world sport psychology sourcebook* (3rd ed.). Morgantown, WV: Fitness Information Technology.

Matveyev, L. (1981). *Fundamentals of sports training*. Moscow: Progress Publishers.

May, J., & Brown, L. (1989). Delivery of psychological services to the U.S. Alpine Ski team prior to and during the Olympics in Calgary. *The Sport Psychologist, 3,* 320-329.

Partington, J., & Orlick, T. (1987). The sport psychology consultant: Olympic coaches' views. *The Sport Psychologist, 1,* 95-102.

Schmidt, R. A., & Wrisberg, C. A. (2004). *Motor learning and performance: A problem-based learning approach* (3$^{rd}$ ed.). Champaign, IL: Human Kinetics.

Tenenbaum, G. (Ed.). (2001). *The practice of sport psychology*. Morgantown, WV: Fitness Information Technology.

Vealey, R. (1994). Current status and prominent issues in sport psychology interventions. *Medicine and Science in Sports and Exercise, 26,* 495-502.

Weinberg, R., & Comar, W. (1994). The effectiveness of psychological interventions in competitive sport. *Sports Medicine Journal, 18,* 406-418.

Weinberg, R., & Williams, J. (2001). Integrating and implementing a psychological skills training program. In J. Williams (Ed.), *Applied sport psychology – Personal growth to peak performance* (pp. 347-377). Mountain View, CA: Mayfield.

Zatsiorsky, V. (1995). *Science and practice of strength training*. Champaign, IL: Human Kinetics.

# CHAPTER 2

# THEORY AND METHODOLOGY OF TRAINING: GENERAL PERSPECTIVES

MICHAEL CARRERA AND TUDOR BOMPA

Ironically, as in so many things in life today, sport training tends to be recycled and re-sold as a new product or concept. For instance, balance training has been around since the 1940s. Many rowers in the 1960s quickly learned that balance is not an ability that needs to be trained in isolation but is integrated in all specific sport movements. For example, balance is necessary for gymnastics and thus is highly practiced in that sport. The same can be applied to tubing/elastic cords and core training. These are not new concepts, but recycled ones that have been passed from one generation to another. In addition, with the advent of sophisticated machines and testing devices sport is becoming much more technical in nature.

The coach and athlete now have more support and information in the form of training. The question to ponder is how much of the new equipment or recycled concepts actually help further training and athlete development? The answer, in accordance to what we have seen over the years, is: very negligible. In this chapter we would like to share a few ideas concerning our beliefs on sport training for both the individual athlete and team sport athlete; they go hand in hand and the theory and methodology of training is similar in both. In our opinion the present and future of sport training depends on properly understanding the meaning of the terms given. Having a grasp of these concepts educates the coach and athlete on the importance of planning, methodology, and aids in determining the value of "new and improved" training methods.

## UNDERSTANDING SPORTS TRAINING

*Training:* Training is a manipulation of methods to induce adaptation. When adaptation reaches high levels, so does performance. Without a continuous increase in an athlete's physical adaptation, improvements are impossible. Consistently look for better training means and methods to induce a superior adaptation.

Training is both science and art. Coaches' knowledge should always be based on the best scientific information available. However, the application of this knowledge is an art, where imagination becomes a great resource.

*The coach* is the only person who can makes it happen. The coach is the artist who applies science to produce a form of art: skill and physical potential displayed by a wonderfully trained athlete.

*Conditioning:* The role of conditioning is to cope with or overcome fatigue – the number one enemy of an athlete. The higher the athlete's level of conditioning, the better his or her rate of recovery. Training is only as good as the athlete's ability to recover from it. Recovery after the game or between workouts, therefore, is as important as the training itself. Pay maximum attention to both.

The winner of an event or contest is often the athlete or team who fatigues last. Therefore, train your athlete(s) to tolerate all forms of fatigue, from central nervous system (CNS) fatigue to lactic acid build-up. If the athlete is able to tolerate fatigue, he or she will function effectively and accurately during the duration of the game/event.

Training for high level conditioning means training all elements according to the needs and complexity of the sport: strength/power, cardiorespiratory, the ability to tolerate the buildup of lactic acid, speed, agility, quickness, and training the energy systems according to your chosen sport's ergogenesis (i.e., the proportion of the contribution of each energy system to the overall energy demand of the game).

*Status quo:* The present state of the art – the level achieved in technical, tactical, and physical training – should not make anyone complacent. On the contrary, the coach should thoroughly examine whether the present training methodology is acceptable, or if a new model should be created based on science and methodology. If this is the case, the coach should:

• Create a technical/tactical model based on the energy systems prevailing in his or her particular sport. Specific training, in the form of technical/tactical drills, must be designed according to the needs and the specifics of energy systems in that particular sport.
• Train for accuracy in passing and shooting, and spiking and throwing under, the conditions of fatigue, when the mechanics of skill break down, as during the last part of a game.
• Technical and tactical corrections should not be made only under conditions of freshness, but rather under conditions similar to the last part of the game – fatigue. This will help your athletes to be truly ready for the game. Teaching for skill acquisition, on the other hand, must be done under conditions of freshness, when the retention of a skill is the highest. Never forget that fatigue affects skill proficiency and skill retention.

*More is better:* This is an old adage based on the idea that if a certain amount of work is good, more work must be better. In the never-ending quest for athletic improvement, some coaches relentlessly push for more and harder work. Inexperienced coaches (those who want to demonstrate their toughness or how hard they can train their players) should be ready for a surprise. In reality, continuous hard, high intensity training may not result in athletic improvement, but rather in performance decline.

As coaches examine the quantity and quality of their training, they should also try to monitor the training effect of their planned work. The tendency to continuously increase intensity is not always the answer. Quite often *less is more* and may, in fact, be more beneficial in the long term. As the coach increases intensity, he or she must also monitor the reaction to the training. How stressful is the training program for your athletes? Do the athletes have enough time to recover, regenerate, super-compensate, and replenish their energy stores before another high intensity training session is planned? Also, were the energy systems used in training properly alternated to avoid high levels of fatigue and physiological and psychological stress?

*No pain, no gain:* This outdated training philosophy is typical of the pre-exercise physiology school of thought. The proponents of this method of training come from an era when two or three training sessions per week was the norm. With few training sessions, these trainers feel it is necessary to train the athlete hard in all training sessions in order to see improvements. High calibre athletes who train only twice per week do not have to worry much about depleting energy stores, overstress, or overtraining; however, they should not expect dramatic improvements either.

When the number of workouts is increased to four or five per week, the whole reality of training becomes more complex and more physiologically and psychologically challenging. Under a heavier training schedule, the philosophy of *no pain, no gain* can become excessive, and even dangerous, pushing the body and mind beyond the capacity to adapt to and tolerate high intensity work. Excessive training, therefore, does not necessarily produce better results or additional improvement. On the contrary, it may lead to chronically depleted energy reserves, which in turn may result in a chronic state of fatigue and staleness, and it may even bring an athlete close to the undesirable effects of overtraining.

*Intensity all the way:* We have seen a coach ruin his team's chances for a bronze medal in a world championship simply because he believed in *intensity all the way*. Because basketball is a high intensity game, the coach constantly demanded high intensity from his players – day in and day out! In addition to gruelling workouts, the team played against another high quality team every three to five days with no regeneration following high intensity workouts or games. High intensity days were not complemented with lower intensity days. The coach had never heard of recovery and regeneration, or of the need to alternate energy systems. Therefore, it was quite easy to predict the outcome of *intensity all the way* applied throughout the pre-championship training camp. The team had reached such a critical level of fatigue – close to overtraining – that the outcome was a total failure; instead of a bronze medal, the team placed in the ninth position.

It is for all the above reasons that theory and methodology of training is so important and vital to sport performance. Planning is a simple concept founded in preparation and foresight. Comprehending the objectives and principles of training will better prepare you for the task at hand.

## SCOPE OF TRAINING

Today athletes prepare themselves for their goals through training. The physiological goal is to improve body function and optimize athletic performance. The main scope of training is to increase the athlete's work and skill capabilities, as well as to develop strong psychological traits. A coach leads, organizes, and plans training, and educates the athlete. Many physiological, psychological, and sociological variables are involved. Training is primarily a systematic athletic activity of long duration, which is progressively and individually graded. Human physiological and psychological functions are modeled to meet demanding tasks.

Paramount to training endeavours for novices and professionals is an achievable goal, planned according to individual abilities, psychological traits, and social environments. Some athletes seek to win a competition or improve previous performance; others consider gaining a technical skill or further developing a biomotor ability as a goal. Whatever the objective, each goal needs to be as precise and measurable as possible. In any plan, short- or long-term, the athlete needs to set goals and determine procedures for achieving them before beginning training. The deadline for achieving the final goal is the date of a major competition.

## TRAINING OBJECTIVES

To improve skill and performance athletes must meet the following training objectives:

### OBJECTIVE #1: MULTILATERAL PHYSICAL DEVELOPMENT
Athletes need multilateral physical development as a training base in addition to overall physical fitness. The purpose is to increase endurance and strength, develop speed, improve flexibility, and refine coordination, thus achieving a harmoniously developed body.

### OBJECTIVE #2: SPORT-SPECIFIC PHYSICAL DEVELOPMENT
Sport-specific development improves absolute and relative strength, muscle mass and elasticity, and specific strength (power or muscular endurance) according to the sport's movement, reaction time, and coordination requirements.

### OBJECTIVE #3: TECHNICAL FACTORS
Technical training involves developing the capacity to perform all technical actions correctly; perfecting the required techniques based on a rational and economical performance, with the highest possible velocity, high amplitude, and demonstration of force; performing specific techniques under normal as well as unusual circumstances (e.g., weather conditions); improving the techniques of related sports; and ensuring the ability to perform all movements correctly.

### OBJECTIVE #4: TACTICAL FACTORS
Tactical factors include improving strategy by studying the tactics of future opponents, expanding the optimal tactics within the athlete's capabilities, perfecting and varying strategies, and developing a strategy into a model considering future opponents.

### OBJECTIVE #5: PSYCHOLOGICAL ASPECTS
Psychological preparation is also necessary to ensure enhanced physical performance. Psychological training improves discipline, perseverance, willpower, confidence, and courage.

### OBJECTIVE #6: HEALTH FACTORS
Strengthening each athlete's health is important. Proper health is maintained by periodic medical examinations, a proper correlation of training intensity with individual effort

capacity, and alternating hard work with an appropriate regeneration phase. Following illness or injury, the athlete must begin training only when completely recovered, ensuring adequate progression.

### OBJECTIVE #7: INJURY PREVENTION

Injuries can be prevented by following all safety precautions, increasing flexibility beyond the level required, strengthening muscles, tendons, and ligaments, especially during the initiation phase of a beginner, and developing muscle strength and elasticity to such a degree that when athletes perform unaccustomed movements accidents will be unlikely. This is achieved by following a disciplined anatomical adaptation phase that focuses on preparing the body for the vigor of maximum load training.

### OBJECTIVE #8: THEORETICAL KNOWLEDGE

Training increases the athlete's knowledge of the physiological and psychological bases of training, planning, nutrition, and regeneration. Coaches should discuss athlete-coach, athlete-opponent, and teammate relationships to help athletes work together to reach the set goals.

This summarizes some general training objectives that a coach/athlete may consider in developing a training program. Specific characteristics of most sports and of individual performance in each sport may require the coach/athlete to be selective or to establish additional training objectives. Training objectives should be pursued in a successive manner. The early program should develop the functional basis of training, then move toward achieving sport-specific goals.

## TRAINING ADAPTATION

A high level of performance is the result of many years of well-planned, methodical, and hard training. During this time, the athlete tries to adapt his or her organs and functions to the specific requirements of the chosen sport. The adaptation level is reflected by performance capabilities. The greater degree of adaptation, the better the performance. Training adaptation is the sum of transformations brought about by systematically repeating exercise. These structural and physiological changes result from a specific demand that athletes place on their bodies by the activity they pursue, depending on the volume, intensity, and frequency of training. Physical training is beneficial only as long as it enables the body to adapt to the stress of the effort. If the stress is not a sufficient challenge, then no adaptation occurs. On the other hand, if the amount of stress is intolerable, then injury or overtraining may result.

### SUPERCOMPENSATION CYCLE

Supercompensation refers mainly to the relationship between work and regeneration as biological bases for physical and psychological arousal before a major competition. All individuals have a specific level of physiological functioning that is predominant during normal daily activities. When an individual trains, a series of stimuli disturb the normal biological state by burning supplementary foodstuff. The outcome of this burning is fatigue and high lactic acid concentration in the blood. At the end of a training lesson, the high level of fatigue temporarily reduces the body's functional capacity. As seen in Figure 1, the abrupt drop of the homeostasis curve illustrates the rapid acquisition of fatigue, which assumes a simultaneous reduction of physical capacity (phase I).

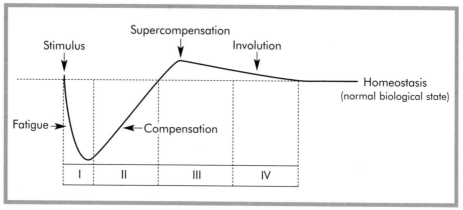

**Figure 1** Supercompensation cycle of a training lesson (Bompa, 1999).

Following training, and between training sessions, the body replenishes the biochemical sources of energy during a phase of compensation. There must always be a balance between energy expenditure and replenishment in an athlete's normal biological behavior. During compensation, what is consumed during training must be replenished and balanced. If not, the depletion of energy stores will result in performance deterioration. As the curve slowly and progressively returns toward a normal biological state (phase II), it is important that the training program not require high intensity bouts that would negatively affect regeneration of the energy stores.

As the curve passes the normal biological state, supercompensation will result (phase III) which in essence is the foundation of a functional increase of athletic efficiency, resulting from the body's adaptation to the training stimulus and the replenishment of glycogen stores in the muscle. If the resulting phase or the time between two stimuli is too long, supercompensation will fade, leading to involution or a phase of little performance improvement (Phase IV).

## TOP 10 PRINCIPLES OF TRAINING

The theory and methodology of training, a distinct unit of physical education and sports, has specific principles based on the biological, psychological, and pedagogical sciences. These guidelines and regulations, which systematically direct training, are known as the *principles of training*. These specific principles reflect the particularities of fulfilling important training goals, namely increasing skill and performance levels. Training principles are part of a whole concept, and though we should not view them as isolated units, we will describe them separately for a more understandable presentation.

### PRINCIPLE #1: ACTIVE PARTICIPATION

It is vital to understand three factors of this principle: the scope and objectives of training, the athlete's independent and creative role, and the athlete's duties during long preparation phases. The coach should promote independent and conscientious development through leadership and expertise. Athletes must perceive the coach's conduct as having the purpose of improving their skills, biomotor abilities, and psychological traits, in an effort to help them overcome the difficulties of training.

Conscientious and active participation in training should be maximized by periodically and consistently discussing with each athlete his or her progress. Athletes can then relate the objective feedback of the coach with the subjective assessment of their performances. By comparing performance abilities with subjective feelings of speed, smoothness, and ease, athletes perceive themselves as strong and relaxed. They will be able to understand the positive and negative aspects of their performance, what they need to improve, and how to do it. Training involves active listening and participation by both the coach and the athletes. Because personal problems may impact performance, athletes should share them with the coach so that they can deal with the problem through a common effort.

The coach should also demonstrate a conscientious attitude toward training by setting precise and achievable objectives for the athletes. This will elevate their interest in training and their desire and enthusiasm to participate successfully in competitions. It will enhance the development of psychological traits, such as willpower and perseverance, for overcoming training difficulties. Objectives should be set so that they are difficult enough to be challenging yet realistic enough to be achievable (McClements & Botterill, 1979). The coach should plan long- and short-term goals for each athlete, in which the latter effectively stimulate the athlete's training interests.

### PRINCIPLE #2: MULTILATERAL DEVELOPMENT

Necessary multilateral or overall development is accepted in most fields of education and human endeavor. Regardless of how specialized the instruction may become, initially there should be exposure to a multilateral development so that necessary fundamentals can be acquired.

You can often observe extremely rapid development in some young athletes. In such cases, it is important that the instructor resist the temptation to develop a specialized training program. A broad, multilateral base of physical development, especially general physical preparation, is a basic requirement for reaching a highly specialized level of physical preparation and technical mastery. Such an approach to training is a prerequisite for specializing in a sport or event.

Athletes should participate in multilateral training throughout their careers, from the early stages of development to advanced levels of competition. Exercise, regardless of its nature and motor requirements, requires the harmony of several systems and various fitness abilities and psychological traits. Muscle groups, joint flexibility, stability, and the activation of all the limbs corresponding to the future requirements of the selected sport should be the focus of attention. In other words, it is necessary to develop to a superior level all anatomical and physiological abilities required to perform efficiently at high levels of technical and tactical skill.

The multilateral principle should be employed primarily when training children and juniors. This does not imply that an athlete will spend all of his or her training time on such a program. On the contrary, training should be more specialized as an athlete matures and elevates his or her level of mastery. Coaches in all sports may contemplate the merits of this principle. The advantage of multilateral development in a training program is that it brings a variety of exercises and fun through playing games, and this decreases the likelihood of boredom.

### PRINCIPLE #3: SPECIALIZATION

Whether training on a field, on ice, or in a gymnasium, from the beginning of an athlete's career the intent and motives are to specialize in a certain sport or event. Specialization represents the main element required to obtain success in a sport.

Specialization and exercises specific to a sport or event lead to anatomical and physiological changes related to the necessities of the sport. Researchers captivated by the uniqueness of athletes' physiological traits have demonstrated that the human body adapts to the activity an individual participates in (Deschenes & Kraemer, 2002; Judge, Moreau, & Burke, 2003). Such adaptation is not only physiological; specialization applies to technical, tactical, and psychological features as well. Specialization is a complex, not a unilateral, process based on multilateral development. From a beginner's first training lesson to a mature athlete's mastery, the total volume of training and the portion of special exercises are progressively increased.

Multilateral development ought to be the basis from which specialization is developed. Carefully plan the ratio between multilateral and specialized training, considering the modern tendency to lower the age of athletic maturation. The age at which athletes can achieve high performance is significantly lower in sports such as gymnastics, swimming, and figure skating. No one is surprised anymore to see children 2 or 3 years old in the swimming pool or on the skating rink, or 6 year-olds in the gym. The same trend appears in other sports: ski jumpers and basketball players start training at age 8. Practicing the same sport regularly for several years, with intensity suited to the athlete, leads to specific adjustments in a youngster's body according to the sport. This creates the physiological premises for subsequent specialized training.

### PRINCIPLE #4: INDIVIDUALIZATION

Individualization in training is one of the main requirements of contemporary training. It refers to the idea that coaches must treat each athlete individually according to his or her abilities, potential, learning characteristics, and specifics of the sport, regardless of performance level. The whole training concept should be modelled according to the athlete's physiological and psychological characteristics in order to naturally enhance training objectives.

Often, coaches apply an unscientific approach in training by literally following training programs of successful athletes, completely disregarding his or her athlete's individual personality, experience, and abilities. What is even worse is that coaches sometimes implement such programs into the training schedules of juniors. This can lead to injury and ineffectiveness in the training outcome.

**PRINCIPLE #5: PLAN ACCORDING TO TOLERANCE LEVEL**

It is of paramount importance that a coach know and understand each individual athlete's tolerance level. The coach should plan the training loads accordingly. Each individual's effort capacity depends on the following factors:

- Biological and chronological age, especially for children and juniors whose bodies have not yet reached maturity. Training for them should be more broad, multi-lateral, and moderate in nature.
- Experience or the starting age of sport participation. The work the coach demands of the athlete should be proportional to his or her experience. If athletes train in groups, the coach must be aware of each athlete's potential and capacity.
- Training and health status. Training status dictates the content, load, and rating in training. Athletes with the same performance level have different levels of strength, speed, endurance, and skill. We strongly recommend individualization for athletes who experience illness or accidents. The coach should work closely with the physician or sport physician.
- Training load/intensity and the athlete's recovery rate. This factor may be influenced by outside factors such as school, homework, or family. The coach must be familiar with the lifestyle and emotional situation of the athlete.

**PRINCIPLE #6: INDIVIDUALIZE TRAINING**

Training adaptation is a function of the individual athlete's capacity. Child athletes, compared to adult athletes, have unstable nervous systems, so their emotional states sometimes alter quickly. This phenomenon requires a harmony between their training and other involvements, especially their schoolwork. Furthermore, athletes' training must have variety in order to keep up their interest and concentration. Also, to enhance a good recovery rate from injuries, a correct alternation should be maintained between training stimuli and rest. This is especially so for intense exercise – the coach should be cautious about the method used in training.

**PRINCIPLE #7: ACCOUNT FOR GENDER DIFFERENCES**

Sexual differences play an important role in performance and individual capacity in training, especially during puberty. A coach should be aware that individual motor performance relates to gender as well as to chronological and biological age. Anatomical differences of the lower body in particular (e.g., women have wider hips) must be taken into consideration, along with endurance capabilities. Males and females tend to tolerate the same quantity of training, but males tolerate a higher intensity of training (Lewis, Kamon, & Hodgson, 1986).

**PRINCIPLE #8: VARIETY**

Doing the same activity over and over with the goal of fostering adaptation can become frustrating and boring. To overcome monotony and boredom in training, a coach needs to be creative, with knowledge of a large resource of exercises that allow for periodic alteration. Coaches can enrich skills and exercises by adapting movements of a similar technical pattern or those that develop the biomotor abilities that the sport requires. Athletes who intend to improve leg power for volleyball or high jumping, or for that matter any sport requiring a powerful takeoff, do not necessarily have to spike or jump every day. A variety of exercises are available, such as half squats, leg presses, jumping squats, step-ups, jumping, or stair-bounding exercises, exercises with benches, and depth jumps. These exercises allow the coach to alternate periodically from one to the other, thus eliminating boredom while maintaining the same training effect. The coach's capacity to create, to be inventive, and to work with imagination is an important advantage for successful variety in training.

### PRINCIPLE #9: MODELING

We have a strong conviction that modeling will progressively become one of the most important principles in training. It is already becoming more popular in team sports. As we learn more about the particular physiological, mechanical, and psychological demands of the selected sport, there will be a desire and a logical need to imitate and model the specifics of a sport in training. By doing so, training will become very precise, resulting in a specific adaptation.

In general terms, a coach uses model training to organize training lessons so that the objectives, methods, and content are similar to those in a competition. Under these circumstances, the competition represents a strong component of training, and not just a reference point. The coach must fully understand the specifics of the work structure, such as volume, intensity, complexity, and number of games or periods. Similarly, it is extremely important that the coach knows the ergogenesis (from the Greek word ergo, meaning to work, and genesis, meaning generation, production) of his or her sports or events. Familiarity with the contribution ratio of the aerobic and anaerobic systems for a sport or event is important in understanding which aspects to emphasize in training.

### PRINCIPLE #10: LOAD PROGRESSION

Improvement in performance is a direct result of the amount and quality of work the athlete achieves in training. From the initiation stage up to the elite-class athlete, workload in training must increase gradually according to each individual's physiological and psychological abilities.

The physiological basis of this principle is that as a result of training the body's functional efficiency, and thus capacity to do work, gradually increase over a long period. Any drastic increase in performance requires a long period of training and adaptation. The athlete reacts anatomically, physiologically, and psychologically to the increased demand in training load. To improve the athlete's nervous system function and reactions, neuromuscular coordination, and psychological capacity to cope with the stress of heavy training loads, time, and competent training leadership are required.

There are three main types of load progressions:

## (1) STANDARD LOADING

A standard loading method is presented in Figure 2. In several sports, athletes maintain the same load in training throughout the year. For instance, in most team sports the number of hours of training stays the same throughout the year, at approximately 6 to 12 hours per week. A similar situation exists in many clubs in track and field. If power is the dominant ability in events, then athletes use power training with similar exercises and loads throughout the preparatory phase and decrease them during the competitive phase. In both cases coaches use standard loading.

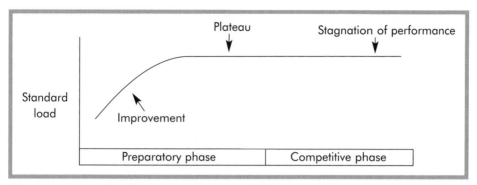

***Figure 2*** Standard loading method (Bompa, 1999).

We should state clearly that the repetition of standard loading results in improvements in the early part of the annual plan, followed by a plateau and stagnation of performance during the competitive phase. As a result, performance may deteriorate during the latter part of the competitive phase because the physiological basis of performance has decreased, and expected improvements from year to year will not occur. Only constantly increasing the training load from year to year will create superior adaptation and thus superior performance.

## (2) OVERLOADING

The overloading principle simply states that athletes must continuously work at loads that are higher than those they are accustomed to (see Figure 3). Rest and regeneration are not

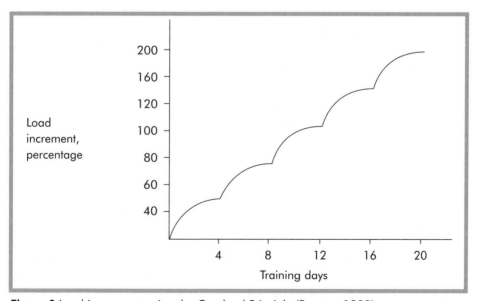

***Figure 3*** Load increments using the Overload Principle (Bompa, 1999).

really seen as priorities. This principle finds its origin in bodybuilding, where the main scope of training is muscle exhaustion, recovery, and muscle growth. This is not the scope of sports training. On a short-term basis, an athlete may be able to cope with the stress of overloading. On a long-term basis, however, overloading will lead to critical levels of fatigue, burnout, and even overtraining, because when rigidly applied it does not allow phases of regeneration and psychological relaxation to take place.

## (3) STEP LOADING

In the past, several studies have investigated methods of increasing the work in training. Researchers found that overloading was less efficient than the step approach (Harre, 1982; Ozolin, 1971). As opposed to the overload approach, the step method fulfills the physiological and psychological requirements of following a training load increase with a phase of unloading, during which the athlete adapts and regenerates, as can be seen in Figure 4.

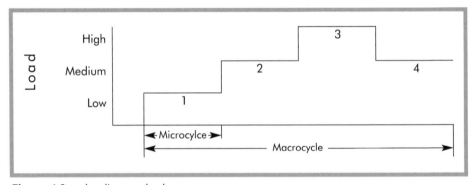

**Figure 4** Step loading method.

The step approach does not mean that the load has to be increased with every training session. One training lesson is insufficient to provoke visible physical or mental changes in the athlete that will lead to adequate adaptation. To accomplish an adaptation, it is necessary to repeat the same type of training lessons or training stimulus several times. Often, training lessons of the same characteristics may be planned for an entire microcycle, followed by another increase in the training load. The training load increases in a macrocycle, which is a phase of training lasting 2 to 6 (usually 4) weeks. In Figure 4, each vertical line represents a change in training load, and the horizontal line represents the phase of adaptation the new demand requires.

The load increases gradually in the first three microcycles, followed by a preparatory decrease or unloading phase, allowing the athlete to regenerate. The purpose of regeneration is to allow the athlete to accumulate physiological and psychological reserves in anticipation of further load increases. Improvement in the degree of training usually occurs following a regeneration phase. The unloading regeneration phase, or the fourth cycle in this example, represents the new, lowest step for another macrocycle. This step is not the same magnitude as the previous low, but it is equal to the medium one, because the athlete has already adjusted to the previous loads.

## VARIABLES OF TRAINING

Any physical activity leads to anatomical, physiological, biochemical, and psychological changes. The efficiency of a physical activity results from its duration, distance, and repetition (volume); load and velocity (intensity); and the frequency of performance (density). All the variables of training should be modelled in accordance with the physiological characteristics of the sport. As a rule, intensity for sports of speed and power, and volume for endurance sports, should be emphasized.

### VOLUME

As a prime component of training, volume is the quantitative prerequisite for high technical, tactical, and physical achievements. The volume of training, sometimes inaccurately called the duration of training, incorporates the following integral parts:

* The time or duration of training
* The distance covered or weight lifted per unit of time
* The repetitions of an exercise or technical element an athlete performs in a given time.

Volume implies the total quantity of activity performed in training. Volume also refers to the sum of work performed during a training lesson or phase. When referring to the volume of a training phase, the number of training lessons should be specified and the number of hours and days of work should be required.

As an athlete becomes capable of high levels of performance, the overall volume of training becomes more important. For elite athletes, there are no shortcuts for the high quantity of work they must perform. A continual increase in training volume is probably one of the highest priorities of contemporary training. High training volume has a clear physiological justification: athletes cannot physiologically adapt without it. An increasing volume of work is paramount in training for any aerobic sport or event. A similar increase is also necessary for sports requiring the perfection of technical or tactical skills. Only a high number of repetitions can ensure the quantitative accumulation of skills necessary for qualitative improvements in performance.

To accurately evaluate the volume of training, a unit of measurement should be selected. For some sports (running, canoeing, cross-country skiing, and rowing), the appropriate unit seems to be space or distance covered during training. The load in kilograms seems to be appropriate for weightlifting or weight training for strength improvement. Time, which regulates other sports (boxing, wrestling, judo, gymnastics, team sports), seems to be a common denominator for most sports, although a coach often must use two measuring units, time and distance, to express the volume correctly (i.e., to run 12 km in 60 min).

## INTENSITY

Intensity, the qualitative component of work an athlete performs in a given time, is also an important component of training. The more work the athlete performs per unit of time, the higher the intensity. Intensity is a function of the strength of the nerve impulses the athlete employs in training. The strength of a stimulus depends on the load, speed of performance, and variation of intervals or rest between repetitions. Muscular work and CNS involvement through maximum concentration determine intensity during training or competition. Even sports requiring a low level of physical exertion, such as shooting, archery, and chess, have a certain level of intensity.

Intensity can be measured according to the type of exercise. Exercises involving speed are measured in meters/second (m/s) or the rate/minute of performing a movement. The intensity of activities performed against resistance can be measured in kilograms or kgm (a kilogram lifted 1 meter against the force of gravity). For team sports the game rhythm determines the intensity.

Intensity varies according to the specifics of the sport. Because the level of intensity varies in most sports and events, varying degrees of intensity in training should be established and used. Several methods are available for measuring the strength of the stimuli and thus the intensity. For example, with exercises performed against resistance or exercises developing high velocity, a percentage of the maximum intensity, in which 100% represents best performance, should be used. In a 100-m dash, however, best performance signifies the mean velocity developed over that distance (i.e., 10 m/sec). The same athlete may generate a higher velocity (i.e., 10.2 m/sec) over a shorter distance. We regard this velocity as 105% of maximum. For exercises performed against resistance, 105% represents a load that the athlete cannot move through the whole range of movement, but may attain isometrically. According to this classification of intensities, a distance runner (i.e., 5,000 or 10,000 m) may train at 125% or more of the maximum, because the maximum is his or her race pace.

During training, athletes experience various levels of intensity. The body adapts by increasing physiological functions to meet the training demand. Based on these changes, especially heart rate (HR), the coach may detect and monitor the intensity of a training program. To develop certain biomotor abilities, the intensity of a stimulus must reach or exceed a threshold level beyond which significant training gains take place. Peterson, Rhea, and Alvar (2004) conducted a meta-analysis and reported that strength gains among athletes at the collegiate or professional level elicited the greatest increases in strength when they trained at an average intensity of 85% of one repetition maximum (1RM).

In training theory, there are two types of intensities: (a) absolute intensity, which measures the percentage of maximum ability necessary to perform the exercise, and (b) relative intensity, which measures the intensity of a training lesson or microcycle, given the absolute intensity and the total volume of work performed in that period. The higher the absolute intensity, the lower the volume of work for any training lesson. Athletes may not extensively repeat exercises of high absolute intensity (greater than 85% of maximum) in a training lesson. Such training lessons should be no more than 40% of the total lessons per microcycle, with the remaining lessons using a lower absolute intensity.

## INCREASING VOLUME AND INTENSITY OF TRAINING

Increasing the volume and intensity of training always provides a challenge to coaches and athletes. When and how much to increase can either be determining factors of strength and endurance or can contribute to overtraining and performance decrements. We suggest that the following rules be followed when attempting to increase either volume, intensity, or both.

### VOLUME OF TRAINING
- Increase the duration of a training session. If 3 sessions of 60 min is your present volume of work per week, then increase it to 3 x 90 min and later to 3 x 120 min.
- Increase the number of training sessions per week. Take the 3 x 120 min to 4 x 120. 5 x 120, and so on.
- Increase the number of repetitions, drills, or technical elements per training lesson.
- Increase the distance or duration per repetition or drill.

### INTENSITY OF TRAINING
- Increase the velocity to cover a given distance, the rhythm (quickness) of performing a tactical drill, or the load in strength training.
- Increase the number of repetitions the athlete performs with this intensity.
- Decrease the rest interval between repetitions or tactical drills.
- Increase the number of competitions per training phase (only if this is not at a desirable level for your athletes or sport).

## PERIODIZATION

Periodization is one of the most important concepts in training and planning. The term originates from *period* which is a division of time into smaller, easy to manage segments called phases of training. Regardless of popular belief, periodization is not a new concept that has miraculously settled into the minds of coaches and fitness trainers across North America and abroad. As introduced by Flavius Philostratus (AD 170-245), a Greek philosopher and sporting enthusiast, periodization has been used in simple forms since the ancient Olympic Games. In his six manuals on training, Philostratus wrote extensively about the methods used by the Greek Olympians.

The term *periodization* has been borrowed from history, where it refers to the specific periods of time of human development. In sports and fitness training, periodization refers to dividing the yearly training plan into smaller, and therefore easier to manage, training phases. Basically, the periodization of an annual plan has three major phases: preparatory – or pre-season, competitive – or season, and transition – or off-season (see Figure 5). In fact this is what Philostratus mentioned concerning the way the ancient Olympians organized their own periodization, except that they used slightly different terms: preparation, Olympic Games, and relaxation. The first group of modern Olympians from the U.S.A. used exactly the same periodization plan: preparatory, competitive – culminating with the Olympic Games, and off-season (transition).

| The Annual Plan | | | |
|---|---|---|---|
| Training Phases | Preparatory phase | Competitive phase | Transition |
| Macro-Cycles | | | |
| Micro-Cycles | | | |

**Figure 5** The periodization of an annual plan.

As illustrated by Figure 5, each training phase is subdivided into smaller phases, such as macrocycle (macro = bigger, and cycle = a phase which repeats itself several times throughout the annual plan) and microcycle (smaller phases lasting 1 to 2 weeks). A macro-cycle is usually 3-6 weeks. The only training phase smaller than the micro-cycle is the training session or workout. Therefore, looking from the top of Figure 1 to the bottom, you realize that a periodized annual plan progressively becomes shorter. The shorter the phase, the easier it is to manage a training program. However, an overall guideline of training is necessary: a periodized annual plan.

The effectiveness of periodization models is so high that coaches virtually around the world have attempted to adopt the many concepts and theories of periodization that the second author has spoken about for the past 50 years. He first implemented his personal version of periodization in the early 1960s, with phenomenal success, when a javelin thrower under his direction shattered the world record in the Rome Olympic Games.

There are five reasons why periodization is a must in sports training:

**1. PHYSIOLOGICAL ADAPTATION TO TRAINING**
The scope of training, especially during the preparatory phase, is to create a training program that will result in the highest fitness adaptation possible. A higher adaptation to training, which inevitably increases an athlete's potential, is the main determining factor in reaching peak performance during the competitive phase. The program that is organized during the preparatory phase, and the development to the highest level possible of the motor abilities necessary in a specific sport (strength, speed, and endurance), are fundamental requirements for improving an athlete's working potential, physical abilities, and, as a result, performance from year to year. The beauty of periodization is that the principles of training can be manipulated for all ages and fitness levels.

**2. PEAK PERFORMANCE**
Although peak performance is normally reached during the competitive phase, it cannot be maintained forever. This is why during the preparatory phase the scope of training is to improve an athlete's work capacity and ability to cope with the fatigue of training and competitions, but not necessarily to reach the highest performances of the year. This is normally achieved during the competitive phase by progressively planning more specific training programs: specific speed, power, and endurance. By specific we mean choosing exercises that closely mimic the movements used in the sport.

### 3. SKILL DEVELOPMENT

The rate of improving and perfecting an athlete's technical and tactical skills is directly dependent upon how the training programs are periodized. During the preparatory phase, when the stress of competitions is almost nonexistant, skill acquisition is maximal. The preparatory phase is the time to develop skills and to perfect the ones acquired during the past year. An athlete's skill improvement during the preparatory phase will be most beneficial during league games and official competitions. The longer the preparatory phase, the better the athlete's chances to improve motor skills. In team sports, martial arts/contact sports, and racquet sports, any technical improvements will directly assist in developing the athlete's tactical proficiency. In other words, the better the technique, the easier it will be for the athlete to apply these skills to a tactical plan.

### 4. PSYCHOLOGICAL QUALITIES

An athlete's psychological behaviour, degree of motivation, and ability to remain focused are directly related to the physical potential acquired during the preparatory phase. It is obvious that motivation and belief in one's ability to succeed is heightened with positive results from training. An athlete's psychological well-being is directly related to the level of fatigue. When an athlete is physically exhausted it directly affects his/her visualization, concentration capabilities, focusing, and motivation. An exhausted athlete is not a highly motivated athlete. But an athlete's psychological behavior is also negatively affected by the volume (quantity) and intensity used in training (e.g., high loads in weight training, the abuse of maximum speed, the daily employment of only high intensity drills in team sports/racquet sports/martial arts, etc.). The higher the intensity of training the higher the stress, and the more it taxes the body. The consequence of constant high intensity training is high psychological fatigue. A properly planned periodization program provides adequate cycling of phases, volume, and intensity, which give the athlete both a physical and psychological means of regeneration.

### 5. CLIMATIC CONDITIONS

The duration of the sport season in a given geographical region also dictates the way the periodization plans are organized. Often the duration of a given training phase, such as the duration of the outdoor season, clearly dictates how long the league games for outdoors team sports can be. Climatic conditions, therefore, directly dictate the periodization of all the outdoor sporting activities, and of seasonal sports such as skiing, rowing, kayaking/canoeing, running, cycling of any type, triathlon, sailing, golfing, etc. The power of periodization is the flexibility in applying the many principles to all sports, regardless of geographical locations, climate, or competitive schedules. ˙

## VARIATIONS OF PERIODIZATION/ANNUAL PLANS

Obviously, the time of the ancient Olympic Games has long since passed, and, along with many other improvements in human society, periodization of training has evolved as well. In addition to the basic periodization plan of three main phases (see Figure 5), there are also variations to the plan. The requirements of certain sports have motivated the push from an annual plan with only one peak (monocycle) to an annual plan with two or more peaks. Consequently, different sports with specific domestic and international calendars of competitions employ other types of periodization plans. Two examples are track and field, which has two major competitions per year – indoors and outdoors competitions, and short and long course championships in swimming. The plan used for these two sports is called a bi-cycle, or double-peaking (see Figure 6). Other sports, such as wrestling, boxing, or martial arts, use either triple-peaking, also called tri-cycle, or multi-peaking plans, where the athletes have to peak several times per year (see Figure 7).

| Month | 1 | 2 | 3 | 4 | 5 | 6 | 7 | 8 | 9 | 10 | 11 | 12 |
|---|---|---|---|---|---|---|---|---|---|---|---|---|
| Period-ization (phases) | Preparatory 1 | | | Competitive 1 | | | T1 | Preparatory 2 | | | Competitive 2 | | T2 |
| | General Preparatory | Specific Preparatory | PC | Competitive | | U | M | Gen Prep. | Specific Preparatory | PC | Competitive | U | |

**Figure 6** Bi-cycle of annual training plan (Bompa, 1999).

Figure 6 shows a bi-cycle annual plan with its training phases, and the specific objectives for each training phase. Note that both preparatory one and two offer phases dedicated to general and specific preparation for the main competition(s).

LEGEND: T=transition phase: the first one of only two weeks, while the second one (Transition 2) is 4-5 weeks long
　　　　PC=pre-competitive, or exhibition competitions/games/matches
　　　　U=unloading/tapering for the major competition of the year
　　　　M=maintenance of a 40-50% of the previous training load

| Month | 1 | 2 | 3 | 4 | 5 | 6 | 7 | 8 | 9 | 10 | 11 | 12 |
|---|---|---|---|---|---|---|---|---|---|---|---|---|
| Perio-dizaton | Prep 1 | Competitive 1 | | T1 | Prep 2 | Competitive 2 | | T2 | Prep 3 | Competitive 3 | | T3 |
| | GP | SP | | | GP | SP | | | GP | SP | | |

**Figure 7** A tri-cycle, or a periodized annual plan with three main competition seasons, or three major peaks.

LEGEND: Prep.1=preparatory for the first competitive phase
　　　　T= transition of two weeks duration, following the first competitive phase
　　　　GP=general preparatory-type of training
　　　　SP=sport-specific training

## PERIODIZATION OF BIOMOTOR ABILITIES

Periodization does not apply only to the training plan or type of training used in a phase. Periodization is also used as a method of planning the training for the dominant biomotor abilities of a given sport. Biomotor abilities comprise the primary elements of fitness required in sport, such as strength, endurance, speed, and power. For the purpose of this chapter, we will take a closer look at the periodization of strength.

### PERIODIZATION OF STRENGTH

Before you can run you must learn to walk. The periodization of strength is simply a systematic progression that matches the body's anatomical and physiological rhythm. Metaphorically speaking, one must first develop the foundation of the house before the other small, intricate components can be fully realized and utilized. Let's take a closer look at the phases of training.

ANATOMICAL ADAPTATION

During the preparatory phase an athlete undergoes an Anatomical Adaptation phase (AA).The main objective of this phase is to involve the largest number of muscle groups possible so as to prepare the muscles, ligaments, tendons, and joints to endure the more strenuous phases of training that follow. The focus of AA is "prehabilitation" – to decrease the need for rehabilitation after an unnecessary injury. During this phase all muscle groups are worked in every possible angle. For example, solely performing a flat bench press movement would not suffice in this phase. The athlete should also be encouraged to perform an incline and decline press to facilitate angle-specific training. Strength adaptations are angle specific; therefore, all possible angles must be utilized during this phase of training.

The loads should be kept low to moderate in this phase – between 55 and 65% of the maximum. As well, exercise selection must be general, not sport specific. Finally, training of the individual's core region should be emphasized, especially the abdominal and lower back areas. The amount of time spent in this phase depends on the age, fitness level, experience and sport-specific needs of the athlete.

MAXIMUM STRENGTH

The AA phase is followed by a Maximum Strength phase (MS). At this time, the objective is to develop the highest possible level of force. This is achieved by increasing the total number of motor units involved in the action, while also increasing the ability to synchronously recruit the maximum number of muscle fibers. This will eventually enable an athlete to develop optimum levels of power or muscular endurance. The loads used during this phase should range between 80% and 95% of the athlete's maximum contraction. As well, rest periods between sets should be longer (three to six minutes), to allow for nervous system recovery. Mainly, compound movements or multi-joint exercises should be used, where the objective is to move the weight as quickly as possible; this will facilitate maximum nervous system adaptation. Such an adaptation will allow the athlete to lift heavier loads by tapping into a strength reserve that was not otherwise utilized. Note that while the individual is attempting to quickly move the load, the actual barbell movement will be slow due to the high resistance. It should be kept in mind that power is the product of strength X acceleration. This phase concentrates on the strength component of the equation while the upcoming phase (if power development is the key) will develop the acceleration component of the equation.

CONVERSION

The Conversion phase follows the maximum strength phase. This represents a very integral part of the athlete's training regimen. It is in this phase that the prior gains in maximum strength are converted into competitive, sport-specific combinations of strength, such as power and muscular endurance. During this phase the athlete is forced to utilize all the physiological gains which were achieved in the previous phases.

If the main scope of the program is power development, then the athlete is urged to attempt to move the weight as quickly as possible. A greater number of explosive-type exercises, which allow the athlete to explode through the full range of movement (e.g., medicine ball tosses, jump squats), should be used in conjunction with traditional weight training strategies to guarantee that the deceleration phase of a particular movement is not overemphasized. For instance, simply performing explosive yet breaking bench press movements in which the athlete stops the weight at the top of the lift may actually further aid in the development of the deceleration phase. It should be kept in mind that acceleration is an important key in maximum power development.

If the main scope of the program is the development of muscular endurance, then the athlete should concentrate on slowly increasing the number of repetitions to a total volume which closely approximates that which is required in his or her particular sport. Once again, a gradual progression is the key to achieving optimal performance and athletic shape. The number of exercises should be kept to a minimum, with a greater emphasis placed on performing the movement in a consistent and controlled manner.

The above shows why it is important to classify one's sport. Knowing the physiological or biomotor breakdown of the sport enables you to plan the training to optimize the required skills and components. Thus the gap is bridged between the requirements of a sport and an athlete's physical abilities. It's quite simple – if the sport primarily involves power, then the training program should be geared toward maximum power development using periodization.

### MAINTENANCE

The conversion phase is followed by the maintenance phase, where strength work must continue. This will eliminate a detraining effect such as a loss in speed, power, strength, or neural adaptations. The main objective is to maintain the sport-specific standards achieved during the previous phases. The volume of training should be decreased, however intensity should be decreased only slightly so as to maintain optimal physiological adaptation.

### CESSATION

Finally, we have the cessation phase. This phase of training begins five to seven days prior to the main competition of the year. All strength training should be stopped in order to facilitate full recovery and overcompensation as the athlete prepares for peak performance. The periodization of strength is simply one example of phase based training.

| Dates | June | July | Aug. | Sept. | Oct. | Nov. | Dec. | Jan. | Feb. | Mar. | Apr. | May |
|---|---|---|---|---|---|---|---|---|---|---|---|---|
| Compe-titions | | | | | | | | Div. champ. | Nat. champ. | World champ. | | |
| Period-ization | Preparatory | | | | Competition | | | | | | Transition | |
| Period-ization | General prep. | | Specific prep. | | Pre-comp. | | Main competition | | | | Transition | |
| Period of end | General end. (run, bicycle) | | Specific endurance (run, skate) | | | | Specific endurance | | | | General endurance | |
| Period of strength | Anat. adapt. | Maximum strength | | Convers. to power | | Maintenance (maximum strength and power) | | | | | Regeneration | |

**Figure 8** Periodization of dominant abilities for figure skating with one peak (Bompa, 1999).

Other components, such as endurance and speed, must also be included in an annual plan model. Figures 8 and 9 provide examples of periodization models for figure skating and baseball, respectively.

| Dates | Nov. | Dec. | Jan. | Feb. | Mar. | Apr. | May | June | July | Aug. | Sept. | Oct. |
|---|---|---|---|---|---|---|---|---|---|---|---|---|
| Compe-titions | | | | | | | | League games | | | | |
| Period-ization | Preparatory | | | | | | Competitive | | | | Transition | |
| | Gen. prep | | Specific prep. | | | | Prec. | League games | | | Transition | |
| Period of strength | Anatomical adaptation | Maximum strength | | | Conversion – Musc. end. – Power | | Maintenance Power Musc. end. | | | | Regeneration | |
| Period of speed | Aerob. end | Anaerob. end. | Specific speed | | | Specific speed, reaction time and agility | | | | | ———— | |
| Period of endurance | Specific endurance | | | | | Perfect specific endurance | | | | Aerobic endurance | | |

**Figure 9** Periodization of dominant abilities for a baseball team with one peak   (Bompa, 1999).

## CONCLUSION

This discussion was simply an introduction to the many variables inherent in the theory and methodology of training. Bear in mind that many variations are available and nothing is written in stone. Our hope is that coaches can begin to question their training methods and continually improve, so as to provide their athletes with the best programs possible.

## REFERENCES

Bompa., T. (1999). *Periodization: Theory and methodology of training* (4th ed). Champaign, IL: Human Kinetics.

Deschenes, M. R., & Kraemer, W. J. (2002). Performance and physiologic adaptations to resistance training. *American Journal of Physiological Medical Rehabilitation*, 81, S3-S16.

McClements, J., & Botterill, C. (1979). Goal setting in shaping of future performance in athletics. In P. Klavora & J. Daniel (Eds.), *Coach, athlete and sport psychologist* (pp. 81-96). Toronto: Twin Offset.

Harre, D. (Ed.). (1982). *Trainingslehre*. Berlin: Sportverlag.

Judge, L. W., Moreau, C., & Burke, J. R. (2003). Neural adaptions with sport-specific resistance training in high skilled athletes. *Journal of Sports Sciences*, 21, 419-427.

Lewis, D. A., Kamon, E., & Hodgson, J. L. (1986). Physiological differences between genders. Implications for sports conditioning. *Sports Medicine*. Sep-Oct.3(5):357-369.

Ozolin, N. (1971). *Sovremennaia systema sportivnoi trenirovky* [Athletes training system for competition]. Moscow: Fizkultura i Sport.

Peterson, M. D., Rhea, M. R., & Alvar, B. A. (2004). Maximizing strength development in athletes: a meta-analysis to determine the dose-response relationship. *Journal of Strength and Conditioning Research*, 18, 377-382.

# CHAPTER 3

# PSYCHOLOGICAL FACTORS OF PHYSICAL PREPARATION

DAVE COLLINS AND ALAN MACPHERSON

These are interesting times for those who are interested in physical fitness. Promotion and maintenance of a physically active lifestyle are world-wide concerns. As the population Body Mass Index (BMI) continues to rise at alarming rates, so do health costs. There is no doubt that physical fitness (PF) is an important commodity. In this chapter, however, we are concerned with the challenge of raising PF to improve performance. While many overlaps with the "health" literature exist, the picture for the training athlete[1] is often subtly but crucially different. PF is essential for performance in many arenas of human endeavor, and even though psychological factors are often a better predictor of performance levels than fitness per se (e.g., Gould, Guinan, Greenleaf, Medbery, & Peterson, 1999; Kilcullen, Mael, Goodwin, & Zazanis, 1999), this may be because the athlete has to possess the mental skills in order to complete the training load necessary for success (Abbott & Collins, 2004). In short, one needs to be able to push him/herself hard in order to achieve. Accordingly, using the various "factors" of PF, we consider both the generic and psychological issues which pertain to the pursuit of physical excellence through training.

There is one other important issue, however, which relates to the motor control perspective. Over the past two decades, a distinction has grown between sport psychology and motor control. We believe this to be an unfortunate and dysfunctional split. All too often, performance suffers due to specific control problems that sport psychologists try to ameliorate through the use of mental skills. It seems much better, however, to consider the control parameters within training, and to promote transfer from practice to competition, while also inoculating against the inevitable stressors. Accordingly, where appropriate, we also consider motor issues from the central to the neurological, and place them in a context for the psychology practitioner.

Our chapter expects a reasonable level of knowledge in exercise physiology and training methods. Just as educational psychologists need to be teachers and organizational management specialists should know something about business, sport psychologists must be sport scientists, coaches, and fitness trainers as well (at least to a reasonable level).

## PSYCHOLOGICAL ASPECTS OF SPECIFIC FITNESS COMPONENTS

As we mentioned earlier, there are a number of generic mental components to being a top class trainer. The psychological characteristics of excellence, identified over the years by Orlick and colleagues (Kreiner-Philips & Orlick, 1993; Orlick & Partington, 1988), work in

---

[1] In this chapter, we will use the term "athlete" to describe any participant in a physically active challenge. As such, we encompass games players, climbers, dancers, etc. within this term.

part by equipping the high-achieving athlete to execute the level and quality of physical and technical work required. More recently, our own research (e.g., Abbott, Button, Pepping, & Collins, 2005) has shown these factors to be equally crucial for developing excellence. These factors need to be borne in mind throughout this chapter – indeed, though arguably, throughout the whole book. Each component of fitness brings its own particular mental challenges, which, while considerable interaction is apparent, can usefully be considered separately.

## ENDURANCE

The simple rule of endurance training (later comments notwithstanding) is that it takes a long time; comparatively longer sessions, large volumes of time during the day, and several years of effort are implicit to the traditional development of endurance. Fortunately, some research endeavors have been allocated to the mental aspects of endurance; indeed more investigations are apparent in this component than any other.

### EFFORT PERCEPTION

There is little doubt that as a feature of adaptation (getting fit), the athlete gains a more accurate perception of effort. Of course, in absolute terms fitter athletes work harder, but when workload is controlled (usually as a percentage of $VO_2$ Max) fitness effects can be allowed for in determining the "dose" of exercise required. However, fit individuals still show a better relationship between actual workload measures (the physiology) and self ratings of perceived effort (Travlos & Marisi, 1996). The various forms of the Borg Scale, otherwise known as Rating of Perceived Exertion (RPE – Callow et al., 2003; Hollander et al., 2003), offer a convenient measure for setting workloads which apply to most settings; pertinently, it appears that this measure increases its validity (at least accuracy-wise) as increased fitness yields better self-perception. It is worth noting, however, that certain situations may require different approaches. Whereas workload can vary due to external influences, RPE may require some supplementation, since athletes can be lured into training at too high or too low intensity for the physiological requirements of that session. Ice speed skating is a good example; in public ice rinks, where training times may be used by others during open, public skating sessions, the body heat of the crowd can change the ice to slush. As a result, session schedules based on lap times are meaningless. RPE will change differentially, however, since the physical challenge balance of the session (for example, between muscular endurance in the legs and cardiovascular elements of the work bouts) will modify with the conditions. Under these sorts of circumstances, athletes need to learn, acknowledge, and apply a combination of different RPEs (legs, back, breathing, heart rate [HR], etc.) or one particular skill-appropriate index, supplemented perhaps with actual HR measures.

### ATTENTIONAL FOCUS AND OTHER MENTAL SKILLS

Our best clue to the mental sets required for efficient endurance training comes from the various studies conducted with marathon runners, starting with the original work by

Schomer (1986, 1987). More recently employed in other endurance settings such as triathlon and swimming (e.g., Antonini-Phiulippe, Reynes, & Bruant, 2003), the combination of "think aloud" and retrospective methodologies offers an insight into the relative frequency of various mental strategies. By extrapolation, this combination also offers some clues into the most effective approaches for performance. The picture has been "muddied" somewhat since the original advice favoring the associative style (focusing on task-relevant components such as breathing) as offering superior results to a self-distracting, disassociational focus (in which the athlete deliberately concentrates on aspects of the environment or aspects of the performance rhythm as a so-called "pseudo mantra"). In a comprehensive review of studies spanning over 20 years of research, Masters and Ogles (1998) supported association for better performance, while suggesting that disassociative strategies seem to result in lower RPE for any given effort. Perhaps the answer lies in the aims of the exercise? Training athletes emphasize performance, and accept the greater mental challenges of association (together with the possible increased risks of injury; Crust, 2003; Masters & Ogles, 1998) in order to optimize achievement. In contrast, recreational/health-focused trainers may wish to achieve their "fix" of aerobic benefits in a less (perceived) painful fashion. In this regard, Wrisberg and Pein (1990) found experienced runners to be more adept at using disassociative styles (e.g., music, surrounding scenery, etc.), perhaps in order to avoid the painful and unpleasant bodily cues inherent in this positive form of body abuse. Consequently, it appears that you can get gain with less pain, but only at the cost of slower progress and lower levels of performance. Figure 1 presents the percentage time spent in various mental sets by elite and non-elite marathoners, based on the study conducted by Stevinson and Biddle (1998, 1999).

At the elite end of endurance, however, distance completed becomes the key factor. When durations and distances get "ultra long," the level of mental intensity may necessitate the use of disassociation just to get through the grind. For example, recent research by

|  | INTERNAL | EXTERNAL |
|---|---|---|
| Task-relevant or "Association" | INWARD MONITORING (40%) (e.g., fatigue, breathing, soreness) | OUTWARD MONITORING (28%) (e.g., conditions, route, strategy) |
| Task-irrelevant or "Dissociation" | INWARD DISTRACTION (8%)=WALL!! (e.g., daydreams, imaging, music, puzzles) | OUTWARD DISTRACTION (26%) (e.g., scenery, environment, runners) |

*Figure 1* Thought content recorded in elite marathon runners.

Richards and Collins (in press) examined the coping strategies used by soldiers undergoing a forty-day endurance challenge which incorporated a ten-day mountain run, a 125 mile canoe race, and an arctic sled pull. Although the performers in this study were not elite athletes but soldiers, and the aim was to survive/complete the event rather than to set a time, the use of disassociation was overwhelmingly the most common strategy. Once again, the aims of participation appear to be key factors in determining the most effective focus strategy.

Whichever attentional focus is preferred, there seems to be little doubt that mental skills training can enhance endurance performance. Early investigations which tended to use single skills were promising, but provided some anomalous results. For example, Weinberg, Bruya, Garland, and Jackson (1987) found that goal setting was effective in improving sit-up performance (and training as well), but that goal difficulty had little or no impact on the size of this effect. More recently, "packages" of skills have shown positive effects on high-level endurance athletes (e.g., triathlon and running; Patrick & Hrycaiko, 1998) and on lower-level performers (e.g., gymnasium triathlon; Thelwell & Greenlees, 2001). Both packages used goal setting, imagery, self talk, and relaxation, but the decisions underlying the combinations used, or indeed the optimization of this mix, were not addressed. As such, these sorts of investigations are good for the athletes concerned, but less useful in guiding our understanding of the mechanisms through which each skill aids performance. As with so many other aspects of sport psychology, the key issue is the customization of the package to optimally address individual needs. If this is done successfully, positive benefits will accrue, and investigators will need to take a more mechanistic line if we are to sort out the logic underpinning the design of the best recipes.

## HIGHER INTENSITY/LOWER VOLUME ENDURANCE

There is one other consideration emerging from the increasing literature on the effects of shorter length, high intensity sessions, which suggests that positive changes in markers of endurance (for example, $VO_2$ Max) can be accomplished in other ways. In typical protocols, subjects work for relatively short periods at high intensity (say 3 minutes at 80% max HR on untrained; Winett et al., 2003), or perform several bouts of very high intensity work with little rest – so-called anaerobic intervals (Glaister, Stone, Stewart, Hughes, & Moir, 2003). This approach can negate some of the "boredom" issues alluded to earlier, and provide several other positive benefits. For a start, and particularly for multiple sprint sports such as team invasion games, the activity is far more specific, ensuring greater transfers for both physical and mental effects. Secondly, through handling the higher psychological pressures inherent to high intensity exercise, athletes gain coping skills which relate to the specific exercise challenge (e.g., Rodgers et al., 2002), but which may also generalize to other stressors such as competition.

This second factor is a significant one for psychology, and is worth considering in greater detail: in short, is it the fitness itself or the experience of coping which is the mechanism for change? Many authors have suggested that aerobic fitness offers some sort of "stress buffering" effect, perhaps by changing the psycho-physiological reactivity of the subject. Indeed, these benefits have often been touted as reasons for increasing aerobic fitness per se as an aspect of health related exercise.

Unfortunately, however, while there is no doubt that aerobic fitness training requires good coping, there is little evidence for a direct reciprocation. A key study by Steptoe, Moses, Matthews, and Edwards (1990) showed no changes to stress reactivity associated with increased aerobic fitness. Ten years later, Dishman and Jackson (2000) also dismissed this much hypothesized link. The picture seems fairly clear: coping with hard training engenders personal growth, but through psychological rather than physiological (or perhaps even psycho-physiological) channels.

## STRENGTH AND POWER

In some ways, the components of strength and power appear to be at the other end of a training psychology continuum. Strength is defined as maximum force application, usually measured as the maximum weight which can be shifted – in training shorthand the one repetition maximum or 1-RM. Power is best thought of as speed-strength and sports-wise; it usually involves shifting smaller but still significant resistances (for example, your body or an implement) at maximum speed.

### EMOTIONS AND STRENGTH/POWER PERFORMANCE

As with endurance, attentional focus is key to performance. In strength-power, however, we are talking about high levels of arousal – indeed some would suggest as high as the athlete's skill level will permit (e.g., Rushall, 1977). This position is a little extreme, but holds for most closed skill activities (Cratty, 1973), with very well-learned, motorically simple movements such as power lifting (actually a test of strength) and tameshawari (breaking) in karate facilitated by very high arousal. This finding is so well accepted it is almost apocryphal, and little discussion seems necessary. As an example, Figure 2 presents data from one of our ongoing studies, in which we examined the roles played by different emotions on performance. Building on work which shows the impacts of emotion on neural control (e.g., Kandel & Schwartz, 1985), we manipulated mood in a group of highly motivated military recruits before testing them on a simple power test, the standing vertical jump (VJ).

We standardized each individual's mean of five efforts under normal ("just do your best") conditions, then manipulated mood through the use of false feedback on their performance (pass = happy, failure = sad) or by showing them an extreme propaganda film (anger). The resulting changes in performance on the VJ clearly demonstrate the importance of setting mood for effective training and performance.

Thus, strength/power training, from a psychological perspective, is largely a matter of appropriate and effective self-regulation (Collins, 1999). For practical purposes, this relates to an initial identification of the most appropriate mental set for each individual performer. In this regard, Hanin's Zone of Optimal Functioning (Hanin & Stambulova, 2002) concept offers an excellent underlying rationale. Practically, one needs to work out the emotions that can be used to "set" the optimum single-minded focus for the session. This process is essential for two reasons. Firstly, strength development by definition requires

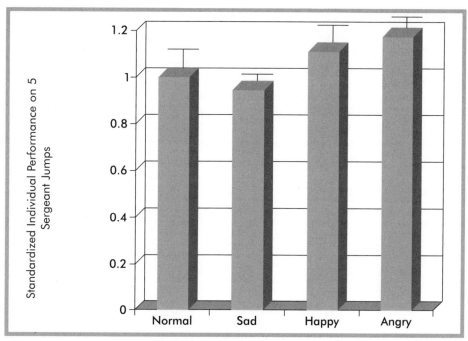

**Figure 2** Impact of emotions on power performance (n=16).

a training load at, or in excess of, maximum limits. This just can't be achieved without adequate mental preparation. Training with lower loads will result (almost by definition) in less training effect on maximum strength. Secondly, and also as a result of these high loads, strength-power work can be very hazardous, with high potential for injury from mistakes, poor technique, or just loss of control.

Caution should be exercised, however, when relating to the "social constructivism" of the performance environment. In fact, our two earlier examples were deliberately chosen to highlight this concern, which relates to peoples' expectations and the social norms for a particular activity. Following the dictates of the mores in their sport, power lifters will often raise themselves to an intensity of emotion. Smelling salts, physical abuse, and face slapping are combined to generate an (apparent) extremity of anger, with the lifter's shouts and screams "demonstrating" his or her readiness to perform. In contrast, the traditional martial artist displays no emotion, with a relaxed but fixed and unblinking stare as he or she calmly and with inner focus prepares for a break. Only one sound is usually uttered — the Ki ai yell as the break is completed. So which is right? Both are extreme strength/power performances, but the preparative behaviors are often completely in contrast. Individual differences are crucial, and we re-emphasize our earlier comments on the need for experimentation in identifying the optimum emotional state. However, there are also social pressures at work, and many performers prepare in a certain way because that is what everybody else is doing; perhaps in an attempt to look "right." An important consideration for athletes and their coaches/psychologists: just make sure that how you prepare is the best way for your needs.

## PREPARATION, TIMING, AND RECUPERATION

Since the psychological demands of strength/power training are high, we need to take care with the preparation for, timing of, and recovery from the sessions. Overtraining and recovery issues are specifically addressed elsewhere in this book (see chapter 8). For the present purposes, however, we need to acknowledge the mental costs of achieving the necessary focus for high quality training, and cater to these in a way that ensures the intermediate training status of the athlete and his or her long-term health. Of course, these issues also pertain to other fitness components. We will address them here purely because the intensity of strength and power training makes them a particular concern.

Firstly, preparation and timing. Athletes, whether training full time or fitting their training in with a job, are busy people and typically rush from one activity to another. This raises a particular investment/return trade-off, which must be addressed in order to form an optimum plan. The sections above show the need for a psychologically intense approach to training; without it, training returns are lowered. Therefore, it is essential to take the trouble to arrive in good time and enable a steady cycle of preparation. In fact, our experience is that without this 10- to 15-min "time out" to get one's "training head" on, you just can't train consistently at a high enough level. In short, take time from the session if necessary to ensure that the training effort is of sufficient quality. Given the well documented impact of circadian rhythm, investigating the most suitable time of day for the session is also worth considering. Obviously, there are considerable variations in daily rhythms, so optimum timing will vary from athlete to athlete.

Another timing consideration is when the athlete will perform. There is little point in placing the most intense session of the day at 3 p.m. if the event is timed for 7 p.m. During the preparation of our athletes for the Athens Olympics, the earlier morning heats necessary for some events (9 a.m.), coupled with the lifestyles and timing preferences of some of our track and field athletes, led us to place medium intensity circuits at 8 a.m. as a feature of their specific preparation phase. Not a popular move, but at least the guys were used to performing at an hour when, come the summer, they would be required to complete their warm-ups.

Finally, consider the level of recuperation and regeneration within the training weeks and months. If we have managed to lift the training quality of each session through various psychological manipulations, there is a parallel need to improve the quality of "R & R" to counter this. Parasympathetic overtraining (the sub-species associated with overtraining in strength/power athletes) and staleness will result if the training load and recovery are not balanced. Educating the athlete to do this is an essential process for the psychologist and other support professionals.

As with other sections, we seem to have just "scratched the surface" with this overview. There is a great deal of other literature that the interested reader may want to consider. However, since much of this work has been done on sub-elite or recreational trainer samples, the best advice for elites or aspiring elites is to test the veracity of individual preference, then stick to it.

## Neurological and Other Control Concerns

The concerns of optimizing transfer fall under this category, as do further issues relating to maintaining sufficient intensity. The important concern of transfer – making sure that improvements in strength/power from gym exercises actually result in improved performance. This is a big issue for strength and conditioning specialists everywhere, and probably offers the best argument for the increasing predominance of free weights, sandbags, medicine balls, and other implements over machines. However, even matching exercises more closely to the actual movement doesn't always do the trick. There are several studies that demonstrate the annoying fact that improvements in weight training exercises don't always transfer to the actual movement; for example, rugby league players getting stronger on the bench press but weaker on their hand-offs. For this and other reasons, specialists are increasingly using an approach known as "combination" training, in which the athlete does a set of high intensity exercises (usually with weights), immediately followed by a set of lighter, often sport-specific movements. Thus, for example, judo players can combine bench pulls or power cleans with a set of six to eight throw-like pulls at a jacket. Even combining heavy exercises with a lighter, faster set seems to offer positive benefits (Baker, 2003a). The key issue is to educate the athlete so that the power set is truly completed (or is at least attempted) at high intensity. The impact of this training style is far reaching, relating not only to the level of neurogenic control, but also down to the biochemistry of the muscle (e.g., Liu, Schlumberger, Writh, Schmidtbleicher, & Steinacker, 2003).

In fact, the specificity of the exercise is very dependent on the temporal coupling of the motor units – put simply, the equivalence of the firing order between the exercise and the performance movements it is designed to enhance. Accordingly, getting units to fire in realistic "tempo" is good practice, and there is increasing evidence that this process is, in turn, enhanced by priming with mental simulation of movement (MSM – the more correct term for mental practice in such settings) of the sports skill itself. Thus, javelin throwers will often mentally run through the throwing action, then do an exercise – a process which promotes the fit of the muscle recruitment to the pertinent skill.

Over and above this priming/transfer effect, thinking through the movement may also have a direct benefit on strength itself. We now know that contrary to previous thinking, MSM can play a role in strength promotion, probably through its impact on central and recruitment parameters (Smith, Collins, & Holmes, 2003). Even though these effects may only be important in the early stages of training with a new movement, it seems impractical to ignore the positive benefits.

Even though this "target movement specificity" is desirable, athletes should not completely avoid a bit of variation. Keeping some "functional variability" in exercise movements provides useful resources for future movement modification (Collins, Morriss, & Trower, 1999), as well as the ability to cope with variations induced by pressure or injury (Collins, Jones, Fairweather, Doolan, & Priestley, 2001). Practically, this means training with movements which match, but not too closely, the types of movements involved in performance. Thus, javelin throwers may well train oblique abdominals using sandbags, shifted from a low to a high platform. Rugby and American football players also benefit from using sandbags; it trains the grip and offers them a good fixator workout as the load shifts during movements. Even very closed-skill athletes like Olympic weightlifters may use part movements, generally termed assistance exercises, both as training stimuli in their own right but also to offer effective strength gains over a broader range of movement.

The second motor concern in strength and power training relates to the maintenance of sufficient intensity. Of course, the emotional and other psychological ideas mentioned earlier are crucial to getting and keeping the training athlete in a sufficiently aroused state. Even with this tight focus, however, simple fatigue effects may limit the athlete's ability to keep working at a high enough quality. It is worth remembering that slower or less intense movements may well result in a slower, less intense, or at the very least less than optimally-trained athlete. Accordingly, sufficient rest and recovery must be built into the session procedures to keep things firing at a high enough level. Figure 3 shows the drop off in force generation that can occur in a simple exercise like bench press, when inter-rep intervals are varied (Tidow, 1990).

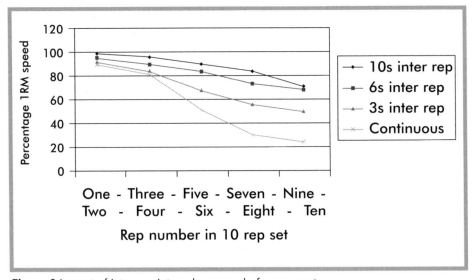

**Figure 3** Impact of inter-rep interval on speed of movement.

To put this in perspective, Tidow offers the example of a shot putter with a personal best of 20 metres. Under conditions of continuous movement (which is, of course, physically easier) or with a short inter-rep interval, the athlete drops to 80% of his speed after three or four reps. In a ten rep set, this means that six of the ten repetitions are "training" him to be a sixteen meter thrower – a somewhat different class.

In fact, strength trainers increasingly use measures of speed/force to ensure that if the criterion quality is not achieved, the athlete stops until recovery permits more, high intensity reps. Use of equipment such as "Musclelab" (www.ergotest.com) in this fashion is a good example; quality is maintained and training return is optimized. In the absence of such hardware, it is essential that the athlete appreciates the need for quality, and takes appropriate action to maintain this while not using it as an excuse. Developing this awareness is a key psychological concern for effective training.

Finally, there is a need to employ movements and patterns which ensure maximum recruitment of the targeted muscle fibers; almost always these will be harder to recruit than Type 2 or fast twitch fibers. Large blocks of fast twitch fibers fire best from big, sudden, intense demands. The movements may be clumsy, but this is a tolerable necessity if we are to train the right systems. "Big bang" recruitment (see Kunnemeyer & Schmidtbleicher, 1999b; Schmidtbleicher, 1992), in which large blocks are "kicked" into action, is the method of choice. Once again, the athlete must be taught the need for this approach, and offered ways in which to achieve it. So, for example, low step ups can use a "claw, stamp, and drive" key phrase to encourage the muscles to fire in the right way. Of course, achieving the correct mental set up prior to the session is the key to effective training. Once again, athletes often need a change in attitude to make sure that they don't fall back into traditional and often more comfortable or accepted methods. For example, consider the motivations for body image which are associated with many athletes from different sports. As a result, they will often request the inclusion (or just do it themselves) of some "body building" style hypertrophy exercises, even using these as a feature of their normal strength-power sessions. They need to accept the literature's position that such hypertrophy work has a very negative impact on the quality (and therefore the return from) their strength/power conditioning (Baker, 2003b). As with so many other training settings, athletes must be educated and won over as to what is really good for them.

## Speed

To a very large extent, speed depends on power, so many of the comments in the previous section apply. Just to add to the complexity, speed also depends on flexibility and agility, so the next section is pertinent as well.

Over and above the excitation effects, and their facilitation through appropriate emotional settings, speed will have a control component and, in all but closed-skill sports, will also involve perceptual and decision making components. Finally, and yet again, speed training carries its own potential transfer issues, which are particularly pertinent for games players and, in a very different way, martial artists.

Control-wise, the key issue is to get the system ready to fire at the right speed, a process which requires the muscle fiber recruitment to be in top form. Increasingly, coaches and athletes are using very intense exercises to generate Maximum Voluntary Contractions (MVCs) as an important part of their warm-up for competition. The idea is that using MVCs provides a short-term potentiation of the muscles, which means that when required to perform, they are capable of greater force contractions at an earlier stage (see, for example, Guellich & Schmidtbleicher, 1996). Physiologically, we still need to identify how long before the actual performance such MVCs should be completed. It would be no surprise if this, like almost everything else, was a highly personal effect. Psychologically, therefore, this needs to be fitted into the preparation schedule, with the resulting excitation effects perhaps maintained and focused by MSM and other procedures. Finally, if such benefits accrue in competition, surely they could be used to raise the quality of training as well. Earlier comments on recuperation/regeneration quality are also pertinent here, but the use of MVCs as part of the setting procedures for high quality sessions should be considered. These quality issues become even more important when one considers that muscle changes may be speed-specific (see, for example, McBride, Triplett-McBride, Davie, & Newton, 2002). Consequently, even though heavy weights are the best way to recruit and develop fast twitch muscle fiber, it may be that some fast movements are needed in the schedule as well, especially if speed rather than power per se is the aim. Interestingly, many sprint coaches now insist that their athletes do some fast movement exercise every day, even on their day off. It seems like the mind-body system can rapidly lose the ability to move very quickly, hence the need for avoiding a post rest day (comparative) slump. Of course, in order to meet the recuperation aspects of the rest day, such work can be usefully done in a non-weight bearing fashion, for example using an exercise bike, so that the total loading on the body is kept low.

The second speed issue relates to perception and decision making – the anticipation which makes the elite player look so smooth and, apparently, have so much time. The technical and tactical aspects of this are dealt with in other chapters (see Chapters 4 and 5, respectively). Suffice it to say, however, that some promotion of simple reaction time is a very useful adjunct to this work, and this is described in more detail in the next section.

And finally... the by now almost traditional consideration of transfer effects; once again, the equivalence of the exercise to its "target" performance skill. Firstly, running: Many sports, particularly team games, have increasingly employed athletics sprint coaches to work on the athletes' speed – no problem when such knowledge relates to the scheduling of training, although some care still needs to be taken. Competing every week throughout a season is rather different from achieving an annual peak for a major championship (Black & McKenzie, 2004).

All this may be far from sufficient, however, when the coaching develops the running action of, say, a rugby player towards the technical model of a track sprinter. The two running actions are different, no doubt, and the rugby player's performance will improve when measured on the track. That is the issue though: training a games player to run like a sprinter and he or she will do better *in that environment*. Before using this approach, coaches need to check the equivalence (if any) of the pitch and track running actions. We know that running actions will differ between quite similar surfaces such as hard wooden treadmills and gym floors (e.g., Wank, Frick, & Schmidtbleicher, 1998). Surely the greater difference in surfaces between pitch and track, coupled with the different demands of the sprint action (flat, straight-line speed versus balanced, "change of direction" running) will involve an even greater difference. If so (and biomechanical analysis is currently underway), the potential for less than optimum training return, or even negative transfer (recall the rugby league hand off cited earlier), means that speed work should be done in the environment and with the kit which is needed for the eventual performance.

A parallel challenge exists for the martial artists who must increase hand and (in some disciplines) leg speed. Until recently, shadow sparring was used to build speed, with speed ball work supplementing this. However, athletes will never punch "full tilt" without a target. Rather, they slow the final part of the punch, usually finishing with a bent elbow (or leg) in order to avoid joint pain from the forced hyperextension inevitable without a target to "use up" the kinetic energy generated. This action is obviously different from the full punch (kick) and results in negative transfer. Indeed, shadow sparring can result in slower hands because the "holding back" can become ingrained as part of the skill. If, however, full power movements are employed, then a few sessions with the physiotherapist may be booked up front, because elbow/knee problems will surely result. Strangely, these can also occur at the other extreme, when athletes make too much use of a heavy bag as a target. The answer is to use a target which reproduces the resistance of an opponent. Focus pads are ideal, permitting the athlete to unleash at full speed but without the risk of injury.

## AGILITY AND FLEXIBILITY

In our experience, agility is the most neglected component of fitness, at least in US and UK gyms. We make this distinction because examination of the types of schedules typically employed in the old Eastern bloc reveals agility as a distinct heading, with a large volume of work allocated to the promotion of this component. Fortunately, the situation is changing. However, too many coaches still confuse speed work with general agility, believing that only sport/activity-specific agility is required and that this accrues from technical work. This myth needs squashing. Following the ideas at the end of the previous section, there is an increasing literature which shows the difference between straight-line speed and gross motor agility (e.g., Young, McDowell, & Scarlett, 2001). This finding has implications for both the testing and training of sport-specific speed, which may well have a large but neglected agility component. Furthermore, extending the ideas presented in the strength section of this chapter, it may well be that general agility development serves as an inoculation against overuse injuries, while also offering a broader basic vocabulary which the athlete can use for movement modification. In short, agility is the key element, and all schedules, even those for more mature athletes, should incorporate some generic agility work at some time in the periodized year.

In contrast, and especially in some sports, flexibility can tend to be overdone, especially in warm-up. Advice on stretching used to be so simple: stretching prior to exercise "clearly" prevented musculoskeletal injury (Best & MacAuley, 2002). It was part of what any sports performer did prior to training or competition. Athletes from such diverse disciplines as rugby, soccer, and track could be observed contorting themselves into various elongated poses. It was (and continues to be in some sports) the done thing – but what does the evidence suggest?

Muscle strain injury is cited as the most frequent injury in sport (Glick, 1980; Salter, 1983) and, until recently at any rate, conventional wisdom dictated that the best way to prevent acute musculo-tendon injury was to stretch prior to commencing exercise. However, in a systematic review conducted by Weldon and Hill (2003) to investigate the efficacy of stretching as a measure for preventing injury, evidence was found to the contrary: the data suggested that pre-exercise stretching may in fact increase the likelihood of injury (Young

& Elliot, 2001). Similar findings were arrived at by Herbert and Gabriel (2002). From their analysis they extrapolated that the effect of stretching was so marginal it could be summarized in the following terms: one hundred people stretching for twelve weeks to prevent one injury. Of course, such ratios become important when you are the one who is injured, but it does rather challenge conventional wisdom. In yet another systematic review, Thacker, Gilchrist, Stroup, and Kinsey (2004) concluded that there was not enough evidence to either endorse or advise exercisers to discontinue routine stretching. What the systematic reviews have in common is that they all request that more rigorously controlled trials be conducted to fully investigate the effect of stretching in minimizing the likelihood of the occurrence of muscle injury.

One other area of contention is the impact that flexibility has on athletic performance. For example, do one-hundred-meter runners have to be superbly flexible in order to maximize their performance? If you were to observe a warm-up area at a major athletics meet, you might be forgiven for thinking that it is the crucial component in performance preparation. Once again, however, the support for the previously accepted "clear" need for flexibility in warm-up is being questioned. Indeed, there is evidence to suggest that static stretching prior to exercise can result in a decrement in performance (Nelson & Kokkonen, 2001). In this study, performance on 1 RM squats was reduced as a result of a thorough period of stretching prior to task execution.

Interestingly, Schilling and Stone's (2001) observation of strength and power lifters' warm-up behavior (including elite weightlifters and track and field throwers) suggests that these athletes, prior to competition, do little in the way of general stretching and conventional warm-up. The types of movement used by these athletes are specific to the exercise they are about to execute; pre-event routines mainly include using light resistance at reduced velocity. The advantage of this approach is that these athletes are combining a light practice session with the rehearsal of elements of the skill they are about to execute, thereby combining the mental and physical components in tandem.

Of course, while we eagerly await further research to completely clarify the pros and cons of flexibility work, it is worth considering the psychological side of this issue. Whether or not flexibility work aids injury prevention, or pre-event "hard" stretching enhances performance, is only part of the puzzle. Athletes' perceptions also play a substantial role, and there is no doubt whatsoever that flexibility-related activities are part of the essential behavior pattern for some individuals, and perhaps the main reason for their common occurrence in some sports. Unless/until the evidence is clear or the athletes are completely open to change, individual beliefs must be taken into consideration when deciding on the best practice. In short, as with so much else in sport and physical activity, if you believe it does some good it probably does. Changes should be made cautiously, with steps taken to ensure athlete buy-in.

This section shouldn't be taken as "open season" on flexibility. It obviously is an essential component of the fitness mix for many sports, and an element of the total training package for every type of physical activity. Our contention is that, through a combination of received wisdom, folklore, and misunderstanding, it has taken on a far more central role than it merits. The literature increasingly highlights the need for a critical reconsideration of common practice. For example, another contradiction of common understanding in relation to flexibility relates to individuals who use free weights. Some might expect that these individuals would be less flexible as compared to regular trainers who use other forms of resistance training. Yet again, common understanding is in error. Kunnemeyer and Schmidtbleicher (1997a) found that individuals using free weights to strength train have more flexibility than athletes following a stretching protocol. In another study designed to investigate flexibility characteristics among athletes who weight train across a spectrum of sports (Beedle & Stone, 1991), it was found that Olympic lifters and the control group (who did no training) were significantly more flexible than the other athlete groups that participated in the study (body building, gridiron football, weight training). What this demonstrates is that static strength is helpful in improving flexibility.

We offer two crucial take-home messages from this section. Firstly, do more agility work in your training schedule; benefits are wide-ranging (including some for specific flexibility), but it seems that this component is badly under-represented in the programs of most athletes. Secondly, and with a constant regard to the emerging picture from research, the coach should be prepared to challenge the common practices apparent in his or her sport. Resist the "it's always worked well this way" argument, ask challenging questions, and require well thought-out answers. Benefits are inevitable from this critical process, which in fact is typical of elite performers and coaches the world over. Flexibility in thinking is arguably more important than in the body.

## PUTTING IT ALL TOGETHER: PSYCHOLOGICAL TECHNIQUES FOR TRAINING BALANCE

We have already alluded several times to the need for careful consideration of psychological factors, and this has several components. As an example, consider the relationship between PF and lifestyle. There is a simple assumption that high levels of physical activity are associated with a healthy lifestyle. This simply isn't true. For example, Special Forces soldiers, who pride themselves on PF and for whom high levels of daily physical challenge are virtually a given, can display extremely dysfunctional lifestyle patterns, including high levels of social drug use (Sridhar et al., 2003). A surprisingly similar "unexpected relationship" can exist between PF and psychological factors. Put simply, high levels of PF can frequently be associated with dysfunctional psychological behavior, a feature well recognized in appearance-related exercise but less researched in performance-focused groups. One big reason for the existence of these problems relates to the individual's commitment to an "athletic identity" and the closely related construct of self-reinforcement.

If you are an athlete, or working with an athlete, the importance of appraising performance realistically in training and competition cannot be underestimated. Youngsters are notoriously unrealistic in appraising their levels of effort and performance. As an athlete's career progresses, performance gain can become even more difficult to achieve, with more and more effort required for less and less achievement reward –

personal bests become harder to realize, records are more rarely broken. As a result, individuals (especially those focused solely on winning) can get de-motivated and drop out of the sport, or even from physical activity altogether. For this reason, developing ways in which athletes can reward themselves following a good session or performance is crucial. Sport at the top level demands that athletes constantly scrutinize their performance. Being self-critical and analyzing deficiencies is part of pursuing peak potential. So is realistically appraising performance.

There are multitudes of factors that contribute to successful performance. Having these factors in the right place, in the right order, at the right time, is the key. Yet to attain peak performance, athletes must cope with the knowledge that realistically, the synchronicity required in bringing together the legion of components that constitute peak performance – to be at your best – can rarely be summoned on demand. So what keeps an athlete going? One aspect of motivation is to examine an athlete's reward structure.

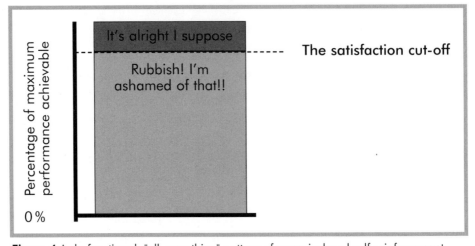

**Figure 4** A dysfunctional, "all or nothing" pattern of appraisal and self reinforcement.

If an athlete's evaluation of his or her performance resembles the pattern shown in Figure 4, then there is little scope for reward. Setting an almost unachievable cut-off for self satisfaction may sound like good sense (desire to be the "best of the best," winners never quit, etc.), but is the sort of "bad for performance" attitude beloved of certain sportswear manufacturers. If this situation is allowed to perpetuate, a number of negative factors may influence future performances (e.g., increased frustration levels, reduced levels of motivation to train, and self-damning or attributing blame to others). We present a healthier approach in Figure 5.

This three-level goals approach employs percentages of personal bests, each of which is accorded specific feedback. It includes an implicit realization that breaking personal targets is, at the very least, unlikely to occur at every performance opportunity. Importantly, the athletes' core construct – how they view themselves as performers – does not get tarnished whenever they fail to meet their previous performance targets. Rather, they are able to recognize and act on sliding scales of achievement, which more realistically reflect real life. With practice, athletes will start to self-manage these goals, adjusting them each day to reflect other challenges, such as weather, their own condition, etc. As a result, they take increasingly greater, but still reasonable, responsibility for their own self-management.

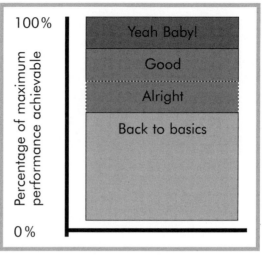

Finally, and once again a factor which is subject to massive influences from the athlete's patterns of self-reinforcement and perceived expectation, make sure that they work on exactly what is needed. We have already pointed this out in the strength section. A great example is the tendency of power/strength athletes, especially those in the more "macho" sports, to

**Figure 5** Performance appraisal and self-reinforcement based on "three-level goals."

indulge in a little bout of "beach weights" rather than the prescribed exercise regime. This can have quite disastrous results. Even a simple, "3 sets of 10" hypertrophy bout can negatively affect power levels, and result in a restriction of training return (Baker, 2003b). The fact that this impact is most marked in the most powerful (i.e., best) athletes is even more reason for keeping them to the schedule. The answer is simple: every session should be supervised, or even better (and as we suggest elsewhere in this chapter), athletes should be educated into understanding why as well as what they have to do.

These are just some of the things that can go wrong, but what about the flip side? What about using psychology to aid performance? The most sensible place to start with is training. In most sports, training represents a greater part of the time commitment than does performing. Accordingly, it always seems odd to us that psychologists don't spend a lot more time focusing on training behavior. Certainly, the psychological (as opposed to the motor) issues will transfer well, while raising the game in training will yield additional benefits in terms of performance potential and mental toughness. Some psychological work seems key, since adherence to set training programs, perceived by strength and conditioning specialists as high, is often very low indeed, with athletes often "faking" their training diaries to keep the trainers happy (Palmer, Burwitz, Smith, & Collins, 1999).

In fact, the relationship between training behavior and achievement may be much closer than was previously imagined. Some data from one of our ongoing studies makes this apparent. We used video analysis and assessment of behavior in gym training sessions with a diverse group of professional and semi-professional athletes (n=67, observations per athlete >6). The results of our observations, coded by investigators blind to the conditions and/or aims of the study, are shown in Figure 6.

The key point is the close association between active involvement in the session and actual training behavior – another good reason to explain "what" as well as "why!" When

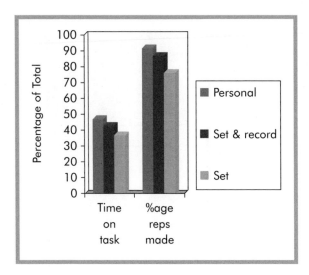

**Figure 6**
Percentage time on task/set repetitions completed, accomplished by athletes with different approaches to training.

athletes perform the set schedule they do work hard. There are significant differences in their performance, however. Both time on task (time spent actually working/preparing for a set rather than resting, chatting, etc.) and the percentage of reps actually completed are higher when athletes actively record their performance (in a training diary, for example) or when they set personal targets for their achievement within the session.

At one level this is very interesting – personal "buy in" to the session has demonstrable benefits. Some may perceive this as less crucial, however, seeing the relationship as merely due to personal commitment. Accordingly, the really interesting finding is that changing attitudinal behavior results directly in improvements in training behavior. These results are shown in Figure 7.

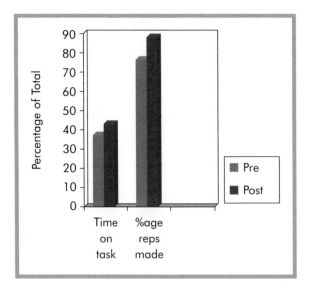

**Figure 7**
Changes in training behavior resulting from a psychological intervention.

Using 23 professional and semi-professional athletes, including some from the "underachieving" group in the previous study, we offered a two-part intervention. Firstly, all athletes were asked to set a single performance goal for each session. Following a good practice, this goal was varied between preferred and less well-liked exercises. The participants were also encouraged to make a "head change" of five minutes, again once per session, in which they consciously tried to lift their levels of focus, commitment, and emotional energy. Evaluation of changes by independent assessors (more than five observations both pre and post) demonstrated the changes.

## SUMMARY

It is increasingly evident that effective support for elite athletes requires a genuinely interdisciplinary approach, and this obviously requires that the practitioner possess a broad knowledge of other subjects which complements her or his particular specialty. We would contend that such interdisciplinarity also underpins effective practice in health-focused exercise environments, and we have tried to reflect some of these ideas as well in this chapter. The bottom line is that effective support in training requires just as much knowledge of psychology as physiology; in fact many successful trainers would contend that the "psychology stuff" is the most important (Black & McKenzie, 2004). Accordingly, we hope that people from every discipline will find something useful in this chapter.

## REFERENCES

Abbott, A., & Collins, D. (2004). Eliminating the dichotomy between theory and practice in talent identification and development: Considering the role of psychology. *Journal of Sports Sciences*, 22, 395-408.

Abbott, A., Button, C., Pepping, G-J, & Collins, D. (2005). Unnatural selection: Talent identification and development in sport. *Nonlinear Dynamics, Psychology and Life Sciences*, 1, 61-88.

Antonini-Phiulippe, R., Reynes, E., & Bruant, G. (2003). Cognitive strategy and ability in endurance activities. *Perceptual and Motor Skills*, 96, 510-516.

Baker, D. (2003a). Acute effect of alternating heavy and light resistances on power output during upper-body complex power training. *Journal of Strength and Conditioning*, 17, 493-497.

Baker, D. (2003b). Acute negative effect of a hypertrophy-oriented training bout on subsequent upper-body power output. *Journal of Strength and Conditioning*, 17, 527-530.

Beedle, C. J. B., & Stone, M. H. (1991). Flexibility characteristics among athletes who weight train. *Journal of Applied Sport Science Research*, 5, Sept/Oct, 15-154.

Best, T. M., & MacAuley, D. (2002). Reducing risk of injury due to exercise: stretching before exercise does not help. *British Medical Journal*, 325, 451-452.

Black, S., & McKenzie, A. (2004). *Blackie: The Steve Black story*. London: Mainstream.

Callow, N., Hardy, L., Rowlands, A., Worth, S., Cook, M., Kendall, B., Parfitt, G., & Thompson, K. (2003). The effects of dehydration status on cognitive functioning and perception of effort. *Journal of Sports Sciences*, 21, 264-265.

Collins, D. J. (1999). The psychology of power training. *Faster-Higher-Stronger*, 3, 28-29.

Collins, D., Jones, B., Fairweather, M., Doolan, S., & Priestley, N. (2001). Examining anxiety associated changes in movement patterns. *International Journal of Sport Psychology*, 31, 223-242.

Collins, D. J., Morriss, C., & Trower, J. (1999). Getting it back: A case study of skill recovery in an elite athlete. *The Sport Psychologist*, 13, 288-298.

Cratty, B. J. (1973). *Psychology of contemporary sport*. Englewood Cliffs, NJ: Prentice Hall.

Crust, L. (2003). Should distance runners concentrate on their bodily sensations, or try to think of something else? *Sports Injury Bulletin*, 30, 10-12.

Dishman, R. K., & Jackson, E. M. (2000). Exercise, fitness and stress. *International Journal of Sport Psychology*, 31, 175-203.

Glaister, M., Stone, M. H., Stewart, A. M., Hughes, M., & Moir, G. (2003). Reliability of power output during short-duration maximal intensity – Intermittent cycling. *Journal of Strength and Conditioning Research*, 17, 781-784.

Glick, J. M. (1980). Muscle strains: Prevention and treatment. *Physician and Sportsmedicine*, 8, 73-77.

Gould, D., Guinan, D., Greenleaf, C., Medbery, R., & Peterson, K. (1999). Factors affecting Olympic performance: Perceptions of athletes and coaches from more and less successful teams. *The Sport Psychologist*, 13, 371-394.

Guellich, A., & Schmidtbleicher, D. (1996). MVC-induced short-term potentiation of explosive force. *New Studies in Athletics*, 11, 67-81.

Hanin, Y. L., & Stambulova, N. B. (2002). Metaphoric description of performance states: An application of the IZOF model. *The Sports Psychologist*, 16, 396-415.

Herbert, R. D., & Gabriel, M. (2002). Effects of stretching before and after exercising on muscle soreness and risk of injury: systematic review. *British Medical Journal*, 325, 468- 473.

Hollander, D. B., Durand, R. J., Trynicki, J. L., Larock, D., Castracane, V. D., Herbert, E. P., & Kraemer, R. R. (2003). RPE physiological adjustment to concentric and eccentric contractions. *Medicine and Science in Sports and Exercise*, 35, 1017-1025.

Kandel, E., & Schwartz, J. (1985). *Principles of neural science* (2nd ed.). New York: Elsevier.

Kilcullen, R. N., Mael, F. A., Goodwin, G. F., & Zazanis, M. M. (1999). Predicting U.S. Army special forces field performance. *Human Performance in Extreme Environments*, 4, 53-63.

Kreiner-Phillips, K., & Orlick, T. (1993). Winning after winning – the psychology of ongoing excellence. *The Sports Psychologist*, 7, 31-48.

Kunnemyer, J., & Schmidtbleicher, D. (1997a). Development of joint mobility by rhythmic neuromuscular stimulation. *Sportverletzung Sportschaden*, 11, 106-108.

Kunnemeyer, J., & Schmidtbleicher, D. (1997b). Modification of reactivity by rhythmic neuromuscular stimulation. *Sportverletzung Sportschaden*, 11, 39-42.

Liu, Y., Schlumberger, A., Writh, K., Schmidtbleicher, D., & Steinacker, J. M. (2003). Different effects on human skeletal myosin heavy chain isoform expression; strength vs. combination training. *Journal of Applied Physiology*, 94, 2282-2288.

Masters, K. S., & Ogles, B. M. (1998). Associative and dissociative cognitive strategies in exercise and running: 20 years later, what do we know? *The Sport Psychologist*, 12, 253-270.

McBride, J. M., Triplett-McBride, T., Davie, A., & Newton, R. U. (2002). The effect of heavy vs. light-load jump squats on the development of strength, power, and speed. *Journal of Strength and Conditioning Research*, 16, 75-82.

Nelson, A. G., & Kokkonen, J. (2001). Acute ballistic muscle stretching inhibits maximal strength performance. *Research Quarterly for Exercise and Sport*, 72, 415-419.

Orlick, T., & Partington, J. (1988). Mental links to excellence. *The Sports Psychologist*, 2, 105-130.

Palmer, C. L., Burwitz, L., Smith, N. C., & Collins, D. J. (1999). Adherence to fitness training of elite netball players: A naturalistic enquiry. *The Sport Psychologist*, 13, 313-333.

Patrick, T. D., & Hrycaiko, D. W. (1998). Effects of a mental training package on an endurance performance. *The Sport Psychologist*, 12, 283-299.

Richards, H., & Collins, D. (in press). Coping consistency in ultra endurance challenge. *Journal of Personality and Individual Differences*.

Rodgers, W. M., Blanchard, C. M., Sullivan, M. J. L., Bell, G. J., Wilson, P. M., & Gessell, J. G. (2002). The motivational implications of characteristics of exercise bouts. *Journal of Health Psychology*, 7, 73-83.

Rushall, B. S. (1977). A study of interval training. *International Swimmer*, 13, 11-13.

Salter, R. B. (1983). *Textbook of disorders and injuries of the musculoskeletal system.* Baltimore: Williams & Wilkins.

Schilling, B. K., Stone, M. H. (2001). Stretching: Acute effects on strength and power performance. *Strength and Conditioning Journal*, 22, 44-47.

Schmidtbleicher, D. (1992). Training for power events. In P. V. Komi (Ed.), *Strength and power in sport* (pp. 381-395). Oxford: Blackwell.

Schomer, H. H. (1986). Mental strategies and the perception of effort of marathon runners. *International Journal of Sport Psychology*, 17, 41-59.

Schomer, H. H. (1987). Mental strategy training program for marathon runners. *International Journal of Sport Psychology*, 2, 133-151.

Smith, D., Collins, D., & Holmes, P. (2003). Impact and mechanism of mental practice effects on strength. *International Journal of Sport Psychology*, 1, 293-306.

Sridhar, A., Duester, P-A., Becker, W. J., Coll, R., O'Brien, K. K., & Bathalon, G. (2003). Health assessment of US Army Rangers. *Military Medicine*, 168, 57-62.

Steptoe, A., Moses, J., Mathews, A., & Edwards, S. (1990). Aerobic fitness, physical activity, and psychophysiological reactions to mental tasks. *Psychophysiology*, 27, 264-274.

Stevinson, C. D., & Biddle, S. J. H. (1998). Competitive orientations in marathon running and "hitting the wall." *British Journal of Sports Medicine*, 32, 229-224.

Stevinson, C. D., & Biddle, S. J. H. (1999). Competitive strategies in running: A response to Masters and Ogles (1998). *The Sports Psychologist*, 13, 235-236.

Thacker, S. B., Gilchrist, J., Stroup, D. F., & Kinsey, C. D. (2004). The impact of stretching on sports injury risk: a systematic review of the literature. *Medicine and Science in Sports and Exercise*, 36, 371-378.

Thelwell, R. C., & Greenlees, I. A. (2001). The effects of a mental skills training package on gymnasium triathlon performance. *The Sport Psychologist*, 15, 127-141.

Tidow, G. (1990). Aspects of strength training in athletics. *New Studies in Athletics*, 5, 93-110.

Travlos, A. K., & Marisi, D. Q. (1996). Perceived exertion during physical exercise among individuals high and low in fitness. *Perceptual and Motor Skills*, 82, 419-424.

Wank, V., Frick, U., & Schmidtbleicher, D. (1998). Kinematics and electromyography of lower limb muscles in overground and treadmill running. *International Journal of Sports Medicine*, 19, 455-461.

Weinberg, B., Bruya, L., Garland, H., & Jackson, A. (1987). Goal difficulty and endurance performance: A challenge to the goal attainability assumption. *Journal of Sport Behavior*, 10, 82-92.

Weldon, S. M., & Hill, R. H. (2003). The efficacy of stretching for prevention of exercise-related injury: A systematic review of the literature. *Manual Therapy*, 8, 141-150.

Winett, R. A., Wojcik, J. R., Fox, L. D., Herbert, W. G., Blevins, J. S., & Carpinelli, R. N. (2003). Effects of low volume resistance and cardiovascular training on strength and aerobic capacity in unfit men and women: A demonstration of a threshold model. *Journal of Behavioural Medicine*, 26, 183-195.

Wrisberg, C. A., & Pein, R. L. (1990). Past running experience as a mediator of the attentional focus of male and female recreational runners. *Perceptual and Motor Skills*, 70, 427-432.

Young, W., & Elliot, S. (2001). Acute effects of static stretching, proprioceptive neuromuscular facilitation stretching, and maximum voluntary contractions on explosive force production and jumping performance. *Research Quarterly for Exercise and Sport, 72,* 273-279.

Young, W. B., McDowell, M. H., & Scarlett, B. J. (2001). Specificity of sprint and agility training methods. *Journal of Strength and Conditioning Research, 15,* 315-319.

# CHAPTER 4

# PSYCHOLOGICAL FACTORS OF TECHNICAL PREPARATION

THOMAS SCHACK AND MICHAEL BAR-ELI

When looking at the practice of sport it becomes obvious that the success of an individual athlete or a team is highly dependent on how well the essential techniques of the sport are applied and mastered. Michael Jordan always impressed people with his sure and accurately mastered shots. Dick Fosbury paved the way to entirely new dimensions in high jumping by developing a whole new run-up and jumping technique. As a result of their amazing technical diversity, Brazilian soccer teams are very successful at the top international level. In contrast, certain athletes and teams repeatedly fail as a consequence of technical problems, while others never perform to their full potential due to insufficient technique. For these reasons, technical training plays a central role in competitive sports. It can be claimed that the effect rather than the technique of a movement ought to be the decisive criterion for success in sport, and therefore for individual movement organization. One must agree with this. Hence, it is crucial for athletes to target their objectives and strive to achieve them in practice as well as in competition. Within certain limitations, the motor system of an athlete organizes itself in relation to this aim. Yet, it is usually too costly and also too risky to wait until this self-organizing system selects the optimum movement variant from the multitude of available variants on its own. Therefore, technique training serves as a means to stimulate learning processes in athletes that assist them in using their body, so that the desired effects can be accomplished in the most effective manner.

Technical preparation has hardly been the focus of scientific literature within the Anglo-American linguistic boundaries. There, the relevant topics were rather titled skill learning, skill acquisition, and skill training. However, a more precise look at different studies in this field reveals that research was usually concerned with movements of low complexity in laboratory settings. Furthermore, technique training is closely connected with the question of how body coordination can function optimally in competition and under practice conditions, and how the targeted technique is structured. As early as 1985 Newell criticized the fact that all issues in the skill acquisition domain focused on the problem of movement control (Newell, 1985). Thus, substantial questions that made up the scientific basis of technical preparation were mostly left out. Newell (1991, p. 109) states: "The study of the establishment of structure in movement and the learner's search for stable modes of coordination has not been an issue for traditional theories of motor skill acquisition." Questions such as how the structure of movement is shaped and how stable modes of coordination for the solution of movement tasks evolve represent a central theme of technical preparation. This chapter focuses on the acquirement of technologies in this field.

Intensive study of different fields of technical preparation is traditionally to be found in the scientific literature from Eastern Europe (e.g., Starosta, 1991; Sučilin, 1980) and later more frequently from Germany (e.g., Daugs, Mechling, Blischke, & Olivier, 1991; Martin, 1992; Mechling & Carl, 1992). Yet even here a closer look at the status of research reveals that accounts of technical preparation are often contradictory and not concrete, or they remain reduced to partial analyses from a biomechanical standpoint. Therefore, an anthology by Nitsch, Neumaier, de Marées, and Mester (1997) took the first steps in the direction of an interdisciplinary regeneration of this field for German-speaking researchers. As technical preparation is always connected with the optimization of motor learning processes, a host of other prominent research topics established in areas of sport psychology are relevant, in addition to the formerly mentioned central field of technical preparation. These include, for example, feedback research (Magill, 2001; Salmoni, Schmidt, & Walter, 1984; Wulf, 1994; Wulf, Schmidt, & Deubel, 1993), the acquisition of learning strategies (e.g., Lidor, Tennant, & Singer, 1996; Singer, 1988; Singer, Lidor, & Cauraugh, 1993), the direction of attention during motor learning (Wulf & Prinz, 2001), and the establishment of routines (Schack, 1997; Schack, Whitmarsh, Pike, & Redden, 2005). However, these more psychologically-oriented approaches have not yet been systematically applied to technique training.

In coaching practice, technical preparation plays an important role. Therefore, interdisciplinary models which provide concrete starting-points for the improvement of techniques are substantial for practical work. Coaches or practical sport psychologists would like to know how to stimulate stable modes of coordination in the athlete, how to stabilize proper techniques, and how to change previously acquired, inefficient movement patterns during training. All of these questions cannot be answered merely through biomechanical analyses or through detailed movement observations. In this context, relevant methods are rather those which comprehend and illuminate the cognitive-coordinative background of technique execution. This means that previous works regarding technique training have to be complemented through the addition of practice-relevant models and usable technologies and methods. This chapter will provide a contribution to this issue.

Thus, regarding the next section "Theoretical background of technical preparation," several steps have to be taken. After an initial clarification of terms regarding the field of technical preparation, model imageries concerning the construction of complex movements have to be created. It is important that these model imageries clarify at which levels of movement technique training starts and which role psychological factors play. After all, the aim is to provide the option to relate the formerly mentioned sport-psychological approaches – for instance, the establishment of learning strategies – through such a model. A further step will introduce current research methods which are particularly applied to the shaping of stable coordination modes, and thus become crucial for a central area of technical preparation. On this basis, an integrative perspective of technical preparation can be developed. This perspective shows how psychological factors are integrated into technical preparation. The section "Theoretical background of technical preparation" concludes with a display of a variety of starting points for the manipulation and optimization of psychological factors in technical preparation.

## THEORETICAL BACKGROUND OF TECHNICAL PREPARATION

### TECHNICAL PREPARATION – DEFINITIONAL ISSUES

All technical achievement is built on diverse factors. In addition to psychological factors, further components are important. In Figure 1, technical performance is divided into three substantial basic components: mental control, coordination, and physiological basis. Respective factors are assigned to each of these basic components. In this sense, physiological, coordinative, and psychological factors are of primary importance for technical performance.

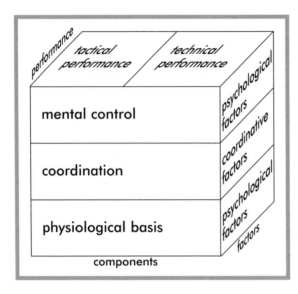

**Figure 1**
Decisive factors for technical performance.

Each of these basic components can be learned. This means that diverse factors can be developed. However, through this means of presentation (see Figure 1) it also becomes obvious that physiological, coordinative, and psychological factors cannot be discussed as completely separate issues, but that these factors interact in the bounds of technical and tactical performance. If, for example, Michael Jordan performs an optimal shot, these different factors have interacted in an effective fashion. Therefore, not only are single factors developed in the bounds of technical preparation, but their interaction is also optimized.

Although biomechanical analyses describe how a technique is performed, they do not provide valid claims about what an athletic technique is. Similarly, a comparison and separation of cognitive, physiological, and other components of technique organization doesn't seem helpful. After all, various factors interact during the execution of a technique (see Figure 1). Due to these and other concerns, we approach our definitions of athletic techniques coming from the movement task that is to be solved. Athletic techniques are optimum solutions for movement tasks. Accordingly, athletic action is something like the process of problem-solving, during which techniques are applied to achieve movement aims (see Bernstein, 1947, 1967, 1988, 1996a; Schack, 2002; 2004b). Thus, based on these works, it can be formulated that athletic technique represents a coordinative structure which is suitable for solving a concrete movement task. Hence, from a functional perspective, athletic techniques are nothing but approved ways for the achievement of movement aims under defined conditions. The conditions are strongly determined through the match- and competition-system, the environment, and through the athlete's individual disposition (see Newell, 1985; Nitsch, 1985).

Usually there is a technique model or a guiding technical imagery for athletic techniques. Such technique models (target techniques) can be found in textbooks, curriculums, and usually also in the minds of athletes and coaches. Technique models include the best solutions for movement tasks according to the current standards of knowledge. Yet one has to reason that an "ideal technique" can neither be achieved nor scientifically described (see Nitsch & Neumaier, 1997). The history of sport has shown that there have always been totally unanticipated new solutions for existing movement tasks (see, for example, the Fosbury Flop; Bar-Eli et al., 2006; Goldenberg et al., 2004). Therefore, established technique models (target techniques) are only useful as long as they help the athlete achieve an optimum coordinative structure for solving movement tasks. Hence, we propose to functionally incorporate target techniques into technique training, but not to treat them as normative factors in the training process.

What, in fact, are the functions of technique training? The essential function of technical preparation is to acquire motor skills and skill elements, to connect them structurally, and to apply them in solving a specific movement task. Further functions of technical preparation are to enable the variegation of learned techniques in a situation-appropriate manner, and to execute them in a stable fashion. The automation of technical processes is often referred to as another goal of technique training (see Martin, Carl, & Lehnertz, 1991; Mechling, 1988; Neumaier, 1997). Technical preparation is a process of several temporal-functional phases. Since techniques emerge gradually, the execution of a technique should improve with each phase in relation to the previous one. Bernstein (1947, 1996 a, b) has said that such motor learning is actually something like "repeating without a repetition." This means that technical preparation represents neither a repetition of the same motion sequence nor a facilitation of a particular technique. Technical preparation is rather a process, in which composition and structure of a movement develop. For this reason, technical preparation repeats the solution of the movement task in different variations and different stages, and the utilized means (motion elements) are gradually modified and improved (see Bernstein, 1996a). The next section will provide a concrete understanding of the functioning and construction of complex movement techniques.

For the acquisition and storage of complex movements, various usages of memory are important (Schmidt & Lee, 2005; Singer, 1980). During technical preparation, the memory serves the function of a referential system. Thus, learning is linked to the correction of memory structures and to the modification of neuronal structures (Jeannerod, 2004). In current studies, it became obvious that the structure of movement representations systematically changes during technique training (Schack, 2003b, 2004a, b). While a high variation and openness of memory structures is to be found in the initial phases, movement representations approach a temporally and spatially more ordered structure in advanced phases of technical preparation. Thus, an increasing amount of order can occur in movement memory. This order meets the requirements concerning movement execution. The cognitive reference structure in the memory increasingly resembles the movement structure of an optimally executed technique. Current neurophysiological studies add to these reflections and research results in a specific manner (Georgopoulos, 2002; Hoffmann, Stoecker, & Kunde, 2004; Jeannerod, 1997; 2004; Koch, Keller, & Prinz, 2004; Schack, 2004a, b). Overall, this provides empirical evidence for the claim that in the bounds of technique training, a structure of the movement and a structure in the memory

| First Phase | Second Phase | Third Pase | Fourth Phase |
|---|---|---|---|
| • Learning of movement elements<br>• Basic-Structure-Learning | • Automation<br>• Basic-Structure-Learning | • Variable Adaptation<br>• Automation<br>• Basic-Structure-Stabilization | • Development of technical styles and technique variation<br>• Variable Adaptation<br>• Automation<br>• Basic-Structure-Stabilization |

**Figure 2** The four phases of technique training.

are gradually established. Therefore, it is reasonable to think about phases of technique training.

Figure 2 provides a distinction of the four phases of technique training. The first phase is about the acquisition of the basic structure of a technique. Therefore, it is to some extent necessary to learn and practice single elements of motion. Besides basic structure learning, the second phase of technical preparation is predominantly concerned with automation of motion sequences. For this reason, attention capacities become more available and applicable for differential learning strategies (see Lidor, Tennant, & Singer, 1996). In the third phase, the focus lies with the stabilization of the technique and its variable application. For the technique to be applicable under various situational conditions, the conditions are purposefully variegated in this phase of training. For instance, in volleyball training, different indoor facilities and different balls are used, and different levels of illumination and artificial soundscapes are produced and incorporated into practice. In the fourth phase of technical preparation, the previous training phases can be extended through the development of technique styles. Thus, on the basis of secure and variable use of techniques, certain modifications of these techniques can be developed. Completely new and supplemental technical solutions are imaginable as well. If novel technical solutions are now sought for the same movement problem, technique training for the new technique starts over with the first phase. As an example, in the 1980s the Eastern Germans aimed at new technical solutions for jumping techniques on the vaulting horse, based on the variable mastery of traditional jumping techniques. Among other things, these new techniques already included the execution of somersaults in the first phase of the jump. Due to the high load on the athlete who had to land on the vaulting horse and depart from it, these techniques did not win recognition (see Krug, 2004).

However, the sequence of technique training must not be imagined as a one-way street. It is often necessary to take a step back and, for instance, return from basic-structure stabilization to basic-structure learning. This becomes particularly important when technical flaws have crept in.

In response to these phases of training one can distinguish among three different forms of technique training: (1) technique acquisition training (phases 1 and 2); (2) technique application training (phases 3 and 4); and (3) technical supplementary training (see Martin, 1991). Technique acquisition training aims at the basic structure of the technique. In contrast, technical application training is oriented towards stabilization and variable application of the technique. In this stage of training, situation-appropriate anticipations play an increased role. Accordingly, the technique acquired in technique acquisition training is increasingly incorporated into match situations and tested therein. These newly-learned techniques are subsequently connected to already existing techniques. For example, new offensive techniques in volleyball can be acquired with no connection to concrete match situations (technique acquisition training). Yet technique application training is concerned with the application of these techniques in concrete match situations, their variable application – depending on actions taken by one's own team and the opposite side, and their combination with existing techniques. For example, anticipatory capacities, which play only a subordinate role during technique application training, become necessary for this aim. In technical supplementary training, coordinative abilities (such as the ability to rhythmic organization in dance and gymnastics), which are essential for the execution of movement training, can be trained. Moreover, forms of mental training such as imagery training must be counted towards this kind of training (see chapter 6 in this book), as well as the application of learning- and attention-strategies (Singer, 1985; Singer, Lidor, & Cauraugh, 1993, 1994; Wulf & Prinz, 2001), or the development of routines (Schack et al., 2005). Psychological factors are decisive in all three forms of technical training. To be able to mark the function of these psychological factors regarding the establishment and maintenance of technical performance more precisely, the construction of movement techniques will be discussed in the next section.

## THE CONSTRUCTION OF MOVEMENT TECHNIQUES

In the last section it became obvious that movement techniques are not "ground in," but rather systematically built up within the bounds of technique training. This assumption is based on works discussing neurophysiological stages of movement organization (Bernstein, 1947; 1996a, b; Gurfinkel & Cordo, 2002; Jeannerod, 1995). Another group of research was able to show that cognitive-perceptual structures play a remarkable role in motor learning (e.g., Mechsner, Kerzel, Knoblich, & Prinz, 2001; Prinz, 1997; Schack, 2002, 2003b; Schmidt & Lee, 1998; Singer, 1980; see also Schack & Tenenbaum, 2004a, b). With reference to these works, the construction of movements will be further clarified at this point, especially regarding psychological factors. For this purpose, we will deal mainly with the question of how structural components of psychology are integrated into the construction of techniques, and which functional role they play in the maintenance of technical performance.

As known from practice and as described by Eastern (Bernstein, 1947; Luria, 1992; Vygotsky, 1992, orig. 1929) and Western (Ach, 1921; Rosenbaum, 1985; Singer, 1980) scientists, one major property of complex movements is their volitional character. Human volition (or will) can be analyzed functionally and broken down into its main components. From the functional perspective taken here, we shall call this ability (volition) *mental control*. One major functional component of mental control is the encoding of the intended action goal. Such a coding is needed before an action goal can adopt the function of a cognitive benchmark for the further process. This intention-related coding is followed by the generation of a *mental model of the future* to which all control and monitoring processes can be related. Strategies like inner speech strategies (Schack, 1997), learning strategies (e.g., Singer, 1985; Singer, Lidor, & Cauraugh, 1993, 1994), and attentional strategies (Wulf & Prinz, 2001) are a further functional component of mental control. These are applied particularly when difficulties emerge in action performance. They are a means of stabilizing activities leading toward the goal. Hence, they are important for the development and maintenance of movement techniques. This is the reason why such strategies have to be developed in the bounds of technical (supplementary) training. If we provisionally locate these functional components of voluntary movement regulation on a *level of mental control*, we still have to ask in what form the knowledge is integrated into behavior control. This is because knowledge plays a central role in storing the movement structure. The development and stabilization of functional coordination structures are regarded as the central task of technical acquisition and technical application training. These stable coordination modes utilize memory structures. The decisive question is how technique-related memory structures are integrated into the whole system, how they can be volitively addressed, and which role they play in the automatization of technical processes.

From our perspective, conscious mental functions can be assumed to emerge on the basis of elementary functions. Hence, whereas elementary functions (e.g., automated processes, reflexes) are influenced directly by stimulus constellations, mental control functions are guided intentionally – the self regulates them. This points to the *vertical dimension of cognitive control*. It is assumed that the functional construction of actions is based on a reciprocal assignment of performance-oriented regulation levels and representational levels (see Table 1). These levels differ according to their central tasks on the regulation and representation levels. Each level is assumed to be functionally autonomous.

*Table 1* Levels of Movement Techniques

| Code | Level | Main function | Subfunction | Means |
|------|-------|---------------|-------------|-------|
| IV | Mental control | Regulation | Volitional initiation control strategies | Symbols; strategies |
| III | Mental representation | Representation | Effect-oriented adjustment | Basic-action concepts |
| II | Sensorimotor representation | Representation | Spatial-temporal adjustment | Perceptual effect-representations |
| I | Sensorimotor control | Regulation | Automation | Functional systems; basic reflexes |

The function of the *mental control level* (IV) has already been sketched for voluntary movement regulation and the coding or the anticipated outcome of movement. The level of mental representations (III) predominantly forms a cognitive benchmark for the mental control level (IV). It is organized conceptually and is responsible for transferring the anticipated action outcome into a model of the movement structure it requires. Because an action is "no chain of details, but a structure subdivided into details" (Bernstein, 1988, p. 27, translated), movement organization has to possess a working model of this structure. The corresponding abilities for using movement representations have been acquired stepwise during technical preparation. These movement representations hold the knowledge that relates directly to performance. However, the model also clearly reveals that these representations are functionally embedded in further levels and components of action organization. Therefore, the functioning of the lower levels (I and II) will also be sketched. The *level of sensorimotor control* is linked directly to the environment. In contrast to the level of mental control (IV), which, as explained above, is *induced intentionally*, the level of sensorimotor control (I) is *induced perceptually*. This can be illustrated in studies of patients whose range of movement is restricted through injury or illness (see, e.g., Leontjev & Zaporoshets, 1960; van der Weel, van der Meer, & Lee, 1991). Leontjev and Zaporoshets studied patients whose elbow and shoulder movements were limited because of peripheral nerve injuries. They found that the ability to move the dominant arm differed as a function of the concrete feedback obtained from the environment. For example, these patients could move their arm further when their eyes were open than when their eyes were closed. Their range improved even further when they had to touch a point on a screen. However, their range was greatest when they had to grasp an object. This study reveals vividly that the execution of movements can only be considered in the context of the intended sensory effect. Several studies concerned with the focus of attention in motor learning (e.g., Maddox, Wulf, & Wright, 1999; Wulf, Lauterbach, & Tool, 1999; Wulf & Weigelt, 1997) point in a similar direction.

The reason why a level of sensorimotor representation is necessary in this context is obvious. It can be assumed that this is where, among others, the modality-specific information representing the effect of the particular movement is stored. As we know from practice the relevant modalities change as a function of the phase of technical preparation and as a function of the concrete task. Representations involving the kinesthetic modality should also be assigned to this level. Such representations play an important role in the development and improvement of the feeling for movement, especially for water, balls, or a ski. This level involves the representation of perceptual patterns of exteroceptive and proprioceptive effects that result from the structure of the particular movement and refer back to the goal of the action. Empirical evidence for such a perspective can be found particularly in recent studies on bimanual coordination (Mechsner, Kerzel, Knoblich, & Prinz, 2001) and in experimental studies on complex movements (Schack, 2002, 2003a; Schack & Mechsner, in press).

As the stage of mental representations plays a special role in the development of stable coordination modes in technical preparation, cognitive units of such representations shall now be examined more closely. The task of movement concepts is to classify movement stages that lead to certain effects, and thus it lies in the spatiotemporal control of movements. Drawing on experimental studies, these concepts have been labeled *basic action concepts* (BACs; see Schack, 2002). BACs are cognitive compilations of movements based on their shared functions in the attainment of action goals. They refer to perception-linked invariance properties of movements. Their characteristic set of features results from the perceptive and functional properties of movement effects. In this way, they ultimately serve to maximize the control of actions with the lowest possible cognitive and energetic effort.

In every technique a variety of submovements have become available for attaining intended action effects, and these can also vary in, for example, joint amplitudes. For instance, when learning to write, children solve the problem of equivalent submovements in a very simple way. They "freeze" their distal joints and thereby reduce the amount of equivalent movements and, finally, the degrees of freedom of the entire system (see Heuer, 1994). One can observe similar strategies in adults when forced to write with the non-dominant hand (Newell & van Emmerik, 1989). The set of possible movements for attaining the goal is initially restricted to prevent control demands from being too high. Once cognitive units have been formed to control the movement, further, more complex, but nonetheless equivalent movements are permitted—the breadth of the concept is extended step by step. Accordingly, movements are functionally equivalent when one can substitute one for the other within the context of a behavior, without this threatening the behavioral goal. This is the case, for example, in volleyball, when the movement concept "extending leg" summarizes all movements that complete a take-off and prepare the hit. However, the relevant movements vary as a function of the player's position on the court, the positions of the opponents, and the current course of play. Hence, the movement concept "extending leg" summarizes all movements that *functionally* fulfill the same purpose when generating the hit. See additional examples concerning BACs in the following sections.

As we know from practice and from special studies, improvement in the domain of technical preparation is accompanied by order formation. In general, movement representations improve when problem-solving-related classifications (concepts) are formed. Hence, one can judge the technique-related order formation of movement knowledge. Such structures in action knowledge can be assessed and judged with the help of specific methods.

## New Methods for Measuring Psychological Factors in Technical Preparation

There are several psychological training practices which can be utilized in supplementary training (e.g., see chapter 6 in this book). However, during the acquisition and stabilization of coordination modes in technical acquisition, psychological factors usually receive little attention. Nevertheless, even in these fields, a functional link of motor learning and the development of suitable attentional and learning strategies (e.g., see Lidor et al., 1996; Wulf & Prinz, 2001) would be recommended. From our perspective, a substantial, previously unused resource lies in the field of psychological factors, which are directly involved in the construction of coordination modes of an athletic technique. If athletic techniques with a functional relation build up, stabilize, and change according to these memory structures, the key to motor learning processes in technical preparation is located right at this point. For instance, based on corresponding methods, the causes for incorrect techniques could be detected in memory scripts. Concrete consequences for further development of performance, and therefore for the next step of technical preparation, could be derived from such memory scripts.

When studying such kinds of movement knowledge in technical preparation, it is important to know their properties. One major property of knowledge in general and movement (tacit) knowledge in particular is that the structures of this action knowledge cannot be explicated directly. However, many methodological approaches to ascertaining such knowledge structures disregard this limitation. For example, expert research often studies action knowledge with survey methods such as interviews and questionnaires. However, this ignores the fact that a major part of movement knowledge cannot be verbalized.

These and other problems with existing procedures led us to develop our own specific method. In line with the assumptions on the structure and dimensioning (feature assignment) of movement knowledge formulated here, this method is conceived as a structure-dimensional analysis-movement (SDA-M) of mental representations in movement organization. The SDA-M is a procedure that attempts to present the structure-dimensional relations of conceptually ordered knowledge psychometrically, for both single cases and groups (Lander, 1991; Schack, 2002). The following steps are necessary to assess the structure-dimensional relations between the BACs of a movement representation. The SDA method proceeds in four steps:

1. As with the methods discussed above, an SDA of a concept system initially seeks to gain information on the distance between selected representation units (concepts) that are relevant for a problem-solving domain. Because it can be assumed that the structure of movement representations can only be explicated to a limited extent, this is done with a special splitting technique. This is based on the selection and presentation of a group of concepts that are a valid component of that set of concepts that is absolutely necessary for a certain problem-solving or working domain. As in the methods mentioned above, this group of concepts is initially obtained through work analysis, survey, or experiment. This can be illustrated with an example of research in tennis, especially the tennis serve (see, also, the following sections). In a preparatory step, we characterised the task-adequate biomechanical organisation of the tennis serve and established a plausible and workable set of basic action concepts in collaboration with non-players, athletes of different levels, and coaches. The tennis serve consists of three distinct phases, each of which fulfils distinct biomechanical demands. First, in the pre-activation phase, the body and ball are put in position and tension energy is provided in preparation of the strike. The following BACs were identified: (1) ball throw, (2) forward movement of the pelvis, (3) bending the knees, and (4) bending the elbow. Second, in the strike phase, energy is conveyed to the ball. The following BACs were identified: (5) frontal upper body rotation, (6) racket acceleration, (7) whole body stretch motion, and (8) hitting point. Third, in the final swing phase the body is prevented from falling and the racket movement is decelerated after the strike. The following BACs have been identified: (9) wrist flap, (10) forward bending of the body, and (11) racket follow-through.

The experimental procedure took the N elements (in this case, 11) from a given set of concepts and selected one as an anchor to which the other N - 1 elements had to be assigned or not assigned according to an individually given similarity criterion. This procedure (while retaining the original anchor) was repeated with each new positive or negative subset until either only indivisible sets with one object remained, or an individually selected break-off criterion was attained at which the set should not be broken down further.

As each concept took the position of anchor once, we obtained a total of N (11) decision trees whose nodes contained the subsets produced and whose edges had a negative or positive sign, depending on whether the elements were assigned or not assigned to the anchor concept. A measure of the distance between the successively assigned or not assigned elements and the anchor concept (on an interval scale level) was obtained (see Schack, 2001).

2. The structured relations between the N concepts were obtained by compiling a distance matrix through the scaling procedure presented above and subjecting it to a hierarchic cluster analysis.

3. The dimensioning of the set of concepts was performed with factor analysis and a special cluster-oriented rotation procedure. This factor analysis delivered the features (factors) and their weights (factor loadings) according to which the cluster formation (structuring) proceeded in each single case.

4. As cluster solutions could differ interindividually (as a function of expertise) and intraindividually (as a function of learning), it was necessary to subject them to an invariance analysis. This was based on a specially defined structural invariance measure $\lambda$ (Lander & Lange, 1992; Schack, 2001, 2002). When two structures possessed a higher value than the invariance measure $\lambda_0 = .68$, they were held to be invariant.

We would like to expand on this method and go into further detail using the following tennis study. The expert group consisted of eleven males (mean age = 24 ± 3.7 years) who were players in upper German leagues, and ranked between places 15 and 500 in the German men's rankings. The low level group consisted of eleven males (mean age = 26 ± 4.8 years) who were players in lower German leagues (district leagues), without being listed in the German men's rankings. For preparation, the participants were made familiar with the above BACs by way of pictures with a verbal BAC name as a printed heading. During the entire experiment, these pictures were continuously positioned in front of the respective participant. In order to determine subjective distances between the BACs, the participants performed the following split procedure, as the first step of SDA-M. On a computer screen, one selected BAC was continuously presented as an anchoring unit in red-colored written language. In addition, the rest of the BACs were presented in yellow-colored written language, as a randomly ordered list. The participant judged for each of these yellow-colored additional BACs, whether they were "functionally related while performing the movement" to the anchoring red-colored BAC or not. In this way two subsets were created which were submitted to the same procedure, and so on, until the referee decided not to do any further splits. The results of the hierarchical cluster analysis are shown in Figures 3a and 3b.

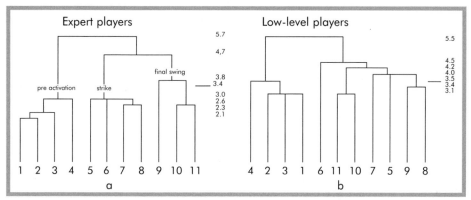

**Figure 3** Dendrograms for the subjective distances of Basic Action Concepts (BACs), resulting from the hierarchical cluster analysis of the means of the three groups, namely experts, low level players, and non-players. [The chosen significance level in all analyses was always p = .05. On the right side of each dendrogram is a scale displaying the extent of the distances between the single BACs in the subjects' long-term memory, measured in Euclidean distances. The smaller the numbers are, the smaller are the distances of the BACs in long-term memory.]

In experts, the cognitive structure comes close to the functional structure of the tennis serve. The three functional phases, namely the pre-activation phase, the strike phase, and the final swing phase, are clearly separated in the dendrograms, in the form of tree-like structured clusters. In experts (Figure 3a), the BACs seem to be grouped in memory according to generic terms which conform to the solution of special movement problems. The results obtained for the low level group look rather different (see Figure 3b). Here, the clustering of the BACs mirrors less well the biomechanically defined phases. In addition, the BACs are less clearly grouped, with no close neighbourhoods, and the partial clusters are usually below the chosen significance level. In individual low level players, significantly separated sub-clusters can also be seen, though not so frequently and clearly as in experts. The biomechanically defined phases, though regularly shining through, are not so properly and uniformly matched. Having gained such information about memory structures, the coach gets a better idea about how to adjust his or her instructions to the individual athlete.

Special computer programs were developed to apply this method so that such experiments could be carried out within a reasonable time (10-15 min; the programs are available from the first author on request). It is possible to measure such structures in athletes directly in the training process with the help of simple laptop computers. On the basis of these and other methods (Schack, 2002), it is possible to economically determine movement knowledge in technical preparation, and to compare persons or groups in terms of the structure of their knowledge. At the same time, such an experimental diagnosis delivers important information for deriving intervention procedures designed to improve technical performance (Blaser, Stucke, Narciss, & Körndle, 2000; Schack, 2002; Schack & Heinen, 2000).

Towards an Integrative Perspective in Technical Preparation

It is already apparent in the comments concerning definitional issues of technical preparation that technical preparation cannot be reduced to the biomechanical analysis of technical output in training or competition. A model description of the construction of movement techniques was set in contrast to this incomplete theoretical idea of technical preparation. This model description shows how different components and levels of movement functionally interact to achieve a particular output. Accordingly, technique training is about the integration and the structuring of input-, throughput-, and output-modules (components) across different levels. These components, for instance, organize anticipation, perception, representation, and motor execution. Thus, depending on the level of expertise and degree of automation, technique training should begin at precisely defined levels and representation structures. Starting with such a model, an integrative perspective of technical preparation is indicated. This perspective is based on a connection of biomechanical accesses to the analysis of a movement task, of kinematic analyses, and the measurement and manipulation of psychological factors in technique training (Schack, 2003b).

According to this perspective, biomechanical movement analysis occurs as one step. This functional movement analysis is meant to more exactly characterize the movement task. At this point the movement is split up into different phases. These phases are more precisely defined regarding their function in the motion sequence, and subdivided into different functional phases (Göhner, 1979; Leuchte, 2004; Rieling, Leirich, & Hess, 1967; Schack, 2004b). Therein, the arrangement of the functional phases is organized according to the movement problems that are to be solved. Rieling et al. (1967), for example, divided the movement into an initial phase, a bridge phase, a main phase, and a final phase (see Leuchte, 2004). The application of this procedure is illustrated using the "end over" in sailing/surfing. Besides this functional movement analysis, kinematic analyses of the actual movement representation are also essential for technical preparation (see the comments on apparatus gymnastics, Schack, 2003b).

As the production of stable and optimal coordination modes represents a central goal of technique training, these biomechanical analyses of the structure of a technique constitute a substantial center of reference for the optimization of psychological and coordinative factors in technical preparation. However, besides these biomechanical analyses, experimental analyses regarding the structure of technique representations are also of central importance (see the previous paragraph). Based on the model imagery concerning the construction of movement techniques, movements are controlled through such representations (level of mental representation). An equally meaningful role must, for example, be attributed to the registration and optimization of strategies for voluntary motor control (such as attention strategies) on the level of mental control. Hence, technical preparation should be based on a perspective which integrates analyses and technologies from different disciplines. The presented model concerning the construction of movement techniques constitutes the crucial pattern for the integration of such information.

## STARTING POINTS FOR MENTAL FORMS OF TECHNICAL PREPARATION

With reference to the model presented to illustrate the construction of movement techniques, mental training designs can be systematically assigned to technical preparation as well. Starting from the stage of mental control, all forms of mental training that are concerned with voluntary strategies are relevant. This includes strategies which aim at an optimization of thoughts during performance (Lidor, Tennant, & Singer, 1996; Singer, 1985, 1988; Singer et al., 1993, 1994), those directed at focusing attention (Abernethy, 1993; Wulf & Prinz, 2001), or those strategies that generally target an optimization of self-management (Meichenbaum, 1979; Schack, 1997). Singer (1985), for instance, developed a specific five-step approach meant to optimize learning processes on different levels of expertise. These five steps deal with reading, imaging, focusing, executing, and evaluating movement techniques. This approach combines awareness- and non-awareness-strategies. Depending on the level of expertise, awareness is allocated to each of these five steps to a different extent, the non-awareness strategy being prioritized. Such techniques are crucial for the acquisition and the stabilization of coordination modes. They become particularly relevant if a technique has previously been acquired, and thus are especially important in technical application training and technical supplementary training.

The establishment of routines (Schack et al., 2005) represents a form of training that should be learned within the bounds of technical supplementary training, but becomes eminently important for technical application training – and particularly for competition – at higher levels of expertise. Routines play a critical role in athletes' preparation for competition and have been shown to be effective pre-competition, during the competition, and post-competition (Boutcher, 1990; Cohn, 1990; Schack, 1997). Most coaches and athletes recognize the value of competitive routines, but they are often unaware of the importance of routines in training. Athletes who develop routines for all aspects of their athletic experience, and adapt them to the specific settings and situations in which they perform, give themselves the best chance of success. Routines form the physical, psychological, and environmental foundation in which technical skills, physical conditioning, and mental skills can be optimally developed in training and used in competition. Between-performance (for sports that involve a series of short performances, such as tennis, golf, and baseball) enable athletes to maintain a high level of performance consistency throughout a competition. Post-competition routines allow athletes to evaluate their performances, learn important lessons from the competition, and use that information to prepare for future training and competitions. When routines are acquired, the levels of mental control and mental representations are heavily involved. In the subsequent training process, the levels of sensorimotor control and sensorimotor representations are increasingly involved before these two levels finally take complete control in the automation stage.

In acquisition and application of stable coordination modes in technical performance, mental representation plays a central role. On this level, the structure of a movement is constituted beyond all learning stages (see Figure 2). Imagery training strongly builds on this level. Movement imageries are formed in structural relation with movement representations in long-term memory (see Schack, 2002). Therefore, it is useful to utilize information about the structure of the movement representation in long-term memory if the goal is an individualized imagery training. For this purpose, we have developed a specific Mental Training based on Mental Representation (MTMR) (Schack & Heinen, 2000).

Furthermore, information about the structure of movement representations is of central importance regarding the acquisition of suitable modes of coordination as well as their stabilization. The structure of movement representations constitutes a functional component of technical performance and, in addition, is meaningful for coach-athlete interactions in technical preparation. As we know from numerous studies, coaches (as experts) and athletes (beginners) often do not use the same information at a specific stage of motor learning of an athlete, namely, the athlete develops an "intuitive" feeling for the water, a "feeling for movement," etc., and the originally applied instructions are no longer valid for the cognitive structure of the learning athlete. Such divergences within the coach-athlete interaction represent a specific reason to obtain a closer insight into the construction and change of cognitive structures in technical preparation and technical performance. As to this domain, examples are provided in the two following sections. Therein, it becomes apparent how technical preparation can be pursued from an integrative perspective.

## INDIVIDUAL SPORTS

### SPECIAL ASPECTS/INTRODUCTION

In individual sports, technical preparation plays an essential role in the training process as well as in competition. In comparison with team sports, the relevance of tactical and social factors within the team is limited at first. Oftentimes, especially in individual sports, conceptions of ideal technique executions (desired values) exist. However, in areas of higher performance, such desired conceptions are only of limited value. For this reason the aim is to display how starting points for an individualized technique training can be derived using the presented methods. Hereto, movements were selected from sailing-surfing and gymnastics. The comparison of these two sports is quite interesting. While well-known techniques have existed in gymnastics for several decades, elite athletes in sailing-surfing sometimes depend on the creation of completely new movement techniques.

### EXTREME SPORTS: THE FRONT-LOOP IN WINDSURFING

Technically sophisticated and novel techniques, for example rotational movements in windsurfing, have proven to be particularly interesting for technical preparation. Until 1986, the possibility of performing an end over in windsurfing (see Figure 4) was only speculated upon. Up to that time, it hadn't been clear how the impulse for forward rotation could be generated out of an ongoing forward motion. In 1985, Cantagalli became the first to perform a forward rotation (which he called a "Cheese Roll") in international competition. This evoked a boom of experimentation with highly complex movement actions in many

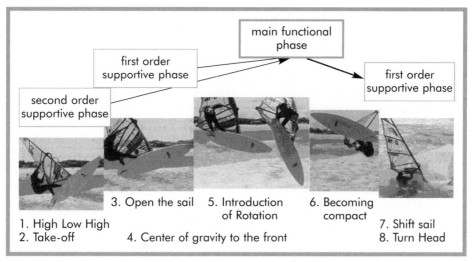

**Figure 4** Movement phases of the front-loop in windsurfing. [The task-related Basic Action Concepts (BACs) are allocated to the respective phases. In the take-off phase, the front-loop can hardly be distinguished from a regular jump. The surfer waits until the angular point of the slope angle and then abruptly pushes the sail's pressure point forward-down. Robby Nash entitled this time lag before the introduction of the front-loop as the "Moment of shock for the spectator" (see Smidt, 1995).]

people interested in the sport. Mark Angulo turned this sideways-rotation into the spectacular front-loop (end over) with the characteristic rotation over the mast top (see Figure 4).

The front-loop represents a mixture of a rotation around the horizontal axis and a rotation around the longitudinal axis. We are dealing with a movement that represents a technical challenge for both highly-skilled hobby-windsurfers and competitive windsurfing professionals. This evaluation is supported by the fact that there are windsurfers with high technical abilities who are unable to perform jumps involving forward rotations. For the execution of this forward rotation, the following subproblems of the movement task have to be solved:

1. The athlete has to execute a sufficiently high jump from the water surface (optimally 5-8 m, but at least as high as the mast) (energizing problem).

2. At the peak of the jump, the athlete has to introduce the rotation. The impulse starts at the sail's pressure point, which, after take-off from the water surface, is located above the barycenter of the complete system. At this point, an enormous mass moment of inertia has to be overcome (impulse-introduction problem).

3. During the forward rotation, the windsurfing board system has to be stabilized (stabilization problem).

4. During the entire movement, numerous orientation problems resulting from the rotation have to be solved. For example, a permanent orientation regarding the situation in space is necessary for initiation, stabilization, and completion of the rotational movement. The water, the sail system, and the horizon represent bench marks in this context (orientation problem).

Various movement phases can be distinguished in biomechanical terms. These movement phases can be subdivided into main phase and supportive phases. This subdivision becomes apparent in Figure 4.

BACs were ascertained for the presented functional phases, which contained substantial means to the solution of the movement tasks and the connected movement problems. To permit an allocation to the biomechanically (functionally) determined movement phases, these BACs are already entered in this figure. The concepts relevant for the movement were gained in a process involving several stages. First, a group of athletes consisting of experts ($n = 8$) and beginners ($n = 7$) gave spontaneous descriptions of the movement (front-loop in windsurfing). Subsequently, the subjects were interviewed individually regarding the BACs from their point of view. At this point, it became apparent that BACs were not only verbally labeled, but could also be demonstrated as a specific movement pattern (see Figure 5). Following an active execution of the movement, the formerly gained results were complemented – respectively corrected – using video-based self-confrontation. Later, complementing allocation experiments were conducted (Schack, 2002).

**Figure 5** A windsurfing-expert illustrates a Basic Action Concept (BAC) for the realization of the front-loop.

The acquired BACs for the frontal loop are: (1) high-low-high, (2) take-off, (3) opening the sail, (4) moving center of gravity to the front, (5) introduction of rotation, (6) becoming compact, (7) shifting the sail, and (8) turning the head.

A total number of 40 test subjects (experts and novices) participated in a special study for the preparation of new forms of technical preparation: $n = 20$ experts (all male); mean age = 28.8 years; engaged in windsurfing for 15.8 years on average; execution of *front-loop* on average for 9.4. This group of people consisted of American, French, and German athletes who, at that point, were counted among the world elite in windsurfing. A number of these athletes rank among the pioneers of windsurfing and have been involved in the movement from its beginning. All athletes were participants in international competition (World Cup, Grand Prix, etc.) and professional windsurfers. They were able to perform the front-loop reliably and variably in a competitive setting (some as a double frontal loop). They trained about 30 weeks annually. The fixation of expert status was oriented according to an ability status of at least 7 years duration of front-loop execution on a competitive level.

In the same manner, the group of novices ($n = 20$, 18 males, 2 females; mean age = 22 years; engaged in windsurfing for 8.2 years on average; front-loop on average for 1.6 years) consisted predominantly of German and American athletes. These athletes trained approximately 23 weeks annually. They participated in national and international competitions, yet without rankings worthy of being mentioned and without being able to perform the front-loop under competitive circumstances. Overall, the (potential) course of development for this group was comparable to the expert group. Hence, we are talking about persons who have the capability to reach the level of experts, but haven't gotten there yet. For the underlying study it was mainly of interest that the novices, as compared to the experts, mastered the technical execution of the front-loop far less reliably and variably. The sovereign execution of the movement (according to expert testimony) greatly depends on the experience in windsurfing and on the repeated practical performance of the movement under various conditions. The minimum condition for acceptance into the novice-group was that the subjects had performed that front-loop at least twice (according to their own testimony).

The results of this study are illustrated in the following figures. For this illustration, a is constantly set at 5%; this equals a $d_{krit}$ value of 3.51.

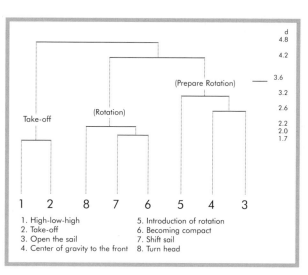

**Figure 6**
Results of the hierarchical cluster analysis of Basic Action Concepts (BACs) of the front-loop in the expert group. [The lower the value of an interconnection between the study units (see the Euclidian distance scale on the right), the lower the distance of the concepts (n = 20; α = 5 %; $d_{krit}$ = 3.51).]

Figure 6 displays the group-structure of the experts (n = 20) as the result of cluster analysis in the form of a dendrogram and contends the factor matrix arranged according to clusters.

Cluster analysis provides three clusters. The ascertained structures of mental movement representation in the expert group show a remarkable affinity to the biomechanical functional structure of the movement. As can be seen in Figure 6 the functional structure of the movement could be divided into several phases. *Take-off* could be classified as a second order supportive phase, *preparation of rotation* as a first order supportive phase, and *rotation* as the main phase. The superordinate concepts acquired on the basis of clusters (take-off, preparation of rotation, rotation) are spatially separate and temporally-sequentially organized. We are assuming that they serve as means to the solution of specific subproblems (energizing, introduction of impulse, rotation).

Figure 7 illustrates the cluster solution of the novice group (n = 20).

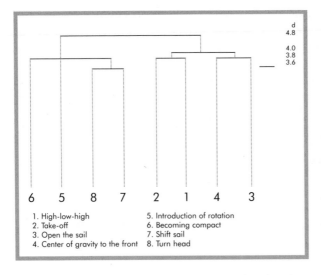

**Figure 7**

Results of the hierarchical cluster analysis of Basic Action Concepts (BACs) of the front-loop in the novice group (n = 20; α = 5 %; d$_{crit}$ = 3.51).

It is characteristic for these cluster solutions that the elements have a weak structural link. The BACs are located slightly above the critical distance (d$_{crit}$ = 3.51). Therefore, no structure can be proven for the whole group. Obviously, the technique-related representational structures are too weak at this point. For technical preparation, especially claims regarding movement, representations in individual cases are interesting.

When comparing the dendrogram of the novice with that of the expert group, a significant difference in the clusters becomes obvious. While the cluster solution of the expert-group follows a functionally-based phase structure of the movement, a comparable structure cannot be found in the novice. As for the novice, the elements are arranged differently and neither a phase-related clustering nor a temporal-sequential structure is noticed. Furthermore, inexpedient mental structures are apparent. Subject 4 (Figure 8) combines elements from different movement phases. As an example, this results in a

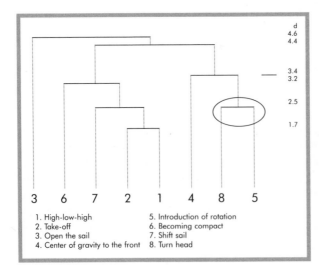

**Figure 8**

An individual novice's solution (subject 4) in the learning stage of rough coordination as the result of hierarchical cluster analysis. [The circular mark denotes the link between two elements that is obviously based on surface features. Explanations in the text (α = 5 %; d$_{krit}$ = 3.51).]

cluster, which consists of elements 5 (rotation) and 8 (head turn). Both elements of the cluster represent rotary motions, yet, regarding functional aspects, have nothing in common. While element 5 plays an important part in the introduction of the rotation, element 8 completes it. Obviously, surface features – and no functional features – were consulted for classification of the elements. The unification of these elements on the representational level is oftentimes linked with typical movement errors on this level of motor learning (rough coordination). In this context, novices often forget to complete the movement with a hand turn, which usually leads to dangerous falls.

In this study, we were able to prove the relation of cognitive representation and performance in a special movement-technique. It is shown that the cognitive structure of persons with a high ability to perform is more differentiated and more strongly function-oriented than is the case with beginners. Experts obviously are better able to apply their knowledge practically to aim for optimal execution of the movement. Furthermore, statements concerning cognitive structures are given, which are of immediate relevance for training processes. Based on these statements the coach is better able to decide the cognitive context which athletes can understand and work on. This statement is particularly relevant for such movements which have to be carried out under extreme time pressure and which assumedly make use of their non-declarative knowledge.

Such analyses concerning representational structures and biomechanical structures of a movement make it possible to derive consequences for technical preparation. Thus, it becomes apparent in which phase of the movement respective representational problems are located. A significant consequence for technical preparation is to train precisely this motion sequence. For this aim, a specific way of teaching was developed (Garzke, 2001; Schack & Garzke, 2002).

Herein, the first step (see Figure 9) consists of the imitation of the whole movement. Firstly, the judo-somersault is perfectly suitable to train the frontal direction of rotation and motion. By executing this movement, the structure of the front-loop can be trained

**Figure 9** Technical preparation using movement execution in the front-loop; the whole movement is trained as well as specific movement phases (Step 1).

and stabilized as a first step. Further focal points in this exercise are the acquirement of coordination and rhythm during rotation. Here, especially those movement components are executed which prove to be poorly structured in representations. The person whose representational structure is illustrated in Figure 9 has to focus his or her training particularly on the rotation phase. Therefore it is crucial that the athlete feels what the optimum movement structure "feels like." This way it can be felt that turning the head is not immediately connected with the rotational impulse. For the person who has difficulties with the execution it thus becomes possible to integrate the intermediate movements *becoming compact* and *shifting the sail* into the movement.

A substantial next step is the execution of the judo-somersault with the rigging. This way the movement structure can be further improved. By also incorporating the rigging, the practiced movement becomes more similar to the targeted movement on the water. Again, this method serves the purpose of working on the tactile movement effects. The athlete is meant to achieve further improvement regarding the movement structure (see Figure 10).

**Figure 10** Judo-somersault with rig (Step 2).

The next step of technical preparation is to perform the exercise with a wooden board and rig (see Figures 11 and 12). This exercise causes the center of gravity to increasingly improve into the direction of the correct movement execution in the water.

The particular movement elements that can be trained are those which have proven to be problematic in the representational structure. From this suboptimal movement structure, the athlete is supposed to move towards an optimal movement structure. This way, the execution of the movement can be trained, for instance under special surveillance of

**Figures 11, 12, 13**
Training of specific key-points
of the movement with rig
and wooden board (Step 3).

shifting the center of gravity to the front (Figure 11), grabbing the sail close (Figure 12), or becoming compact (Figure 13).

When the movement structure has been acquired up to this point of technical preparation, we suggest that the SDA-M method be applied again in order to reveal the athlete's representation structure. Conclusions can be derived from this analysis for deciding on further steps of technical preparation. At this point, the representation structure should be close to the expert's structure, at least regarding its basic organization (see Figure 14). If major problems are still apparent in the representation structure, we recommend moving back in technique execution and movement representation to step 2 or even step 1, depending on the extent of the problem. If movement structure and representation structure prove to be stable, we can proceed to step 4 (see Figure 15). Here, the movement is executed in a dune, with the wind as an additional factor. This exercise aims at stabilization of the movement structure. In particular, utilizing the wind enables the athlete to have the basic technique available in increasing variability. The athlete now has to apply the acquired basic technique under varying environmental circumstances as a means of securing a stable movement. In this step of technical preparation, it is crucial to learn about the functional meaning of the head as the leading instance within the movement. Athletes who do not turn their head over the distal end of their shoulder will land on their back as a result of a lack of rotational impulse. Athletes who turn their head towards their rear neck during initialization of the movement will stop rotating and crash onto the water surface. On the shore, the damage will be limited, but overall, the correct movement of the head is an important cornerstone in the optimal movement structure. It is essential that the head be turned in the rotation phase and the horizon sighted.

**Figure 14** Wooden board with rig, close-up view (see Garzke, 1998).

**Figure 15** Exercises performed under the influence of wind (Step 4).

The next step of technical preparation of the front-loop is practicing it on the water. Here, the speed loop can be performed as the last preparation step. The speed-loop is comparable to a skidding sideways-purler, in which the board is pulled after the body. Similarly, this is only about an increase in the variability of the movement execution. Thus, the aim is a variable accommodation to varying environmental conditions. Herein, we attempt to further stabilize the structure of the movement. After this step, we move back to the direct practice of the front-loop. After a certain practice phase, or if problems show up right after beginning the exercise, we again incorporate the SDA-M method. The representation structures can thus be measured and evaluated.

As made obvious in this representative example of individual sports, the acquisition of representation structures can vastly contribute to the optimization of technique training. As the measurement only takes approximately 15 min and results of the analysis are immediately available, many opportunities arise for technical preparation.

A further step of technical preparation is to conceptualize a mental training that begins with the representational structure of the athlete. In such a mental training based on mental representation, the individual dispositions and concerns of the athlete can be respected.

## TECHNICAL SPORTS: GYMNASTICS

The account concerning gymnastics will particularly illustrate the integrative perspective of technical preparation. Here, we will investigate once more how mental representation and kinematic parameters can be related to one another. The essential question is how mental representation and movement execution are linked.

## MEASURING REPRESENTATION STRUCTURES

In the first step, mental representations were measured in the forward somersault with a full twist. The results of the hierarchical cluster analysis shown in Figure 16 are characteristic of gymnasts who are able to perform a maximum number of half-twists in a layout somersault (novices). With an increasing level of expertise the cognitive structure changes, and comes even closer to a biomechanical functional structure. In both figures we find that some movement phases are separate from each other and are used to solve specific movement problems (e.g., generating energy, initiating rotation). A detailed analysis shows, for instance, that the BAC muscular control of leg joints is connected with the free flight for a novice (Figure 16). In an expert structure of motor representation (see Figure 17), the muscular control of his leg joints is connected with the take-off phase when performing the somersault. Therefore, the gymnast is able to perform a higher flight with a greater amount of angular momentum. In such studies we learned, for

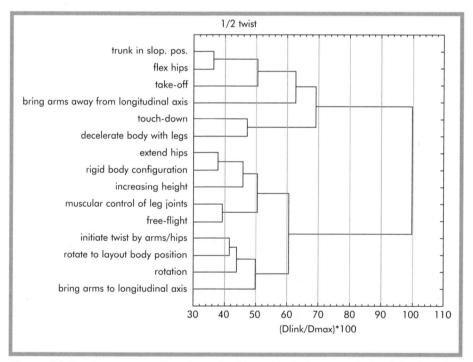

**Figure 16** Dendrogram resulting from the hierarchical cluster analysis of basic action concepts (BACs) in the forward somersault. [The vertically aligned words denote the BACs. The horizontal numbers shows the Euclidean distances of the BACs in LTM in a normalized scale. The dendrogram shows the cluster solutions for gymnasts (novices) who are able to perform a maximum amount of 1/2 twist in a layout somersault (n = 6).]

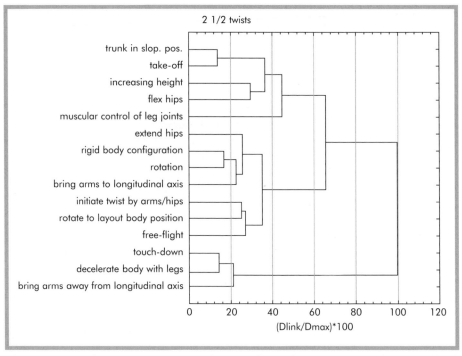

**Figure 17** Dendrogram on conceptual sum: object distances are in the normalized Euclidean distance scale. [The dendrogram shows the cluster solutions for gymnasts (experts) who are able to perform a maximum amount of 2 1/2 twist in a layout somersault (n = 6).]

example, that the occurrence of shifting and focusing of attention according to the muscular stiffening of the leg joints (during the learning process) is increased with a higher level of expertise.

## MEASURING KINEMATIC PARAMETERS (BIOMECHANICAL ANALYSIS)

In order to perform a kinematic analysis, the movements were recorded with two cameras. Movement kinematics were analysed using a computer-based 3D-analysis software (AViP-System; Heinen, 2001). The subjects were asked to perform somersault flights on the trampoline. The amount of twists increased every sixth jump until the individual maximum amount was reached. Only the successful jumps were analysed, using the AViP-method.

When analyzing the movement kinematics, it may be helpful to look at the time of flight and the time-structure of the movement right from the beginning. Table 2 shows the data for the flight time and the time structure of the twisting somersaults.

Take-off was set at 0s and parameters of the time structure (initiating twist and stopping twist) were normalized to the time of flight. With a higher level of expertise (higher amount

**Table 2** Time of Flight and Time Structure of the Twisting Somersaults. [Time of flight is measured in seconds (± SD) and the parameters of the time structure are normalized to the time of flight (take off → 0% $t_{flight}$; touch down → 100% $t_{flight}$).]

| Number of twist(s) | Time of flight [s] | Time structure [% $t_{flight}$] | |
|---|---|---|---|
| | | initiating twist | stopping twist |
| ½ twist | .91 ± .06 | 10.29 ± 4.77 | 63.38 ± 10.60 |
| 1/1 twist | .93 ± .09 | 7.40 ± 3.20 | 70.78 ± 9.51 |
| 1½ twists | 1.02 ± .06 | 6.01 ± 2.51 | 86.25 ± 11.57 |
| 2 twists | 1.02 ± .05 | 4.27 ± 1.11 | 82.01 ± 8.37 |
| 2½ twists | 1.07 ± .06 | 3.74 ± .61 | 84.06 ± 3.58 |

of twists) the moment of initiating the twist comes closer to the take-off and the moment of stopping the twist comes closer to the touch-down. The transition between initiating the twist by an asymmetrical arm/hip-movement and performing a contact twist may not be observable by the trainers' eyes because of the high movement velocity. Even stopping the twist close to the touch-down may result in stopping the twist when colliding with the ground. The trainer has to pay attention to the moment of initiating the twist and the moment when stopping it. Both moments should be during the free flight.

Table 3 shows the angular velocities according to the longitudinal and the lateral axis of the body and the tilting angle when performing the twisting somersaults.

**Table 3** Angular Velocities According to the Longitudinal Axis of the Body ($\omega_{LoAB}$) and the Lateral Axis of the Body ($\omega_{LoAB}$) when Performing the Twisting Motion ($\gamma_{tilt}$ Describes the Tilting Angle.)

| Number of twist(s) | $\omega_{LoAB}$ [°/s] | $\omega_{LoAB}$ [°/s] | $\gamma_{tilt}$ [°] |
|---|---|---|---|
| ½ twist | 569.25 ± 101.77 | 308.73 ± 44.47 | 11.06 ± 3.50 |
| 1/1 twist | 649.60 ± 77.61 | 297.92 ± 21.48 | 11.22 ± 3.03 |
| 1½ twists | 900.35 ± 155.27 | 315.48 ± 38.53 | 12.45 ± 2.61 |
| 2 twists | 965.20 ± 115.34 | 289.54 ± 16.17 | 14.14 ± 1.74 |
| 2½ twists | 1012.50 ± 159.10 | 320.22 ± 37.90 | 14.70 ± 1.75 |

With a higher expertise level (higher amount of twists) we find an increase in the angular velocity according to the longitudinal axis of the body when performing twisting somersaults. The angular velocity according to the lateral axis of the body remains nearly the same. With an increase in twisting velocity we find an increase in the tilting angle. A larger tilting angle induces a greater twisting velocity.

RELATIONSHIP BETWEEN STRUCTURE OF MOTOR REPRESENTATION
AND THE KINEMATIC STRUCTURE OF THE MOVEMENT

According to our ideas concerning the units of movement control, the whole movement is structured and controlled by way of cognitive-perceptual representations. In this perspective movements are organized by means of event-representations. Therefore, the hierarchical structure of movement representations seems to be close to the kinematic events of the movement and far from muscle activation patterns. While investigating the motor representations of the somersault, we learned that this structure is topological in nature, meaning that the structure involves information concerning the space and time of the movement. We also learned about the relationship between the maximum amount of twists and the structure of motor representation. After measuring kinematic parameters we are able to directly study the relationship between structure of motor representation and kinematic parameters.

First, the kinematic parameters and the structure of motor representation of every subject were evaluated. We have seen some results in the previous sections; then the data of every test were related to each other (see Figure 18). Statements concerning the structure of motor representation were gained from the hierarchical cluster analyses of the SDA-M method (Euclidian distance matrix). The relevant parameters here are Euclidian distances between the units of representation (BACs). Now we are interested in learning about the correlation of measured kinematics and the Euclidian distances between relevant BACs. Since we believe that motor representation is of functional significance for movement control, we assume a correlation between the structure of BACs and the structure of movement.

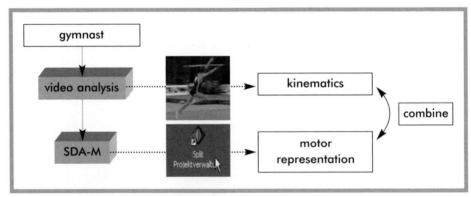

**Figure 18** Design and methodological approaches of our study. (After measuring kinematic parameters and the structure of motor representation separately we are now able to combine the results by means of special forms of data analysis.)

When connecting these two kinds of data, significant correlations between important kinematic parameters (time structure, leg-trunk-angle, tilt-angle, angular velocities, etc.) and structural parameters of the motor representations are found. Figure 19 shows one example of the relation between a kinematic parameter and the Euclidian distance between two BACs. These two chosen BACs, twisting arms and hip and extending hip, are of functional significance for the initiation of the twisting motion. We find a negative correlation ($r=-.97$; $p<.00$) between the angular velocity according to the longitudinal axis of the body when performing the twisting motion and the Euclidean distance of these two BACs.

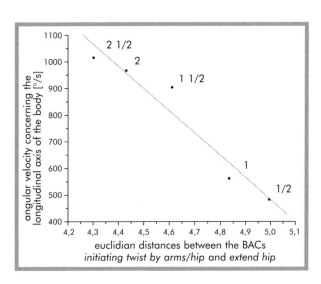

**Figure 19**
Relationship between the angular velocity concerning the longitudinal axis of the body and the Euclidean distance between two relevant BACs; these results are described here with help of the means of each group. Notice the number of twisting somersaults of each group.

These results indicate a direct translation of the Euclidean distance between the BACs twist by arms/hip and extended hip into movement-parameter (angular-velocities). The greater a Euclidean distance, the lesser the angular velocity. A gymnast whose motor representation shows big Euclidean distances between the described BACs is not able to produce a large number of twists. This is interesting, because the two BACs are located in the free-flight phase, where the athlete has to initiate the twist. Hence, we come to the conclusion that during the learning process not only the structure of movement concerning the amount of twists changes, but the structure of representation changes too. In the reported case the Euclidean distances may become smaller and the athlete increases his capability of performing and controlling the movement. Therefore, there might be a direct link between motor representation and biological organisation of movement control. From this point of view we do not need additional motor programs. More probably, motor representations are directly connected to a network of perceptual elements or representation, as described by Mester (2000) and in recent studies by Mechsner et al. (2001). According to this idea the whole movement is structured and controlled by way of these perceptual and conceptual representations.

Results from our study support this perspective. For instance, when correlating the BACs take-off and touch-down with the time of flight, we found a significant correlation ($p <.00$). So even the time of flight seems to be mapped (implicit) in the structure of motor representations. Additionally, we found direct links between special body angles (for instance the angle between the thighs and the trunk during take-off) and the accessory parts of motor representations.

The investigated relationships between the structure of motor representations and the movement kinematics draw far-reaching conclusions. These results support the hypothesis that voluntary movements are planned, executed, and directly stored in memory by means of representations of their anticipated perceptual effects. In this view, representations create a link between the central goal and the biomechanical organization of the movement. For general statements concerning the organization of complex movements in different kinds of sport, further research is necessary.

## TEAM SPORTS

In team sports, technical performance, in addition to a host of other factors such as tactics and team coherence, has a strong influence on a team's overall performance. Yet, suitable action patterns – and therefore stably accessible technique execution – can still be viewed as crucial, basic conditions for performance in team sports. In this regard, technique training serves an important function. In a first step we will present ways to access technique training, implementing the method we developed for top-level volleyball. This is followed by a presentation of soccer.

### VOLLEYBALL

We have chosen as an example a current study conducted in top-level volleyball. The selected movement task is the spike, which is also often called a "hit." Figure 20 presents the volleyball skill.

This movement task is of a structure which can be more closely defined using functional movement analysis (Engel & Schack, 2002; Schack, 2002). For each functionally located

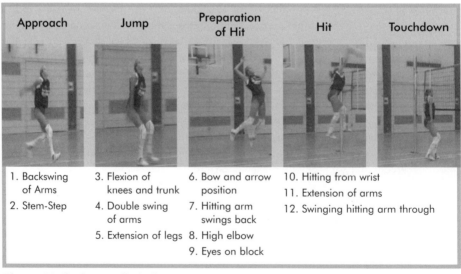

| Approach | Jump | Preparation of Hit | Hit | Touchdown |
|---|---|---|---|---|
| 1. Backswing of Arms | 3. Flexion of knees and trunk | 6. Bow and arrow position | 10. Hitting from wrist | |
| 2. Stem-Step | 4. Double swing of arms | 7. Hitting arm swings back | 11. Extension of arms | |
| | 5. Extension of legs | 8. High elbow | 12. Swinging hitting arm through | |
| | | 9. Eyes on block | | |

**Figure 20** The hit in volleyball.

movement phase, allocated representation units (BACs) were set (see http://www.spormed.de/area/proment/anc/anc.html). Table 4 presents the list of used BACs of the hit in volleyball.

***Table 4*** Basic Action Concepts (BACs) of the Hit in Volleyball

| | | | |
|---|---|---|---|
| 1. Taking the arms back<br>2. Stem-step<br>3. Bending knees and trunk | (Approach) | 6. Bow<br>7. Spiking arm back<br>8. High elbow | (Preparation of hit) |
| 4. Swing both arms forward<br>5. Extending legs | (Jump) | 9. Eyes on block<br>10. Spike emphasizing the wrist<br>11. Whipping extension of arm<br>12. Draw-through of hitting arm | (Execution of hit) |

First, we will illustrate the results using a single case (see Figure 21). Two players of the women's youth National team will serve as an example for a discussion of different *technique profiles* in memory. The results are displayed as "dendrograms", which are based on hierarchical cluster analyses.

**Figure 21**
Technique profile of the "hitting skill" of player A in motor memory.
[The numbers correspond to the numbering in the list of BACs mentioned above. Technique profile "spike" of an expert (ace spiker) from the German National team concerning formerly mentioned quantity of BACs (Distance measures: dmax = 3,5; dcrit = 3,3; α = 5%).
The lower the value of a

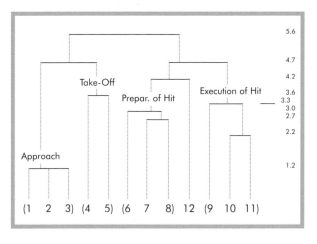

horizontal connection between the BACs (see set of values of Euclidean distance on the right), the lower the distance of the BACs in memory.]

Player A is an ace spiker. Her memory displays clearly structured movement representation (movement imagery) that is an almost ideal type. BACs 1-3 in connection with 4 and 5 constitute the phase of "approach and jump" in the memory of player A. Terms 6, 7, and 8 combine to make up the phase of "preparation for the hit," and terms 9, 10, and 11 represent the "execution of the hit." The truly interesting element at this point is the comparison with player B (see Figure 22).

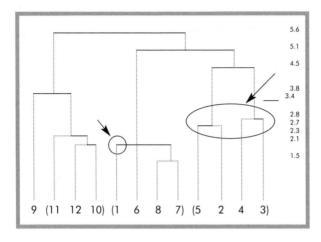

5.6
5.1
4.5
3.8
3.4
2.8
2.7
2.3
2.1
1.5

9 (11 12 10) (1 6 8 7) (5 2 4 3)

**Figure 22** Technique profile "hit" for player B.

She (player B) has been playing the identical position for several years, but has been having difficulties managing an optimal execution of the hit. In her own view, the cause of her difficulties was to be found in her insufficient jumping height. This explanation seemed unreasonable, though, because the measures of her jumping abilities provided excellent results. Her coaches observed difficulties in the backswing of her hitting arm prior to the hit. Our analysis makes a more precise definition of the possible problem (see Figure 22). The BACs making up the approach and jump reveal a structure of less clarity in player B (circled) as compared to player A. One BAC (1) was even allocated to a different phase (preparation of hit). Other than that, approach and jump is broken into two inefficient clusters (5-2; 4-3) while ideal-type clusters (1-3; 4-5) (see Figure 21) become visible in player A as far as biomechanical analyses are concerned.

Accordingly, this led to the conclusion that player B incorporated an inefficient sequence of impulses in approach and jump and that this caused her jumping height to be only suboptimal. This is the origin of the insufficient backswing of the hitting arm (as observed by the coach) and, finally, for the bad hit. As a consequence, technique training was changed, and a training was deducted which focused on an optimization of the sequence of impulses in approach and jump. Moreover, an individualized mental training (imagery training) was implemented which started from the individually acquired mental representations and integrated kinesthetic patterns (the impression of an ideal jump and a proper hit). This way, player B's hit could be improved significantly prior to the 2001 Women's Youth World Championships. She has subsequently managed to get on the roster of Germany's A-National Team.

Our studies in volleyball, and in other sports as well (Heinen, Schwaiger, & Schack, 2002; Schack, 2002; Schack & Heinen, 2000), have proven and underlined the functional meaning of a level of mental representations in motor learning. As a result, further steps for the optimization of motor learning are to be expected in this context. If both coaches and teachers are aware of their athletes'/students' mental movement representations, they will gain a better understanding of how to intervene in the learning process and optimally instruct and address their learners.

SOCCER

Another team sport in which studies regarding technical preparation have been conducted is soccer. Subsequently, we will present a study we engaged in to gain information about mental representations of the heading technique, which is illustrated in Figure 23.

**Figure 23** Sequence of the heading technique in soccer.

In this study we measured the differences in mental representations of the header in an expert who currently plays in the Bundesliga (the top division in Germany), and a subject with a comparably lower expertise level who plays in the fourth division (Oberliga). The expert (Player 1) attended an average of eight practice sessions plus one game per week, whereas the player with a lower level of expertise (Player 2) usually practiced four times a week and participated in one game weekly. Both players were central defenders, a position for which a good heading technique is considered crucial. Moreover, they had very similar anthropometrical data (difference in height: 1 cm, "similar build"). However, observing the two players' repeated performance of an isolated heading drill, it appeared to us that Player 1 – despite not accomplishing greater jumping height – was able to execute the header much more explosively and give the ball a substantially higher pace than Player 2.

Subsequently, the two players were subjects of a study implementing the SDA-M-method. Similar to the previously presented study concerned with the spike in volleyball, allocated representation units (BACs) were set for each of the three functionally located movement phases. The BACs were derived from video analysis of headers executed by professional soccer players, as well as from movement descriptions included in relevant literature (Bauer, 1997; Bisanz & Gerisch, 2001).

**Table 5** Basic Action Concepts (BACs) of the Header in Soccer

| | |
|---|---|
| 1. Stem-step<br>2. Bending knees and trunk<br>3. Swinging arms forward<br>4. Extending legs | (Run-Up/Jump) |
| 5. Upper body is arched back<br>6. Legs swing back<br>7. Drawing chin towards chest | (Preparation of Header) |
| 8. Accelerating forehead towards the ball<br>9. Swinging arms back<br>10. Forehead meets ball<br>11. Bending the trunk | (Execution of Header) |

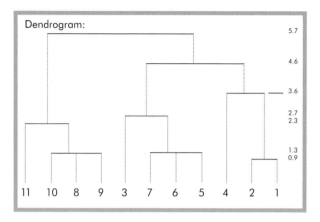

**Figure 24**
Heading technique profile of the expert.
[Distance measures:
rkrit = .457; dkrit = 3.457;
Ckrit = .207; pikrit = .368;
α = 5%). The numbers on the horizontal border of the dendrogram point to the BACs as listed in Table 5.]

Table 5 presents a list of those movement phases (in parentheses on the right) and BACs that were used in this study:

To begin with, we will briefly discuss the results for Player 1 gained through the SDA-M-method. A graphical display of these results as dendograms is presented in Figure 24.

The expert structure displayed for Player 1 reveals a well-organized mental representation of the header. The clusters of BACs in the dendrogram generally correspond well with the functionally ordered phases we proposed in Table 5, although the expert has allocated the BAC *Swinging arms forward* (3) to the phase *Preparation of Header*. However, due to the fact that strictly taken, the forward-swing of the arms takes place across the two phases of *Run-Up/Jump* and *Preparation of Header*, this does not detract from our assessment that Player 1's heading technique remains very close to the movement execution found in respective literature. In a similar fashion, the mental representation structure of Player 2 (see Figure 25), the player with a lower level of expertise, is fairly consistent with respect to the initially determined movement phases. Hence, we can also attest that he has a well-structured heading technique.

However, a slight but potentially crucial difference of Player 2's cluster formation in comparison with the results for Player 1 is to be found in the *Execution of header*-phase, in which especially the BACs *Accelerating forehead towards the ball* (8), *Swinging arms*

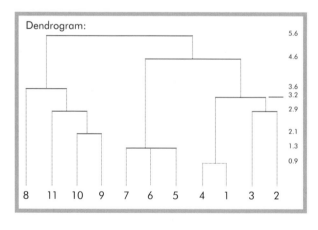

**Figure 25**
Technique profile of the header of the player with a lower level of expertise.
(Distance measures:
rkrit = .457; dkrit = 3.457;
Ckrit = .207; pikrit = .368;
α=5%.)

back (9), and *Forehead meets ball* (10) are organized in remarkably closer affinity in the expert's memory. This supports the impression of a discrepancy regarding the explosiveness of the two players' heading techniques that we had when observing their movement executions, which, in retrospect, had been visible as a less intense backswing of the arms and flexion of the trunk in Player 2.

When attempting to incorporate this newly acquired knowledge into a technique training to improve Player 2's heading technique, we recommended focusing on this latter movement phase. It was important for Player 2 to gain cognitive insight into the lack of explosiveness he revealed when executing the header. For this aim, implementing media for visual feedback might prove to be successful. Simply videotaping a sequence of Player 2's heading technique and subsequently contrasting it to an expert's technique should contribute to a better understanding of the discrepancy in explosiveness (if the two players happened to play on the same team, one could even use computer-based methods such as cross-fading procedures to further illustrate the differences).

Thereafter, we proposed an individualized technique training overemphasizing the sequence of impulses of the Executing the header-phase, namely BACs 8, 9, and 10. This training should first be pursued without the ball and later with the addition of the ball. Furthermore, mental training in the form of imagery training could be used as a further intervention method for Player 2 to acquire the proper kinesthetic pattern[1].

## COMPUTER-BASED METHODS IN TECHNICAL PREPARATION

**Figure 26** Video-cross-fading in downhill skiing competition for comparison of the skiers' lanes.

The development of digital video-techniques opens up a variety of new opportunities for technical preparation in sport (see, for example, the display presented in Figure 26). Besides the mere display of moving images, digital supplementing and analysis of video images can introduce these new perspectives.

---

1 The authors would like to thank Coach Daniel Niedzkowski for the substantial support he provided to the above part of this chapter. We are especially thankful that he contributed his wide-ranging experience in the field of soccer to further illustrate the practical dimension of technique training.

Such procedures can be used particularly well to reveal differences in speed, for instance in downhill skiing. Furthermore, the simultaneous display also shows differences in movement techniques. Through this means, key-points and errors in motion sequences can easily be emphasized and utilized as additional information in technique training.

1) Inserting movement paths adds to the video sequence. By utilizing tracking-procedures (see Intel 2001) which follow objects based on their structure and/or color information, movement paths of athletes or pieces of equipment can be recognized and drawn in the video image. Here, movement paths, which are not directly recognized or are extremely long, are made visible. Figure 27 displays the tracked lanes of two downhill skiers in connection with the cross-fading procedure.

2) With the help of mathematical models and simulated arithmetic, movements and movement paths can be created and visualized on the computer screen (Seifriz, 2001). Starting with tracked movement paths and kinematic analyses, optimized movement solutions can thus also be presented visually and compared with real movements. Figure 28 shows an image taken from an animation of an optimized lane on a slope created via GPS-measurement.

**Figure 27** Tracking of lanes using the cross-fading method.

We have gone further into the question of how a modular measuring set can be constructed, which for the support of motor learning processes combines kinematic analysis of movement technique and analysis of mental parameters, and utilizes those in technique training. This modular measuring set was called the enhanced movement representation analysis inventory (e-BRAIN; Schack & Heinen, 2002).

Module 1 of e-BRAIN is made up of the previously presented method for measuring mental movement representations. These data provide vital information for technique training, and highlight the mental framework of movement organization. On the other hand, the movement can be illustrated, for instance, through the use of biomechanical measurement procedures (Module 2). The parameters thus collected form a complex yet structured web of parameters. It is the aim of e-BRAIN to

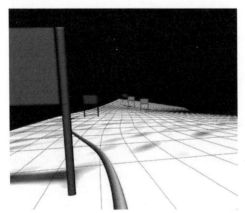

**Figure 28** Visualization (animation) of simulated lanes.

acquire such parameter-webs not separately, but to establish a *connective function* between the mentioned pools of values (representation-related and biomechanical data), to use them as feedback in technique training, and to utilize them for simulations.

Figure 29 shows the measuring set build-up of e-BRAIN. On the left, we find the representation structure of the volleyball hit in an athlete's long-term memory. The center features a 3-D clip of his movement execution. These clips also constitute the basis of the analysis of movement kinematics which is used to report the movement via an animation and to simulate partial aspects of the movement (as in the context of technical errors) (on the right). As a consequence, e-BRAIN, for one, provides data regarding the athlete's movement organization (structure of movement representation, kinematic data, and linkage of both sets of data). Moreover, e-BRAIN also delivers extensive information that can be used as visual feedback.

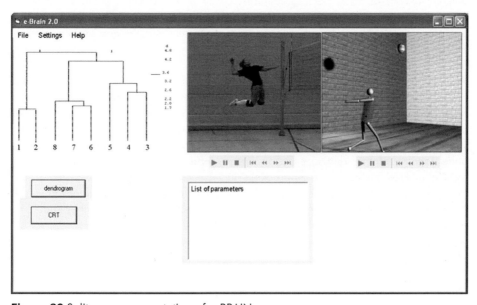

**Figure 29** Split-screen presentation of e-BRAIN.

## CONCLUSION

Based on new and integrative perspectives concerning technical preparation, this chapter introduced various tools that play an essential role in the work of sport psychologists. It is important to note that these tools are always applied in a specific training setting. In this setting, the sport psychologist can work directly with the athlete, for example by means of computer-based methods. However, he or she will also serve as a consultant to the coach. The underlying principle here should be that the person with the highest degree of expertise (coach or sport psychologist) becomes active in the ongoing training session or regarding the athlete's current problem. Thus, it is usually recommended that the sport psychologist advise the coach regarding the set-up of technique training. Experimental analyses using the SDA-M are an example of how this purpose can be served. By means of such methods, it is possible to gain information about the cognitive background of specific difficulties during technique execution. The information thus gained can be utilized for deciding which elements or phases of the technique are to be improved and thus should be targeted through technical preparation.

On the contrary, the sport psychologist takes the active part when it comes to mental training. In this respect, he or she will discuss the structure of movement imagery with the athlete. For this aim, the psychologist can use the SDA-M-data already gained. He or she will also lead the execution of the actual mental training process.

Computer-based methods may be applied by both coaches and sport psychologists as a basis for their work. By means of such methods it is possible to give the athlete insight into different aspects of his or her movement execution and to illustrate the structure of the athlete's movement representation. Such methods are of high practical relevance when we aim at the development of more goal-oriented movement imagery and an improvement of technical performance.

Thus, the essential message of the chapter is that current experimental and media-based methods (tools) can support technique training on a high level. Central aspects regarding these efforts are the technical capabilities and health of the athlete. The presented methods and perspectives have been proven to supplement professional technical preparation, and yet they cannot replace it. Therefore, applying such methods demands a basic understanding of the training situation and a certain idea of the specific movement technique. New methods and approaches in technical preparation can systematically improve technical performance, especially where they enable a better understanding of practical events and the athlete's movement organization. In this respect, they should be regarded as substantial and effective components of our tool kit.

# REFERENCES

Abernethy, B. (1993). Attention. In R. N. Singer, M. Murphey, & L. K. Tennant (Eds.), *Handbook of research on sport psychology* (pp. 127-170). New York: Macmillian.

Ach, N. (Hrsg.). (1921). *Untersuchungen zur Psychologie und Philosophie, Bd.3. Über die Begriffsbildung. Eine experimentelle Untersuchung.* Bamberg: C. C. Buchners Verlag.

Bar-Eli, M., Lowengart, O., Master-Barak, M., Oreg., S., Goldenberg, J., Epstein, S., et al. (2006). Developing peak performers in sport: Optimization versus creativity. In D. Hackfort & G. Tenenbaum (Eds.), *Essential processes for attaining peak performance* (pp. 158-177). Oxford, UK: Meyer & Meyer.

Bauer, G. (1997). *Lehrbuch Fußball: Erfolgreiches Training von Technik, Taktik und Kondition.* München: BLV.

Bernstein (Bernštejn), N. A. (1947). *O postrojenii dviženij* (Über den Aufbau der Bewegungen). Mozkva: Medgiz.

Bernstein, N. A. (1967). *The coordination and regulation of movements.* Elmsford, NY: Pergamon Press.

Bernstein (Bernsteijn), N. A. (1988). *Bewegungsphysiologie* (2.Aufl.). Leipzig: Barth.

Bernstein, N. A. (1996a). *Die Entwicklung der Bewegungsfertigkeiten.* Leipzig: IAT Eigenverlag.

Bernstein, N. A. (1996b). On Dexterity and its Development. In M. L. Latash & M. T. Turvey (Eds.), *Dexterity and its Development* (pp. 3-23). Mahwah, NJ: Erlbaum.

Bisanz, G., & Gerisch, G. (2001). *Fußball. Technik, Training, Taktik.* Reinbek: Rowohlt.

Blaser, P., Stucke, C., Narciss, S & Körndle, H., (Hrsg.). (2000). *Auswirkungen eines Leistungstrainings im Brustschwimmen auf den Zusammenhang von Bewegungsrepräsentation und Bewegungsausführung.* Köln: Sport und Buch Strauß.

Boutcher, S. H. (1990). The role of performance routines in sport. In J. G. Jones & L. Hardy (Eds.), *Stress and performance in sport* (pp. 231-245). New York: Wiley.

Cohn, P. J. (1990). Preperformance routines in sport: Theoretical support and practical applications. *The Sport Psychologist, 4,* 301-312.

Daugs, R., Mechling, H., Blischke, K., & Olivier, N. (Hrsg.). (1991). *Sportmotorisches Techniktraining und Lernen,* Band 1 (Schriftenreihe des Bundesinstitutes für Sportwissenschaften, Bd. 76). Schorndorf: Hofmann.

Engel, F., & Schack, T. (2002). Knowledge and performance in volleyball. *Proceedings of 7th Annual Congress of the European College of Sport Science* (p. 123). Athens: ECSS.

Garzke, P. (1998). *Der Frontloop beim Segelsurfen* [Diploma Thesis]. Köln: Deutsche Sporthochschule Köln.

Garzke, P. (2001). Frontloop. So lernt ihn jeder. [special]. *Surf,* (7).

Geourgopoulus, A. P. (2002). Bahavioral and neural aspects of motor topology: Following Bernstein's thread. In M. L. Latash (Ed.), *Progress in motor control* (Vol. 2, pp. 1-12). Champaign, IL: Human Kinetics.

Göhner, U. (1979). *Bewegungsanalyse im Sport.* Schorndorf: Hofmann.

Goldenberg, J., Lowengart, O., Oreg, S., Bar-Eli, M., Epstein, S., & Fosbury, R.D. (2004). Innovation: The Case of the Fosbury Flop. *Marketing Science Institute (MSI) Reports – working papers series*, Issue 1 (Report No. 04-106), 153-155.

Gurfinkel, V. S., & Cordo, P. J. (2002). The scientific legacy of Nikolai Bernstein. In M. L. Latash (Ed.), *Progress in motor control* (Vol. 1, pp. 1-19). Champaign, IL: Human Kinetics.

Heinen, T. (2001). *Rotationsbewegungen im Gerätturnen – Mentale Strukturen und kinematische Parameter* [Diploma Thesis]. Köln: Deutsche Sporthochschule Köln.

Heinen, T., Schwaiger, J., & Schack, T. (2002). Optimising gymnastics training with cognitive methods. *Proceedings of the 7th Annual Congress of the European College of Sport Science* (p. 608). Athens: ECSS.

Heuer, H. (1994). Koordination. In H. Heuer & S. W. Keele (Hrsg.), *Psychomotorik* (Enzyklopädie der Psychologie: Themenbereich C. Theorie und Forschung: Serie 2. Kognition: Bd. 3, S. 147-222). Göttingen: Hogrefe.

Hoffmann, J., Stoecker, C., & Kunde, W. (2004). Anticipatory control of actions. *International Journal of Sport and Exercise Psychology*, 2, 346-361.

Intel (2001). Open Source Computer Vision Library. http://developer.intel.com (23.04.2003).

Jeannerod, M. (1995). Mental imagery in the motor context. *Neuropsychologia*, 33(11), 1419-1432.

Jeannerod, M. (1997). *The cognitive neuroscience of action*. Oxford, UK: Blackwell Publishers Ltd.

Jeannerod, M. (2004). Actions from within. *International Journal of Sport and Exercise Psychology*, 2, 376-402.

Koch, I., Keller, P., & Prinz, W. (2004). The ideomotor approach to action control: Implications for skilled performance. *International Journal of Sport and Exercise Psychology*, 2, 362-375.

Krug, J. (2004). 20 Jahre Stützsprungforschung in Halle – ein Beitrag zum Technik- und Messplatztraining. *Institutszeitschrift zur Tagung Sportmotorik – Konzepte, Repräsentationen und Visionen* (S. 29-42). Martin-Luther-Universität Halle-Wittenberg.

Lander, H.-J. (1991). Ein methodischer Ansatz zur Ermittlung der Struktur und der Dimensionierung einer intern-repräsentierten Begriffsmenge. *Zeitschrift für Psychologie*, 199, 167-176.

Lander, H.-J., & Lange, K. (1992). Eine differentialpsychologische Analyse begrifflich strukturierten Wissens. *Zeitschrift für Psychologie*, 200, 181-197.

Leuchte, S. (2004). Zur strukturellen Systematik der Übungen des Gerätturnens und dem Stellenwert für die Theorie, Methodik und Praxis. *Institutszeitschrift zur Tagung Sportmotorik – Konzepte, Repräsentationen und Visionen* (S. 6-15). Martin-Luther-Universität Halle-Wittenberg.

Leontjev, A. N., & Zaporoshets, A. V. (1960). *Rehabilitation and hand function*. London: Pergamon.

Lidor, R., Tennant, K. L., & Singer, R. N. (1996). The generalizability effect of three learning strategies across motor task performances. *International Journal of Sport Psychology*, 27, 23-36.

Luria (Lurija), A. R. (1992). *Das Gehirn in Aktion*. Reinbek: Rowohlt.

Maddox, M. D., Wulf, G., & Wright, D. L. (1999). The effect of an internal vs. external focus of attention on the learning of a tennis stroke. *Journal of Sport and Exercise Psychology*, 21, 78.

Magill, R. A. (2001). Augmented feedback in motor skill acquisition. In R. N. Singer, H. A. Hausenblas, & C. M. Janelle (Eds.), *Handbook of sport psychology* (2nd ed., pp. 86-114). New York: Wiley.

Martin, D. (1991). Merkmale einer trainingswissenschaftlichen Theorie des Techniktrainings. In R. Daugs, H. Mechling, K. Blischke, & N. Olivier (Hrsg.), *Sportmotorisches Lernen und Techniktraining Band 1* (Schriftenreihe des Bundesinstitutes für Sportwissenschaft, Bd. 76, S. 53-77). Schorndorf: Hofmann.

Martin, D. (1992). Training science: Technique training – An aspect of training theory. In H. Haag, O. Gruppe, & A. Kirsch (Eds.), *Sport science in Germany – An interdisciplinary anthology* (pp. 241-262). Berlin: Springer.

Martin, D., Carl, K., & Lehnertz, K. (1991). *Handbuch Trainingslehre*. Schorndorf: Hofmann.

Mechling, H. (1988). Zur Theorie und Praxis des Techniktrainings: Problemaufriss und Thesen. *Leistungssport*, 1, 39-42.

Mechling, H., & Carl, K. (1992). Technik, sportliche (technique). In H. Becker, K. Carl, D. Kayser, & R. Prohl (Hrsg.), *Sportwissenschaftliches Lexikon* (6. Aufl., S. 504-506). Schorndorf: Hofmann.

Mechsner, F., Kerzel, D., Knoblich, G., & Prinz, W. (2001). Perceptual basis of bimanual coordination. *Nature*, 414, 69-72.

Meichenbaum, D. (1979). *Kognitive Verhaltensmodifikation*. München: Urban & Schwarzenberg.

Mester, J. (2000). Movement control and balance in earthbound movements. In B. M. Nigg, B. R. Macintosh, & J. Mester (Eds.), *Biomechanics and biology of movement* (pp. 223-238). Champaign, IL: Human Kinetics.

Newell, K. M. (1985). Coordination, control and skill. In D. Goodman, R. B. Wilberg, & I. M. Franks (Eds.), *Differing perspectives in motor learning, memory, and control* (pp. 295-317). Amsterdam: North-Holland.

Newell, K. M. (1991). Augmented information and the acquisition of skill. In R. Daugs, H. Mechling, K. Blischke, & N. Olivier (Hrsg.), *Sportmotorisches Lernen und Techniktraining Band 1* (Schriftenreihe des Bundesinstitutes für Sportwissenschaft, Bd. 76, S. 96-116). Schorndorf: Hofmann.

Newell, K. M., & van Emmerik, R. E. A. (1989). The acquisition of coordination: preliminary analysis of learning to write. *Human Movement Science*, 8, 17-32.

Neumaier, A. (1997). Trainingswissenschaftlicher Ansatz zum Techniktraining. In J. R. Nitsch, A. Neumaier, H. de Marées, & J. Mester (Hrsg.), *Techniktraining* (Schriftenreihe des Bundesinstituts für Sportwissenschaft, Bd. 94, S. 173-225). Schorndorf: Hofmann.

Nitsch, J. R. (1985). The action-theoretical perspective. *International Review for Sociology of Sport*, 20, 263-282.

Nitsch, J. R., Neumaier, A. (1997). Interdisziplinäres Grundverständnis von Training und Techniktraining. In J. R. Nitsch, A. Neumaier, H. de Marées, & J. Mester (Hrsg.), *Techniktraining*. Schriftenreihe des Bundesinstituts für Sportwissenschaft (Bd. 94., S.37-49). Schorndorf: Hofmann.

Nitsch, J. R., Neumaier, A., de Marées, H., & Mester, J. (1997). *Techniktraining.* Schriftenreihe des Bundesinstituts für Sportwissenschaft, Bd. 94. Schorndorf: Hofmann.

Prinz, W. (1997). Perception and action planning. *European Journal of Cognitive Psychology, 9,* 129-154.

Rieling, K., Leirich, J., & Hess, R. (1967). Zur strukturellen Anordnung der Übungen des Gerätturnens. In K. Rieling, J. Lierich, & R. Hess (Hrsg.), *Theorie und Praxis der Körperkultur 16* (S. 225-232).

Rosenbaum, D. A. (1985). Motor Programming: A review and scheduling theory. In H. Heuer, U. Kleinbeck, & K.-H. Schmidt (Eds.), *Motor behavior: programming, control and acquisition* (pp. 1-33). Berlin: Springer.

Salmoni, A. W., Schmidt, R. A., & Walter, C. B. (1984). Knowledge of results and motor learnning: A review and critical appraisal. *Psychological Bulletin, 95,* 355-386.

Schack, T. (1997). *Ängstliche Schüler im Sport – Interventionsverfahren zur Entwicklung der Handlungskontrolle.* Schorndorf: Hofmann.

Schack, T. (2001). On the structure of movement representations – Basic assumptions and methodical approach. *Motor Control and Learning* (E-Journal; ISSN 1439-7919 P1-12), 01.05.2004: HTTP://JOURNAL:MOTORIK:SWI:UNI-SAARLAND.DE

Schack, T. (2002). *Zur kognitiven Architektur von Bewegungshandlungen - modelltheoretischer Zugang und experimentelle Untersuchungen.* Unveröff. Habil., Psychologisches Institut, Deutsche Sporthochschule, Köln.

Schack, T. (Hrsg.). (2003a). *Mentale Repräsentation und sportliche Leistung.* Köln: MRI-Verlag.

Schack, T. (2003b). The Relationship between motor representation and biomechanical parameters in complex movements – towards an integrative perspective of movement science. *European Journal of Sport Sciences, 3,* 1-13.

Schack, T. (2004a). Relation of knowledge and performance in motor action. *Journal of Knowledge Management, 4,* 38-53.

Schack, T. (2004b). Cognitive architecture of complex movement. *International Journal of Sport and Exercise Psychology, 2,* 403-438.

Schack, T., & Garzke, P. (2002). *Neue Wege im Techniktraining im Surfen.* Unveröff. Manuskript.

Schack, T., & Heinen, T. (2000). Mental training based on mental representation. In B. A. Carlsson, U. Johnson, & F. Wetterstrand (Eds.), *Sport psychology conference in the new millennium - a dynamic research-practice perspective* (pp. 333-337). Sweden: Halmstadt University.

Schack, T., & Heinen, T. (2002). Messplatz "Mentale Repräsentationen" im Sport. In *Programm- und Abstractband des 5. gemeinsamen Symposiums der dvs-Sektionen Biomechanik, Sportmotorik und Trainingswissenschaft vom 19.-21. Sepmtember 2002 in Leipzig* (S. 42). Sportwiss. Fak.; Uni. Leipzig.

Schack, T., & Mechsner, F. (in press). Representation of motor skills in human long-term-memory. *Neuro Science Letters.*

Schack, T., & Tenenbaum, G. (Eds.). (2004a). The construction of action – new perspectives in science. Special Issue Part I: Perceptual and cognitive control. *International Journal of Sport and Exercise Psychology, 2(3).*

Schack, T., & Tenenbaum, G. (Eds.). (2004b). The construction of action – new perspectives in science. Special Issue Part II: Representation and planning. *International Journal of Sport and Exercise Psychology*, 2(4).

Schack, T., Whitmarsh, B., Pike, R., & Redden, C. (2005). Routines. In J. Taylor & G. Wilson (Eds.), *Applying sport psychology: Four perspectives* (pp. 137-150). Champaign, IL: Human Kinetics.

Schmidt, R. A., & Lee, T. D. (2005). *Motor control and learning. A behavioral emphasis* (4th ed.). Champaign, IL: Human Kinetics.

Seifriz, F. (2001). Simulation im alpinen Skisport. Germany: Berlin.

Singer, R. N. (1980). Cognitive processes, learner strategies, and skilled motor behaviours. *Canadian Journal of Applied Sport Sciences*, 5, 25-32.

Singer, R. N. (1985). Sport performance: A five-step mental approach. *Journal of Physical Education, Recreation, and Dance*, 57, 82-84.

Singer, R. N. (1988). Strategies and metastrategies in learning and performing self-paced athletic skills. *The Sport Psychologist*, 2, 49-68.

Singer, R. N., Lidor, R., & Cauraugh, J. H. (1993). To be aware or not aware? What to think about while learning and performing a motor skill. *The Sport Psychologist*, 7, 19-30.

Singer, R. N., Lidor, R., & Cauraugh, J. H. (1994). Focus of attention during motor skill performance. *Journal of Sports Sciences*, 12, 335-340.

Smidt, W. (1995). Loopenrein. *Surf* 11/12, 61-63.

Starosta, W. (1991). Eine neue Methode der "Auffrischung" kinästhetischer Empfindungen als Verbesserungsverfahre der Sporttechnik. In R. Daugs, H. Mechling, K. Blischke, & N. Olivier (Hrsg.), *Sportmotorisches Lernen und Techniktraining Band 2* (Schriftenreihe des Bundesinstitutes für Sportwissenschaft, Bd. 76, S. 118-121). Schorndorf: Hofmann.

Sučilin, N. G. (1980). Grundlagen einer perspektivisch-prognostischen Programmierung des Vervollkommnungsprozesses der technischen Reife (Osnovy perspectivno-prognostičeskogo programmirovanija processa soveršenstvovanija tehničeskogo masterstva). Gimnastika, Moskva 2, S. 42-48.

Van der Weel, F. R., Van der Meer, A. L. H., & Lee, D. N. (1991). Effect of a task on movement control in cerebral palsy: Implications for assessment and therapy. *Developmental Medicine and Child Neurology*, 33, 419-426.

Vygotsky (Vygotskij), L. S. (1992, orig. 1929). *Geschichte der höheren psychischen Funktionen*. Münster: Lit.

Wulf, G. (1994). *Zur Optimierung motorischer Lernprozesse* (Beiträge zur Lehre und Forschung im Sport, Bd. 104). Schorndorf: Hofmann.

Wulf, G., Lauterbach, B., & Toole, T. (1999). Learning advantages of an external focus of attentionin golf. *Research Quarterly for Exercise & Sport*, 70, 120-126.

Wulf, G., & Prinz, W. (2001). Directing attention to movement effects enhances learning: A review. *Psychonomic Bulletin & Review*, 8, 648-660.

Wulf, G., Schmidt, R. A., & Deubel, H. (1993). Reduced feedback frequency enhances generalized motor program learning but not parameterization learning. *Journal of Experimental Psychology: Learning, Memory, and Cognition*, 19, 1-18.

Wulf, G., & Weigelt, C. (1997). Instructions about physical principles in learning a complex motor skill: To tell or not to tell. *Research Quarterly for Exercise & Sport*, 68, 362-367.

# Chapter 5

# Psychological Factors of Tactical Preparation

Keith Henschen, Traci Statler, and Ronnie Lidor

Initially, for the reader to understand this chapter, we must clarify exactly what is meant by *tactical* preparation of an athlete. According to Webster's Dictionary (1993, p. 1787), there are actually two definitions that are applicable to the word *tactical*:
   (1) Of or relating to small scale actions serving a larger purpose
   (2) Skillful in planning or maneuvering.

When these two concepts are combined, it is indicated that the objective of tactical preparation is to provide athletes with the strategic knowledge required for them to effectively execute the skills they have acquired and perfected in real life situations, such as in practices, games, or competitions. More specifically, in tactical preparation, athletes are taught how to develop a game plan or competition strategy that best fits their sport and that will increase the probability that they will exhibit superiority over their opponents (Blumenstein, Lidor, & Tenenbaum, 2005; Bompa, 1999). Tactical preparation should be linked to other phases of preparation, such as the physical, technical, and psychological phases. It has been argued by sport theorists (e.g., Bompa, 1999; Matveyev, 1981; Zatsiorsky, 1995; see also chapters 2 and 7 in this book) that effective interaction among the four phases of preparation, namely the physical, technical, tactical, and psychological, will result in better athletic performance.

The purpose of this chapter is to discuss the psychological support needed for an athlete to achieve and master the objectives of the tactical phase. This, of course, infers that the proficient performer must learn to appropriately "use his or her mind" while competing, and that "using" the mind is just as crucial during performance as are the physical and technical aspects of performance. In the history of athletics, tactical or "strategy" preparation has traditionally been the domain of coaches, while athletes have been given a "pass" in this area and allowed just to "play". However, the Renaissance athlete of today is not afforded this luxury (Bompa, 1999; Hoberman, 1992). To be truly competitive, contemporary athletes must become students of their sport and ultimately understand as much as their coaches concerning tactical preparation.

This chapter is composed of five parts. The first part presents a theoretical background of tactical preparation in sport, and the second part introduces a philosophical approach to sport tactical preparation as well as general thoughts on the subject. The third part examines individual sport tactical preparation, and the fourth part team sport tactical preparation. The fifth part presents a short summary on the use of psychological factors in tactical preparation.

## THEORETICAL BACKGROUND OF TACTICAL PREPARATION

From a theoretical perspective, it is logical and essential that psychological preparation be required during the tactical phase of training (Blumenstein et al., 2005). It would seem apparent that the more the athlete knows about strategy, the better he or she will be able to actually perform. A greater amount of information concerning when to use certain techniques will contribute to their becoming better cognitively prepared performers. Although this notion has long been popular among coaches and athletes, it is somewhat questionable. It seems that having more knowledge does not necessarily translate into being a better player. If this premise were accurate, then the brightest individuals would naturally be the best athletes. Obviously, this is not the reality of the situation. Apparently a weak relationship exists between how much a person knows concerning an athletic activity and his or her ability to perform that activity. Yet being exposed to an appropriate strategy, namely effective tactical preparation, is essential for most high-level athletes. What, then, is the solution to this dilemma?

Obviously, athletes need to be well versed in the various strategies of their event, but each strategy must be so ingrained in their being that it becomes a "reflex" instead of a cognitive process. In other words, athletes must understand the event's strategies, but should also be able to employ these strategies without thinking about how to use these tactical plans. This is a difficult scenario to achieve, because individuals are taught at an early age that when confronted with a problem they must analyze the possible solutions, and then utilize the best one to solve it. This analytical technique or style of information processing may be effective in domains such as academics, where time is not of essence, but it can be ineffective in situations where quickness is crucial (Singer, 1995; Tenenbaum, 2003). Coaches are familiar with intelligent athletes who seem to totally understand their sport, but over-think and perform poorly. Effective athletic performance is a matter of using strategy reflexively instead of thinking about how to use knowledge of the activity.

The challenge of acquiring knowledge about an athletic activity and using it without thinking is complicated, because this is a skill in itself (Williams, Davids, & Williams, 1999). During early stages of skill development, the athlete often perceives a need for conscious analytical thought in order to produce an accurate movement pattern. Yet as the skill becomes more autonomous this level of analysis must be abandoned, as the athlete must now attend to issues of accuracy, cue utilization, and strategy (Adams, 1971; Schmidt, 1975; Tenenbaum, 2003). Only when the athlete ceases to think about the movement pattern, allowing him/herself to "trust" in his or her ability, can peak performance be attained. This is a challenging skill to learn, in and of itself, because in many countries around the world the public education system is founded on analytical thinking. Young people are continually reinforced positively if they develop this type of conscious, cognitive processing. Yet, if an athlete uses this type of thinking process, his or her performance will be less than effective – a situation often referred to as "paralysis by analysis."

The psychology of tactical preparation should not only include "reflexive thinking" instead of conscious analysis, but also necessitates the skill of employing appropriate strategies automatically. This requires mastering one particular thinking technique – focusing forward instead of backward. Jerry Sloan, the immensely successful coach of the Utah Jazz professional basketball team, constantly trains his players in this thinking pattern. His interpretation of this concept is that the athlete needs to attend to what is going to happen instead of focusing on what has already occurred. According to this view, the past is already history and cannot be changed, but the future can be altered by focusing appropriately on what has previously happened. Learn from what has already happened, make the necessary adjustments, and get focused on what has to happen next. Thinking backwards is, in essence, bringing in baggage from the past into the present. Thinking is unavoidable during performance, but the challenge is to think effectively at all times.

## A PHILOSOPHICAL APPROACH AND GENERAL THOUGHTS ON SPORT TACTICAL PREPARATION

The psychological factors of tactical preparation for individual and team sports are virtually identical, but the nuances of application are different. Broadly speaking, athletes need to be in control of their cognitions, and subsequently their emotions, if they are to have a chance to perform optimally (e.g., Brown & Burke, 2003; Mikes, 1987). The way a person thinks will ultimately dictate the way he or she behaves in specific situations.

From a tactical point of view, there are only two ways for an athlete to become a good performer:

(1) To be so cognitively impervious that nothing cerebral registers, therefore forcing the athlete to respond in specific, pre-conditioned ways. This type of athlete rarely succumbs to negative emotions, because he or she has been programmed to respond to stimuli in certain patterns. The problem is that opponents soon figure out how this athlete will react, and they will quickly develop a strategy to inhibit the skill responses of the conditioned one. Quite often coaches work with this type of athlete, who is resistant to change, cannot incorporate new tactical techniques, and relies on conditioned reactions to perform. Employing tactical preparation with these athletes actually is an impediment to performance, because thinking slows their reactions and thereby leads to a deterioration in their performance.

(2) To become so psychologically proficient that one's thoughts do not interfere with his or her actual physical performance. This method is the preferred one because the mind and body are working in correlation, and performance becomes a "whole person" endeavor. Athletic performance must be somewhat spontaneous, but there also must be room for tactical input when performance needs improvement. In other words, the athlete must learn to think tactically in an appropriate fashion.

To accomplish such a feat, five "Cardinal Mental Skills" of performance that must be mastered have been identified (Henschen, 2005). In addition to this, athletes must be able to employ them in such a manner that actual performance is not interrupted. The five "Cardinal Mental Skills" are as follows:
    (1) relaxation and activation
    (2) concentration (focusing and shifting attention)
    (3) imagery
    (4) self-talk
    (5) a pre-competition mental routine.

RELAXATION AND ACTIVATION

Relaxation/activation, at the appropriate level, is the foundational skill of the "Cardinal Mental Skills," and therefore is the first that must be learned. Traditionally, relaxation training has been advocated for reducing excessive levels of stress, arousal, and anxiety, all of which can have a negative effect on performance (Henschen, 2005). Even though relaxation training frequently enables the athlete to lower pre-performance apprehension and performance anxiety, it also provides at least one other important benefit: it allows the athletes' mind and body to effectively communicate. It trains the mind and body to listen to each other's signals.

Relaxation is based on the concept that it and tension are opposites and cannot occur simultaneously in the body. In addition, as the athlete masters the skill of relaxation, it becomes possible to control the amount of tension or activation desirable in every muscle group of the body. This necessitates that the athlete become aware of how relaxation and/or tension feel at many different levels. This is a difficult challenge. At first, these levels will be difficult for the athlete to recognize, but the more they practice, the easier they are to recognize and control. Tension levels are intricately connected with tactical preparation, because tension impairs the ability to think clearly about strategy. Relaxation techniques include, but are not limited to, the following: breathing awareness, progressive relaxation, autogenic training, meditation, and yoga.

If athletes can learn to control their thought patterns, then they have the opportunity to control the situation, instead of letting the situation control them. Athletes must find a relaxation technique that works for them – to practice it, master it, and then reap the benefits in the tactical component of their performance.

CONCENTRATION

Concentration is the second "Cardinal Mental Skill" and is dependent on how an athlete can relax and stay within a manageable level of activation. Talk to high level athletes about their tactical preparation for performance, and inevitably the words "concentration," "attention," or "focus" will be part of the conversation. Every athlete quickly recognizes that without appropriate concentration their performances will be inconsistent, error prone, and less than optimal (Moran, 1996, 2003).

Concentration is a skill and must be learned. To complicate matters further, there is not just one type of concentration or attentional style, but rather several different types that can affect performance (Nideffer, 1992). In addition, each type of athletic performance may demand one or more attentional styles, utilized singularly or in concert. Each athletic situation requires specific attentional styles for the athlete to perform adequately (Abernethy, 1987, 1991). Even in the same athletic team, the concentration demands on individual athletes may be quite different. In other words, the skills of concentration are many and vary with the situation at hand. It is imperative for a good athlete to learn to intensify his or her concentration when the situation requires it, and to lower the intensity when appropriate. In order to do this effectively, athletes should master five attentional styles (see Nideffer & Sagal, 2001).

The first attentional style is a *Broad External* focus, where the performer will rapidly assess a situation, taking in a variety of information from the external environment (e.g., a soccer player dribbling the ball toward the opponent's goal). The next is a *Broad Internal* focus, where the athlete will begin to analyze and plan his or her reaction, in essence creating a game plan or strategy (e.g., a point-guard in basketball planning the next offensive maneuver). The next category of focus is *Narrow Internal*. This is where the athlete should be able to center his or her concentration on mentally rehearsing a performance skill, or regulating an emotional state (e.g., a golfer readying him/herself for the swing). This stage of concentration is where an athlete internally prepares to act. The fourth category of concentration is *Narrow External*, where the athlete will focus entirely on one or two external cues in order to actually perform the necessary action (e.g., a free-throw shooter in basketball aiming at the front area of the rim while preparing him/herself for the shooting act). The final attentional style needed for an athlete to perform effectively is referred to as *Shifting*. It is essential for an athlete to have a certain amount of attentional flexibility within any given situation. In essence, they need to be adept at "bouncing" back and forth between these categories to assure that they are picking up all relevant cues and filtering out all the irrelevant ones (e.g., a team-handball player following the path of the ball and at the same time the actions of the opponent players, while being in a defensive position).

The skills of concentration are probably the most important of all the psychological skills for actual performance, but can only be mastered if the athlete has first learned to control his or her anxiety and arousal levels through the skill of relaxation. Concentration, anxiety, arousal, and self-confidence are intricately interwoven, with each of these factors greatly dependent upon effective concentration skills that have become automatic in their deployment (Broadbent, 1971; Jacoby, Ste-Marie, & Toth, 1992). Athletes should remember these facts concerning concentration: (1) as anxiety increases, concentration ability deteriorates; (2) as arousal increases, the ability to focus generally narrows; (3) athletes with high levels of confidence can handle greater arousal without impairing concentration (Anshel, 2005; Moran, 2005).

## IMAGERY

Imagery is the ability to create or recreate an experience in the mind by utilizing all of the senses (Hall, 2001). Imagery is a mental skill that can readily be employed in practicing tactical procedures as well as in enhancing performance. It is trainable through practice and can be perfected with continuous use. Imagery should be a multi-sensory experience: visual, auditory, tactile, olfactory, and kinesthetic (feeling). Most athletes are capable of both visual and kinesthetic imagery, with the latter becoming more dominant as physical skill level increases. Imagery is most effective if the athlete has already mastered the skills of relaxation and concentration (Henschen, 2005). It is an excellent practice technique because it can be performed virtually anywhere. Harnessing the power of imagery will aid an athlete's performance in a number of ways, but is especially effective when practicing tactical strategies.

## SELF-TALK

Epicetus, in the first century A.D., wrote, "Men are disturbed not by things, but by the views they take of them." Do we talk to ourselves? Of course we do, but we don't want anyone else to know it. The truth is that we all have a constant running dialogue in our head. Self-talk is actually just another way of perceiving thinking, therefore tactical thinking is just another form of self-talk.

We are all aware that there are basically two types of self-talk – negative and positive. Negative self-talk is the more damaging to athletic performance but is difficult to avoid or control. Any time negative emotions, such as distress, anxiety, fear, or frustration occur, chances are that the vast majority of athletes will respond by talking to themselves negatively. Tactical preparedness is destroyed by negative self-talk. Negative self-talk and negative thinking are virtually the same thing, and can be caused by fear of failure, fear of success, comparison to others, insecurity, low confidence, or unrealistic expectations. Negative self-talk lessens the control athletes have over themselves, as it inhibits constructive and reinforcing thought patterns. Thus, performance is impaired, since tactical preparedness cannot be implemented.

Positive self-talk, on the other hand, is the type of talk that programs our minds with thoughts that enable us to manage situations more effectively. It is solution-directed, not problem-focused. Positive self-talk concentrates on the process – attuned to the present moment, focused on composure, and designed to be uplifting. It is essential for athletes to learn to talk to themselves from a positive perspective, thus enhancing the probability of consistent and optimal performance. Like any skill, self-talk must be practiced in order to acquire a positive, solution-focused inner dialogue. Habitual positive thinking can become integrated and automated by athletes if they want to utilize their tactical preparation

In the applied literature in exercise and sport psychology (e.g., Henschen, 2005; Moran, 2005), sport consultants, sport psychologists, and coaches who are engaged in individual and team sports can find useful practical information and guidelines for the implementation of techniques such as relaxation and activation, concentration, imagery, and self-talk.

### A PRE-PERFORMANCE MENTAL ROUTINE

The ultimate goal of learning psychological skills is to be able to use them to enhance performance [see Andersen (2000) and Tenenbaum (2001) for a variety of such enhancement psychological techniques]. If an athlete just shows up and hopes to perform well without tactical preparation, the chances are that he or she will be inconsistent and will rarely demonstrate his or her true athletic skills. A pre-performance mental routine is an effective way for an athlete to enter into a competitive state of mind, and still be in control and capable of using tactical preparedness. Pre-performance routines work by helping athletes shift their focus from task-irrelevant thoughts that will interfere with performance, to task-relevant thoughts that will assist them in achieving a high level of proficiency.

A well-planned pre-performance routine eliminates the "randomness" from an athlete's preparation, and allows him or her to choose effective things to do and think about before each performance. It will allow an athlete to proactively incorporate physical and mental actions that have previously proven to be successful, and to set the conditions that promote peak performance experiences (Ravizza & Hanson, 1995). This pre-performance mental routine normally consists of a series of mental activities involving imagery, relaxation, positive self-talk, and, finally, an appropriate level of arousal/activation. These skills are ordered in a well-established pattern that helps the athlete feel comfortable and ready to implement his or her competition strategies. The pre-performance routine allows the athlete to approach each performance in the same way and to become somewhat immune to the stress and pressure of so-called "big performances." The pre-performance routine is an extension of the tactical preparedness, because it *prepares the athlete to perform.*

A specific example of a pre-performance mental routine is a pre-performance routine in a self-paced task. Self-paced acts are those taking place in a relatively stable and predictable environment, where there is adequate time to prepare for the execution (Lidor & Mayan, 2005; Lidor & Singer, 2003). In these, the individual can activate a ritual, a strategy, or a pre-performance routine. A pre-performance routine is defined as a systematic sequence of motor, emotional, and cognitive behaviors that are demonstrated on a regular basis before the execution of self-paced tasks (Cohn, 1990; Moran, 1996). This routine is performed by an athlete when readying him/herself for such tasks as shooting free-throws in basketball, kicking a penalty kick in soccer, or serving in volleyball. Pre-performance routines help performers focus attention during the act, feel under control before and after the act, and effectively plan their performed act.

## INDIVIDUAL SPORT TACTICAL PREPARATION

Participants in individual sports need to be psychologically prepared in the tactical phase differently than athletes in team sports. This is competition of one individual against another individual. Every individual sport competitor is entirely responsible for his or her own actions. The only other person who needs to be considered in this scenario is the opponent. From a psychological perspective, and more specifically from a tactical perspective, the athlete is required to know everything about his or her competitor. He or she needs to be aware of their favorite techniques, tendencies, and weaknesses, especially the psychological ones.

The individual sport participant is engaged in two competitions simultaneously – one against an opponent and one against him/herself. The competition against the opponent involves a specific set of strategies akin to those in a regular competition (e.g., Bompa, 1999). The difficult challenge is to study the opponents' physical and psychological behaviors and understand their tactical tendencies. The second competition, the one against him/herself, is much more difficult. Successful individual sport competitors must first master themselves before they can conquer others. Mastering oneself is a complex process which requires high levels of self-control and self-confidence, and the ability to trust one's own training while reacting to opponents' actions. The psychological "Cardinal Mental Skills" of performance, discussed earlier in this chapter, are essential for individual sport participants. These psychological skills permit the athlete to place the focus where it needs to be – on the competitor. They free athletes to be confident in their own skills while employing specific tactical procedures to ensure the desired outcome – winning the competition.

Individual sport athletes use psychological preparedness to steel themselves mentally, and then they are allowed to shift their emphasis to overcoming the tactical preparation of their competitor. The ideal individual sport athlete has mastered his or her own psychological weaknesses and emotions, and thus is able to concentrate on counteracting the opponent's tactical attempts.

## TEAM SPORT TACTICAL PREPARATION

Athletes involved in team sports have a different challenge concerning tactical preparation than do individual sport athletes. While individual sport participants can focus on an object, time, or single competitor, this is not the case for a member of a team. It is essential that team members develop an "expanded attentional style" if they are to have a chance to succeed. A different set or combination of psychological skills is necessary for the team sport participant. He or she should be aware of themselves, their teammates, and all the members of the opposing team who are playing at the same time they are. This expanded awareness factor is just one of many differences between team and individual sport athletes that impacts their tactical preparation.

Another factor is the sheer volume of strategy, namely strategic information, which must be mastered in order to be effective. The quantity of tactical preparation for team athletes is extraordinary as well as complex. Team sports demand knowledge of group offense and defense, while individual sports, with only a few exceptions, require a greater reliance on offensive strategies.

In addition, tactical preparation for team sports is normally provided in a team atmosphere (i.e., a group setting), which limits one-on-one interactions. Sometimes certain members of a team are too inhibited to ask questions in front of their teammates, because of the social pressure exerted within the group (Henschen & Cook, 2003). The group dynamics operating within all teams influences how team members employ the tactical information provided to them. Two other factors of group dynamics should be mentioned concerning team sport athletes – cohesion and the stage of group development the team is currently experiencing (Eys, Patterson, Loughead, & Carron, 2005).

Cohesion can be thought of as a dynamic process that is reflected in the tendency of a group to stick together and remain united in pursuit of its instrumental objective and/or for the satisfaction of its members' affective needs (Carron, Brawley, & Widmeyer, 1998). The degree of cohesion in a team has a great influence on each member's tactical preparation. If members respect their teammates, have effective communication, have common goals, and are anxious to work with each other, then they will have cohesion, and achieving tactical preparedness becomes fairly easy. Team members will want to be successful for each other, and the team becomes primary instead of secondary in each member's perception. The more connected team athletes are, the more committed they will be to the productivity of the entire team (Brawley, Carron, & Widmeyer, 1988).

The second aspect of group dynamics, which is the stage of group development of the team, also affects how a team member is tactically prepared. The commonly accepted stages of group development are: *forming, storming, norming*, and *performing* (Tuckman, 1965). In the *forming* stage, team members are just beginning to familiarize themselves with each other, engaging in social comparison and assessment of each other's strengths and weaknesses. The next stage, *storming*, is characterized by conflicts – conflict between the team and the leaders, such as coaches, resistance to control by the group, and conflict between members of the group. This is a very turbulent time for a team, as individuals are fighting to establish their roles and expectations. The third stage of group development is the *norming* stage. The hostility experienced earlier is replaced by unity and cooperation. Team members begin to work cohesively, shifting from intra-group competition to inter-group competition. The final stage, *performing*, occurs when team members unite to synergistically challenge their opponents. In this stage, the primary goal is team success.

Depending upon which stage the team finds itself, it will be either easy or difficult to teach tactical preparedness. During the stages of *forming* and *storming*, team members are neither ready for nor receptive to tactical training. Only during the *norming* and *performing* stages will team members "buy into" strategy development.

## SUMMARY

The objective of tactical preparation is to provide athletes with the strategic knowledge required for them to effectively perform (Bompa, 1999). To achieve this objective, a great deal of psychological training must be available for the athletes. The proficient performer must learn "to use his or her mind" appropriately in practice and competition situations. Unfortunately, there is a major problem with theory and tactical preparation. The more knowledge an athlete has concerning a sport does not necessarily translate into making him or her a better player. In fact, some experts believe that no relationship exists between tactical preparation and an athlete's ability to perform. It is thought that the psychology of tactical preparation should include reflexive thinking instead of analysis. Athletes especially need to be taught to think forward instead of backwards. Thinking backwards brings baggage from the past into the present, thereby interfering with a constructive focus on the present.

The psychological factors of tactical preparation for individual and team sport athletes are virtually identical. This means teaching to both types of athletes the "Cardinal Mental Skills" of performance: relaxation and activation, concentration, imagery, self-talk, and having a pre-competition mental routine. Even though tactical preparation for individual and team sports is similar, the nuances of the applications are different. Individual sport preparation focuses on self-control and a narrower field of attention. Team sport tactical preparation requires an expanded attention field, a higher volume of tactical information, and a reliance on group considerations, such as cohesion and stage of group development. The athlete must be a master of all the strategies associated with his or her sport, but at the same time be able to employ these strategies automatically without delaying actions by thinking.

# REFERENCES

Abernethy, B. (1987). Selective attention in fast ball sports: Expert-novice differences. *Australian Journal of Science and Medicine in Sport*, 19, 7-16.

Abernethy, B. (1991). Visual search strategies and decision-making in sport. *International Journal of Sport Psychology*, 22, 189-210.

Adams, J. A. (1971). A closed-loop theory of motor learning. *Journal of Motor Behavior*, 3, 111-150.

Andersen, M. B. (Ed.). (2000). *Doing sport psychology*. Champaign, IL: Human Kinetics.

Anshel, M. H. (2005). Strategies for preventing and managing stress and anxiety in sport. In D. Hackfort, J. L. Duda, & R. Lidor (Eds.), *Handbook of reserach in applied sport and exercise psychology: International perspectives* (pp. 199-215). Morgantown, WV: Fitness Information Technology.

Blumenstein, B., Lidor, R., & Tenenbaum, G. (2005). Periodization and planning of psychological preparation in elite combat sport programs: The case of judo. *International Journal of Sport and Exercise Psychology*, 3, 7-25.

Bompa, T. (1999). Periodization: *The theory and methodology of training* (4th ed.). Champaign, IL: Human Kinetics.

Brawley, L. R., Carron, A. V., & Widmeyer, W. N. (1988). Exploring the relationship between cohesion and group resistance to disruption. *Journal of Sport and Exercise Psychology*, 10, 199-213.

Broadbent, D. A. (1971). *Decision and stress*. London: Academic Press.

Brown, D., & Burke, K. (2003). *Sport psychology library – Basketball*. Morgantown, WV: Fitness Information Technology.

Carron, A. V., Brawley, L. R., & Widmeyer, W. N. (1998). The measurement of cohesion in group sports. In J. L. Duda (Ed.), *Advances in sport and exercise psychology measurement* (pp. 213-226). Morgantown, WV: Fitness Information Technology.

Cohn, P. J. (1990). Preperformance routines in sport: Theoretical support and practical implications. *The Sport Psychologist*, 4, 301-312.

Eys, M. A., Patterson, M. M., Loughead, T. M., & Carron, A. V. (2005). Team building in sport. In D. Hackfort, J. L. Duda, & R. Lidor (Eds.), *Handbook of reserach in applied sport and exercise psychology: International perspectives* (pp. 219-231). Morgantown, WV: Fitness Information Technology.

Hall, C. R. (2001). Imagery in sport and exercise. In R. N. Singer, H. A. Hausenblas, & C. M. Janelle (Eds.), *Handbook of sport psychology* (2nd ed., pp. 529-549). New York: Wiley.

Henschen, K. (2005). Mental practice – Skill oriented. In D. Hackfort, J. L. Duda, & R. Lidor (Eds.), *Handbook of reserach in applied sport and exercise psychology: International perspectives* (pp. 19-34). Morgantown, WV: Fitness Information Technology.

Henschen, K., & Cook, D. (2003). Working with professional basketball players. In R. Lidor & K. P. Henschen (Eds.), *The psychology of team sports* (pp. 143-160). Morgantown, WV: Fitness Information Technology.

Hoberman, J. (1992). *Mortal engines – The science of performance and the dehumanization of sport*. New York: The Free Press.

Jacoby, L. L., Ste-Marie, D., & Toth, J. P. (1992). Redefining automaticity: Unconscious influences, awareness, and control. In A. Baddeley & R. Weiskrantz (Eds.), *Attention: Selection, awareness, and control: A tribute to Donald Broadbent* (pp. 261-282). Hillsdale, NJ: Erlbaum.

Lidor, R., & Mayan, Z. (2005). Can beginning learners benefit from preperformance routines when serving in volleyball? *The Sport Psychologist*, 19, 343-363.

Lidor, R., & Singer, R. N. (2003). Preperformance routines in self-paced tasks: Developmental and educational considerations. In R. Lidor & K. P. Henschen (Eds.), *The psychology of team sports* (pp. 69-98). Morgantown, WV: Fitness Information Technology.

Matveyev, L. (1981). *Fundamentals of sports training*. Moscow: Progress Publishers.

Mikes, J. (1987). *Basketball fundamentals – A complete mental training guide*. Champaign, IL: Human Kinetics.

Moran, A. P. (1996). *The psychology of concentration in sport performers: A cognitive analysis*. East Sussex, UK: Psychology Press.

Moran, A. P. (2003). Improving concentration skills in team-sport performers: Focusing techniques for soccer players. In R. Lidor & K. P. Henschen (Eds.), *The psychology of team sports* (pp. 161-189). Morgantown, WV: Fitness Information Technology.

Moran, A. P. (2005). Training attention and concentration skills in athletes. In D. Hackfort, J. L. Duda, & R. Lidor (Eds.), *Handbook of research in applied sport and exercise psychology: International perspectives* (pp. 61-73). Morgantown, WV: Fitness Information Technology.

Nideffer, R. M. (1992). *Psyched up to win: How to master mental skills to improve your physical performance*. Champaign, IL: Human Kinetics.

Nideffer, R. M., & Sagal, M. (2001). Concentration and attention control training. In J. M. Williams (Ed.), *Applied sport psychology: Personal growth to peak performance* (4th ed., pp. 312-332). Mountain View, CA: Mayfield.

Ravizza, K., & Hanson, T. (1995). *Heads-up baseball: Playing the game one pitch at a time*. Indianapolis, IN: Master's Press.

Schmidt, R. (1975). A schema theory of discrete motor skill learning. *Psychological Review*, 82, 225-260.

Singer, R. N. (1995). Mental quickness in dynamic sport situations. In F. H. Fu & M. L. Ng (Eds.), *Sport psychology: Perspectives and practices toward the 21st century* (pp. 63-82). Hong Kong: Hong Kong Baptist University.

Tenenbaum, G. (Ed.). (2001). *The practice of sport psychology*. Morgantown, WV: Fitness Information Technology.

Tenenbaum, G. (2003). Expert athletes: An integrated approach to decision making. In J. L. Starkes & K. A. Ericsson (Eds.), *Expert performance in sports: Advances in research on sport expertise* (pp. 191-218). Champaign, IL: Human Kinetics.

Tuckman, B. W. (1965). Developmental sequences in small groups. *Psychological Bulletin*, 63, 384-399.

Webster's New Encyclopedia Dictionary (1993). New York: Black Dog & Leventhal.

Williams, A. M., Davids, K., & Williams, J. G. (1999). *Visual perception and action in sport*. London: E & FN Spon.

Zatsiorsky, V. M. (1995). *Science and practice of strength training*. Champaign, IL: Human Kinetics.

# CHAPTER 6

# PSYCHOLOGICAL PREPARATION IN SPORT

DANIEL GOULD AND SARAH CARSON

"I like the Olympics because... there is so much at stake. The more at stake the better." (Greenleaf, Gould, & Dieffenbach, 2001)

"We knew we were there for one purpose and one purpose only... It wasn't to go party... It was for us to be the best that we could be." (Gould, Guinan, Greenleaf, Medbery, & Peterson, 1999)

"Just as physical training is a process, so is mental training, and you can't expect to have an expert come in and do a quick fix." (Gould et al., 1999)

As the above quotes from Olympic competitors show, great athletes and coaches feel that psychological preparation is critical for athletic success. Over the last 30 years, sport psychology researchers have focused much of their research efforts toward a better understanding of how psychological factors influence athletic performance, and on ways to enhance athlete mental preparation. Practicing sport psychology consultants have also added to this wealth of knowledge through summarized lessons from their consulting experiences in the form of professional practice articles and chapters.

This chapter is designed to summarize this literature and outline implications for psychological training and preparation of athletes and teams. The chapter's three purposes are: first, to discuss what research has revealed about psychological preparation in sport and ways mental training can be used to enhance psychological preparation of individual athletes and teams; second, to identify psychological preparation and mental training principles that can be used to guide professional practice; and third, to provide case examples of how these principles can be used to help athletes and teams enhance their mental preparation for sport.

## THEORETICAL BACKGROUND

A major barrier to reviewing the literature on psychological preparation in sport is the expansiveness of the topic. The topic could virtually include all the performance-oriented research in sport psychology. The scope of such a review is well beyond the space available in a chapter such as this. Therefore, we will begin by outlining what psychological preparation for sport performance involves and by defining mental skills training and what it entails. We will then summarize the research on psychological characteristics, differentiating more versus less successful athletes, factors influencing Olympic performance, and psychological factors involved in group or team performance. Finally, the efficacy of athlete and team mental training studies will be examined.

### MENTAL TRAINING AND PSYCHOLOGICAL PREPARATION FOR PEAK PERFORMANCE

Mental skills training has been defined as the systematic employment of "procedures that enhance an athlete's ability to use his or her mind effectively and readily in the execution of sport-related goals" (Gould & Damarjian, 1998, p. 70). This training typically focuses on learning skills and techniques that enhance performance, such as goal setting, stress management, and confidence enhancement. However, in recent years there has been a move towards teaching athletes, particularly young athletes, psychological skills and techniques (e.g., moral development, leadership, goal setting) through sports participation. These skills can then be transferred to other situations beyond sport. This latter area has often been referred to as teaching life skills through sport (see Danish & Nellen, 1997; Hellison, 1995), and is an extremely important movement in the field since it demonstrates how sport can be a tremendous developmental experience in one's life. Because of space limitations, however, this chapter will focus only on the more traditional approach of psychological preparation and training for enhanced athletic performance.

## PSYCHOLOGICAL CHARACTERISTICS OF TOP PERFORMERS AND STUDIES ON PSYCHOLOGICAL DIFFERENCES IN ATHLETES

Over the last 30 years, sport psychology researchers have been studying psychological characteristics of elite sport performers, using both in-depth interviews and formal and informal psychological assessments. For example, Gould, Dieffenbach, and Moffett (2002) gave standardized psychological measures to 10 Olympic champions, and interviewed the athletes, a parent, or a significant other who knew each athlete throughout their career, as well as the athletes' coaches. Results revealed that these outstanding performers were characterized by high levels of confidence, the ability to cope with and control their anxiety, the ability to focus and block out distractions, competitiveness, the ability to set and achieve goals, high levels of optimism, adaptive perfectionism, sport intelligence, and resiliency/mental toughness.

In another recent study, Jones, Hanton, and Connaughton (2002) had 10 highly successful international athletes identify the attributes of a "mentally tough" athlete. Attributes identified included: an unshakable self-belief in one's ability to achieve; having an unshakable belief that one has unique attributes that make him or her better than opponents; an insatiable desire to achieve; the ability to bounce back from setbacks; thriving on competitive pressure; recognizing that competitive anxiety is inevitable and knowing one can cope with it; not being adversely affected by good or bad performances; remaining fully focused in the face of life distractions; the ability to switch sport focus on and off; remaining fully focused in the face of sport distractions; pushing the boundaries of emotional and physical pain while maintaining technique; and regaining control when unexpected or uncontrollable events occur.

Taking a more quantitative approach, Thomas, Murphy, and Hardy (1999) developed the Test of Performance Strategies (TOPS), a measure of the eight psychological skills of goal setting, relaxation, activation, imagery, self-talk, attentional control/ negative thinking, emotional control, and automaticity. The TOPS, unlike previous measures, assesses mental skills in the contexts of both practice and competition. Initial scale development work revealed that international-level athletes used a wider range of psychological strategies than college, regional, and recreational performers. Moreover, with the effects of age removed from the data, these differences were significant for goal setting, imagery, and activation in males, and for self-talk, emotional control, goal setting, imagery, activation, negative thinking, and relaxation in females.

Finally, after carefully reviewing much of the research in this area, Williams and Krane (2001) concluded that a number of specific mental skills and psychological characteristics (e.g., having a well developed competitive routine and plan, high levels of motivation and commitment, coping skills for dealing with distractions and unexpected events, heightened concentration, high levels of self-confidence, self-regulation of arousal, goal setting, and visualization) were associated with peak performance. Highly successful athletes, then, have been shown in the research to have unique psychological skills that help them achieve athletic success.

## PSYCHOLOGICAL FACTORS ASSOCIATED WITH OLYMPIC PERFORMANCE SUCCESS

Another way sport psychology researchers have studied the role psychological factors play in sport success is through studies of athletes participating in the Olympic Games. Orlick and Partington (1988) began this line of research with their ground-breaking study of 1984 Canadian Olympians. Using both interviews and surveys, these investigators found that mental readiness was a significant factor influencing performance at the Games. In particular, athletes who demonstrated superior performance demonstrated a total commitment to excellence, had plans for dealing with distractions, had detailed performance competitive plans and routines, took part in quality training involving the use of goal setting, imagery and competitive simulations, and had the ability to focus attention. Olympians who did not perform up to their expectations reported changing things that work, late team selection, and the inability to focus in the face of distractions.

More recently, a series of studies examining factors influencing the performance of U.S. Olympians over three Olympic Games (Atlanta, Nagano, and Sydney) was conducted (Gould, Diffenbach et al., 2002; Gould, Greenleaf, Chung, & Guinan, 2002; Gould, Greenleaf, Guinan, Dieffenbach, & McCann, 2001; Gould, Guinan, Greenleaf, Medbery, & Peterson, 1999; Greenleaf et al., 2001). Multiple methods were used in these studies, including individual athlete interviews, focus group team interviews, coach interviews, and surveys of athletes and coaches. Medal versus non-medal winning athletes and teams were compared, and a large number of diverse factors were found to influence performance. This led the investigators to conclude that successful Olympic performance was influenced by a number of diverse psychological and physical factors that could easily be disrupted by numerous distractions. While long term preparation is critical for success, athletes and coaches must also exhibit a good deal of flexibility during the Games and react to unexpected events and numerous potential distractions. Psychological factors of particular influence included the quality and length of mental training, the ability to focus, commitment, viewing the Olympics as a time to shine, adherence to performance routines, the ability to deal with distractions, team unity, family/friend support, and strong team chemistry and cohesion.

This line of research, then, clearly demonstrates that Olympic performance is determined by an array of psychological factors. Moreover, mental preparation and training is a key to Olympic performance success.

## TEAM PERFORMANCE RESEARCH

In the previous Olympic studies it was found that team unity, cohesion, and social support were related to Olympic success for both individual athletes and teams. These findings are important in that much of the sport psychological research conducted to date has focused on the individual athlete. Yet many athletes typically train and perform in teams or groups. It is critical, then, that those interested in psychological preparation in sport have an understanding of groups, group processes, and group productivity.

When compared to research attention focused on individual competitors, group research is generally lacking in sport psychology. However, a small but committed group of researchers has focused their careers on looking at the psychology of groups and teams, and much has been learned from their efforts.

In their book, *Group Dynamics in Sport*, Carron and Hausenblas (1998) summarized the research on groups and teams in sport and integrated this literature with the general psychological research on group dynamics. Those engaged in mental training of athletes should be familiar with this work. Carron and Hausenblas have shown, for example, that the group cohesion-athletic performance relationship is more complex than once thought. Increasing team cohesion increases performance, but improved performance also increases cohesion. The cohesion-performance relationship is also mediated by the type of task/sport being performed, with cohesion having a stronger relationship in interactive sports such as basketball and volleyball and less influence on coactive tasks such as bowling and golf. Lastly, different types of cohesion have been identified: task cohesion – the degree to which a team is united in the pursuit of a common goal, and social cohesion, or the degree to which members of a group enjoy each others company and social interaction. In general, task cohesion has been found to have a stronger relationship to performance than social cohesion.

Another important set of findings focuses on the makeup of groups. Citing research on the Ringleman effect (Ingham, Levinger, Graves, & Peckham, 1974), it has been found that group performance is not a simple additive function of individual member abilities. Hence, the five most skilled players do not necessarily make the most effective basketball team; it is the five most talented individuals who can work together with the fewest losses, due to motivation and coordination of efforts. Thus, the team as a whole is more than the simple sum of individual member abilities.

Related to the above findings, group performance researchers have also discovered that social loafing, the phenomenon in which individual group members give less effort as group size increases, can occur in sport groups (Hanrahan & Gallois, 1993). More importantly, social loafing can be prevented if individual group members receive feedback relative to their individual efforts. Therefore, understanding one's roles and being aware of the social loafing phenomenon can help to eliminate it.

Finally, sport psychology researchers have studied effective leadership in groups, and rejected the notion that effective leaders possess the same universal set of personality traits (see Weinberg & Gould, 2003 for a summary of this research). In contrast, leadership is best understood from a person-by-situation perspective, where effective leadership is dependent on leader qualities, leadership style, situational factors, and characteristics of the followers. This implies that leaders must match their style to particular situations that are conducive to that style, or must change their style to match situation and follower needs.


## EFFICACY OF MENTAL TRAINING RESEARCH

For about 20 years practitioners have been implementing mental skills training (MST) programs to enhance performance and enjoyment of participation among athletes from varied sports and competitive levels (Mamassis & Doganis, 2004; Orlick & McCaffrey, 1991). However, only in recent years have investigators turned their attention to examining the utility of these MST programs.

Findings across several studies have shown that MST programs are indeed effective for achieving a variety of desired outcomes, such as decreased anxiety (Buckles, 1984; Elko & Ostrow, 1991; Savoy, 1997), enhanced self-confidence (Bakker & Kayser, 1994; Burton, 1988; Mamassis & Doganis, 2004), and improved performance (Buckles, 1984; Hall & Rodgers, 1989; McCaffrey & Orlick, 1989; Patrick & Hrycaiko, 1998; Savoy, 1993). Savoy and Beitel (1997) tested the efficacy of a MST program on the pre-game state anxiety and self-confidence of a NCAA Division I female basketball team and its individual players (n = 10). The team as a whole received training in centering, focusing, and imagery three times a week throughout a competitive season. After an instruction phase, these three psychological skills were integrated into a routine the athletes performed five minutes prior to each practice session for the remaining six weeks of the competitive season. Three of the ten athletes (one first-year, one second-year, and one fourth-year; two starters and one substitute) were also selected to participate in individualized MST programs. These athletes met individually (for one-half hour a week) with the team's sport psychology consultant to work on positive self-talk, the use of cues to promote concentration, and/or energizing techniques. The athletes each chose two of the three psychological skills to learn and integrate into their personalized psychological skills training (PST) programs, and were also instructed in the use of a logging system to monitor their progress. Pre-game scores on the CSAI-2 (a measure of state anxiety and self-confidence) and post-game evaluations of the use of psychological performance during competition demonstrated that both cognitive and somatic anxiety were significantly reduced in the athletes who received the group PST program and also in those who had received the group and individualized PST programs. However, those athletes in the group/individualized PST program combination exhibited greater and more significant decreases in anxiety levels. These three athletes also demonstrated a positive significant change in self-confidence, whereas the group intervention athletes did not. Thus, while a group PST intervention proved to be effective, a combined group and individualized intervention program exhibited greater positive outcomes.

Another conclusion, in research conducted by Savoy and Beitel (1997), was that the use of logs, game evaluation forms, and individual interactions was particularly useful in reducing state anxiety and increasing self-confidence of athletes. Similarly, other studies have made recommendations for improving the effectiveness of MST programs with athletes and teams. A few practical suggestions have been: to incorporate MST programs throughout an entire season to increase their effectiveness (Mamassis & Doganis, 2004); to help athletes view MST as a standard and useful part of their training for sport, and to train coaches how to better incorporate this training into practices (Nowicki, 1995); to provide athletes with a variety of psychological skills and explain how they can be used in combination (Patrick & Hrycaiko, 1998); and to constantly evaluate MST programs for effectiveness and areas of improvement (Hardy & Jones, 1994).

Although the effectiveness of MST programs has been supported across several research projects, a word of caution is in order. This line of research has proven to have several inherent challenges in its implementation. Firstly, these studies tend to look at the effectiveness of MST programs that occur within intact field situations. In other words, MST interventions are carried out with athletes and teams submerged within a dynamic sport environment. Research conducted in these settings does not allow for strict control of variables, thus relationships between variables might be confounded, and therefore causal relationships cannot be determined. Another difficulty that exists in carrying out research in this area is that the study of MST program effectiveness is not conducive to large scale research projects, and thus the generalizability of the research findings is reduced. The coordination of a large scale MST intervention and assessment would not only be challenging, but it would also be unrepresentative of most MST programs. A final challenge faced by those who study MST effectiveness is the lack of a common conception of what constitutes MST. Some studies have addressed single-skills interventions aimed at outcomes, while others have studied the effectiveness of mental skills packages that encompass a wide range of skills (Mamassis & Doganis, 2004). Additionally, programs that train the same skills use varied methods of MST, making comparisons of programs problematic. In spite of the complexity involved in studying the effectiveness of MST programs, more research is needed in this area to develop a clearer understanding of what MST practices are advantageous for achieving positive outcomes and how to best implement these practices.

## PRINCIPLES OF PSYCHOLOGICAL PREPARATION AND MENTAL TRAINING

The actual process of mental training is similar to that used by teachers, consultants, and coaches. What separates sport psychology specialists from other potential mental skills training program providers is their discipline-specific knowledge of sport psychology. Simply teaching relaxation skills, confidence building strategies, or enhancing group cohesion, and thinking that doing so will enhance athletic performance, is unrealistic.

One must determine which emotional state within an athlete or team is associated with best performance, the type of cohesion needed for best performance, and the levels of sport specific self-efficacy required.

Below are some key discipline-specific principles that should be understood by those engaging in mental training. These are derived from extensive reviews of the research conducted by Hardy, Jones, and Gould (1996), Gould, Greenleaf, and Krane (2001), and Weinberg and Gould (2003), and include principles related to individual athlete and team performance.

## INDIVIDUAL PERFORMER PRINCIPLES

- A substantial body of mental preparation research has shown that each athlete has an individual, specific recipe of feelings and emotions that is associated with peak athletic performance. Often referred to as one's *zone of optimal functioning*, it is critical that athletes learn what this zone entails and how to regulate their states of emotions and feelings in order to reach this optimal zone of functioning.
- Athletes perform best when they develop specific physical and mental preparation routines and adhere to those routines in the face of adversity and challenges. These should be designed to control one's attention, cognitive anxiety (e.g., worry), and physiological arousal.
- Elite athletes experience stress from a variety of physical (e.g., injury), psychological (e.g., meeting others' expectations), social (e.g., playing in front of hostile crowds) and organizational (e.g., sport organization politics) sources. They must learn to manage this stress.
- Stress can be managed in a number of ways. Physical stress management techniques like progressive relaxation, cognitive stress management such as thought stopping and restructuring, multimodal techniques like stress inoculation training, and environmental engineering techniques (e.g., eliminating parents from games to reduce pressure) can be used. Athletes must learn multiple methods of coping with stress, and to be effective these techniques must be fully understood.
- It may be best to tailor the specific type of anxiety techniques used to the particular types of anxiety experienced (e.g., for cognitive anxiety cognitive techniques like thought restructuring; for somatic anxiety a physical technique like progressive relaxation).
- Athletes should set a combination of difficult but realistic long- and short-term goals. These should include performance goals (e.g., increasing the percentage of first serves in tennis), process goals (e.g., having a consistent ball toss on the serve), and outcome goals (e.g., winning a particular tournament). These goals should be specific and measurable versus general and vague.
- Immediately before competition it is best to focus on process goals as opposed to outcome or performance goals, since the athlete has much more control over process goals.
- Mental imagery is an effective technique for enhancing performance but is not a replacement for physical practice. Therefore, it must be practiced and integrated into physical practice.

- Outstanding performers not only need high levels of general confidence, but also specific efficacy expectations for important sport tasks (e.g., fielding in baseball and digging in volleyball).
- It is unlikely that any single coping strategy will work in all situations or that any one strategy will be effective all the time. Thus, athletes should develop a variety of stress-coping techniques.
- Coping strategies must be so well learned that they are executed in an automatic fashion. Competitive simulations should also be extensively used to ensure that mental skills can work effectively in pressure situations.
- If an athlete experiences a performance catastrophe (e.g., totally falls apart as result of excessive stress) he or she must be taken out of the situation, substantially relax, restructure his or her thoughts, and then reactivate to the optimal zone of functioning before performance can be recovered.
- Efforts should be made to eliminate coping misconceptions such as "one can always go it alone." Efforts should be made to seek out appropriate social support.
- High levels of intrinsic and extrinsic motivation are needed for elite performances. Self-motivation is best sustained by providing choice and self-determination for athletes.
- Athletes have multiple motives for participation, including self-improvement, affiliation, winning, and fun. For motivation to be maintained these multiple motives must be satisfied.
- All elite performers should be instructed on the use of positive self-talk and cognitive restructuring, especially when faced with failure or adversity.

## TEAM SPORTS PRINCIPLES

- Efforts must be made to mentally prepare not only individual team members, but the team as a whole. Moreover, the team is more than the simple sum of its parts. Mental training efforts need to address how individual player psychological attributes, goals, motives, and communication patterns come together and interact to form a team.
- Team goals should be set, but they also are not simply the sum of individual member goals. They must be discussed and accepted by all team members. For team success, individual members must be willing to place team goals ahead of individual goals.
- Norms of "high" productivity must be established for teams to be effective.
- Individual player roles must be discussed and accepted by individual team members. Role clarity and acceptance is critical.
- To avoid social loafing coaches and team leaders must delineate individual roles with players, discuss social loafing, develop pride in subunits, and provide individual feedback within the group context.
- Efforts must be made to build both task and social cohesion.

## CONDUCTING MENTAL TRAINING PROGRAMS: KEY STEPS[1]

There are two typical ways in which mental training programs are conducted (Gould, 2000). One is an intervention that is preplanned and is not initiated in reaction to a particular psychological problem an individual athlete or team may have experienced. Much like preventive medicine, this type of approach is carried out in an effort to make athletes and teams psychologically stronger. A second approach is problem-centered. A coach or athlete engages in mental training in an effort to overcome a particular psychological issue such as inability to perform under pressure, lack of confidence, or poor team cohesion. The biggest differences between these two situations is that in the former, some athletes may not be motivated to engage in mental training, and that program leaders are under less time pressure to produce performance results. However, the general steps that a consultant follows are similar in either case.

## STEP 1: CLARIFY PROGRAM PURPOSES AND THE CONSULTANT'S ROLE AND DUTIES

Before starting any mental skills training program, purposes and consultant roles and duties must be clarified and understood by all parties involved. For example, as a consultant, is one working for the team or for an individual athlete? Will the consultant be involved in team selection? In the case that the athlete is a minor, do parents understand and agree to any confidentiality concerns? If it is a team situation, does management expect the consultant to give differential time to starters versus bench players? Questions such as these must be addressed.

In addition to the more philosophical questions, a variety of logistical issues must be understood. What cost will be charged for services, and when will payments be made? How much time is the athlete or team willing to devote to mental training each week? Finally, what facilities are available, and does the consultant have a budget for supplies and materials?

An especially important set of issues to discuss is ethics. A consultant should indicate the type of professional training he or she has had and what this training qualifies him or her to do and not to do (e.g., an educational sport psychology consultant is not equipped to handle clinical issues). Consultant-client confidentiality should also be addressed, as well as any limits to that confidentiality. Lastly, it is especially important for coaches to understand that a consultant may not be able to convey some types of information to interested parties (e.g., coaches, administrators) because of his or her promise of confidentiality to an athlete.

## STEP 2: CONDUCT AN ASSESSMENT TO DETERMINE SPECIFIC TOPICS/NEEDS TO ADDRESS AND BARRIERS TO MENTAL SKILLS DEVELOPMENT

Once a consultant's roles and responsibilities are clarified and understood, he or she needs to determine what specific topics or athlete/team needs must be addressed. This may be done in a formal manner by using some sort of psychological assessment such as the TOPS. Many consultants, however, simply conduct an informational interview with key parties involved in order to develop a sense of what psychological strengths an athlete or

---

1 These steps are presented as a general guide for organizing a mental skills training program to enhance psychological preparation for sport. However, they should not be viewed as invariant and are not time-dependent. For instance, it is not uncommon to do Steps 1-4 in an initial meeting with an athlete. Similarly, as one consults, he or she is constantly employing many of the steps in an iterative fashion.

team possess. Areas of improvement should also be addressed. Even though a consultant may have a good idea of what is needed, it is essential to listen to all parties involved, as some unexpected needs may arise.

During this process it is essential to begin to identify barriers that might interfere with program success. Previous literature (e.g., Pain & Harwood, 2004; Ravizza, 1988) has identified a lack of knowledge of or misconceptions about psychology, a lack of time, the failure of key parties (e.g., coaches) to buy into the program, funding, and unrealistic expectations for immediate or dramatic results, as often experienced barriers. By identifying these barriers, efforts can be made to avoid or overcome them.

## STEP 3: HOLD MEETINGS TO INCREASE AWARENESS AND CONVEY CRITICAL INFORMATION

Once program goals are established, an initial meeting must be held with the athlete or team to discuss the program and how it will be carried out. This is a tricky meeting in many ways, as the consultant must convince the client that mental skills training works, and that it is worth investing his or her time in this process. At the same time, the benefits should not be emphasized so forcefully that participants develop unrealistic expectations and false hopes. A good deal of effective persuasion is needed here, but we have also found that movie clips, activities, and exercises can help make the importance of mental skills come alive for athletes. Finally, research by Orlick and Partington (1987) has emphasized the importance of building credibility and trust in such an initial session. This may come from the way one fits into the particular athletic culture, showing some knowledge of the sport, using practical/concrete examples, and being perceived as a "regular" down-to-earth person versus an aloof academic.

## STEP 4: IDENTIFY ON AND OFF-THE-FIELD STRATEGIES TO IMPLEMENT CHANGE OR DEVELOP SKILLS

Once mental preparation skills training needs are identified, strategies for teaching and practicing mental skills must be derived. For example, for an athlete who is having difficulty dealing with competitive stress and is experiencing considerable cognitive and somatic anxiety, any number of strategies may be taught. These might include the identification of his or her optimal zone of functioning, the development of precompetitive physical and mental preparation routines, thought stopping and replacement, progressive muscle relaxation, centered breathing, and positive imagery. It is important to have multiple strategies as not all strategies will work with a particular athlete or in a particular context, and/or one strategy alone may not be enough to combat the problem at hand.

## STEP 5: IMPLEMENT INTERVENTION STRATEGIES

When studying how coaches use mental skills training (Gould, Damarjian, & Medbery, 1999; Gould, Medbery, Damarjian, & Lauer, 1999), our research group found that knowledge of one particular technique or strategy is not enough. Coaches must understand how to make these techniques come alive for their players and specifically teach them to implement these skills in on-the-field practice and competitive situations. Thus, techniques and strategies must be presented in engaging, practical ways.

For example, we might teach an athlete centered breathing (a slow deep breath to regain composure) in a classroom setting. However, as soon as possible, we will incorporate this skill onto the field by having players "center" during warm-ups and cool-downs. Finally, one must monitor the athletes' centering use, and instruct them to use centered breathing in competitive "pressure" simulations during practices, and ultimately in game situations.

To help the athletes better remember to center we sometimes present it as a "flush" breath, emphasizing the need for the athletes to clear their heads of all waste products such as negative thoughts, worry, and undue tension. In fact, in teams where we have done this, athletes and coaches often told teammates to "flush it" after a teammate had made a mistake, reminding them to take a second to compose themselves before resuming action.

## STEP 6: PROVIDE FEEDBACK AND ADJUST STRATEGIES

Teaching mental skills is an imperfect process, and strategies do not always work. Adjustments must be made, and athletes must provide consultants with feedback as to how their efforts are progressing.

Simultaneously, consultants must help athletes monitor their psychological skills training efforts and provide feedback when needed. So it is a mistake to simply present mental skills to athletes and assume they will be implemented. Consultants need to facilitate adherence and provide critical feedback.

## STEP 7: EVALUATE PROGRESS AND CONSULTANT EFFECTIVENESS, AND MODIFY THE PROGRAM

Mental skills training efforts are not as tightly controlled as monitored research studies. Thus, it is often difficult to determine how successful a program actually is. Improved performance is certainly an important indicant, but it can be affected by numerous other factors. Athlete self-reports are important, but as a consultant you need to work hard to make sure athletes will give you honest feedback about what works and what does not (often, if athletes like a consultant they do not want to hurt his or her feelings by saying something does not work).

Asking coaches to look for performance improvements helps, and simply looking for instances of athletes executing their psychological skills in the field are critical (e.g., using their pre-performance routines, taking flush breaths). The key, however, is to always be looking for ways to evaluate program effectiveness and to use multiple feedback sources for doing so.

## EXAMPLE CONSULTATIONS:
## PREPARATION FOR GAMES AND COMPETITIONS[2]

It has been our experience that psychological preparation programs for individual athletes and teams, while having some common elements, in the end are always somewhat unique and situational dependent. Hence, as a consultant you are constantly customizing your program to the unique needs of the athlete or the team and to the situation in which they train and perform. To illustrate this and other points emphasized in this chapter, two mental training cases are presented. The first involves a problem-focused consultation with an individual athlete who had considerable problems dealing with competitive stress. The second focuses on a preventative team program designed to help a college softball team develop improved group functioning.

### CASE 1: HELPING MICHAEL DEFEAT PERFORMANCE-DEBILITATING ANXIETY[3]

Michael was a 25 year-old power weight lifter with eight years of experience. He approached the first author by the recommendation of his physical conditioning coach. Michael was very dejected after competing in the World Championships. A favorite to win a medal, Michael instead had a disastrous performance. He was eliminated early in the competition after missing three consecutive lifts at relatively easy weights for him.

In the initial meeting with Michael, the first author described his background and training, informed Michael of his consulting capabilities, and discussed confidentiality. Michael informed the consultant that his goal was to lift to his capabilities and that he hoped the first author could help him achieve that goal. No formal assessment was conducted, but during our discussion it became clear that Michael had a highly perfectionistic personality, frequently exhibited emotional control and frustration problems, and had very low self-confidence. Michael based his self-worth entirely on his performance success, and overtrained as a result of his excessive anxiety. Lastly, he experienced considerable stress management problems in competitive performance situations.

Over a 30-month period, Michael and the first author met 27 times, with each meeting lasting between 60 and 90 minutes. Relative to assisting Michael in enhancing his performance and enjoying competition more, the consultant worked continuously on helping this athlete achieve a philosophical change relative to the importance of power lifting in his life. While recognizing that lifting was one of the most important things he did, it was continually emphasized to him that there was more to his life than lifting, and that he should not totally base his self-worth on his lifting performance. For example, he had a wife and son who loved him no matter how he lifted. Moreover, Michael learned to recognize that some bad performance days are normal for any elite athlete, and while they are not desirable, they should not be overanalyzed. Finally, minimizing the importance of

---

2 This case study originally appeared in Gould (2000).

3 Fictitious names have been used in these case examples to protect the identity of the participants.

others' performance expectations and understanding the positive and negative aspects of his perfectionism were continually emphasized.

To help Michael enhance his confidence, a number of strategies were used. Positive statements were written on cards, placed in his lifting bag, and read by him when he started to lose confidence. Michael also visualized lifting, and kept a log where he listed reasons why he should be successful. (e.g., ate right, trained hard). Short-term performance and process goals linked to long-term outcome dream goals (e.g., placing at Worlds) were set. Finally, Michael memorized positive statements to use during competitions.

Strategies Michael used to cope with excessive anxiety included focusing on realistic performance/process goals while downplaying outcome goals (especially during or near competition), centered breathing, and the development of performance refocusing routines. In conjunction with Michael's coach, specific periodization plans were also developed, emphasizing scheduled bouts of rest and relaxation. Particular emphasis was placed on identifying relaxing activities that distracted Michael from thinking too much about his lifting. Finally, strategies for dealing with the "trash" or "junk" talk of competitors were discussed, do's and don'ts of mental preparation were logged after performances, and competitive simulations were emphasized.

Michael's progress was gradual. He first focused on using his newly-acquired mental skills and strategies to lift consistently in regular competitions. Progress was slowly made, and effective strategies were identified, revised, and then used in competitions of greater importance (e.g., National Championships, World Championships). After 18 months, Michael was lifting well, and he finished in the top three in the U.S. nationals and qualified for the World championships. Michael failed to place in the Worlds, but while not having a great performance, he did not lift poorly. Most importantly, he coped well with the outcome. However, the next year Michael won a bronze medal at the World Championships. He retired after doing so.

A vital aspect from the consultant's perspective was the fact that Michael showed transfer from his athletic performance enhancement skills to other life settings. He learned to better control his emotions and frustration outside the gym as well, and seemed to enjoy life more.

CASE 2: TEAM BUILDING WITH A UNIVERSITY ATHLETIC TEAM

For two years the second author worked with a variety of groups, including sport teams, through a program that had the primary focus of aiding these groups in becoming more highly effective. Hundreds of programs like this one operate around the United States and are commonly referred to as adventure education, ropes course, or teambuilding programs. The underlying philosophy guiding these programs is that groups/teams can become more effective if given a common experience in which they are challenged, so that they become aware of their strengths and weaknesses, are educated about skills that highly effective groups/teams possess, and are given the opportunity to practice these skills and to identify ways in which they can be transferred into their everyday lives. The key to this philosophy is that group transformation occurs through a *shared experience*. The approach of learning-by-doing, or experiential education, is supported by studies demonstrating that by directly interacting with nature, people, objects, and tasks, material taught to individuals or groups is learned faster, better retained, and more greatly appreciated and understood than other, more traditional learning methods (Freeberg & Taylor, 1963).

Research has produced evidence suggesting that participation in teambuilding programs is related to positive outcomes, such as enhanced group cohesion, communication, trust, problem-solving, and decision making skills, conflict resolution, increased self-esteem, understanding, and respect for diversity, and leadership skills (Bronson, Gibson, Kichar, & Priest, 1992; Cason & Gillis, 1994; Goldenberg, Klenosky, O'Leary, & Templin, 2000; Goldman & Priest, 1991; Kadel, 1988). In one of the few empirical studies investigating the effectiveness of adventure education in the promotion of positive outcomes in athletic teams, Meyer and Wenger (1998) found that athletes reported increases in sport-related confidence, concentration, trust in teammates, and dedication to the team after their teambuilding experiences. Other common goals that teambuilding programs pursue are increased self-awareness and the development of skills such as goal setting, conflict management, role clarification, trust building, and creative thinking.

Following is a case example of how a teambuilding program (Adventure Inc. – a pseudonym) created and ran a teambuilding program for a university sport team (the Titans). Much of the work in setting up an adventure education program is done by the program's staff members (i.e., facilitators) before coming into contact with the athletes and coaches. In this case the facilitator was a doctoral student in applied sport psychology.

The Titan's teambuilding experience began when Coach Johnson contacted Adventure Inc. to schedule a program. In order to tailor the teambuilding experience to meet the needs and wishes of the Titans, information about the group (e.g., its size, member composition, performance history), the reasons the team was interested in teambuilding training (e.g., to set the tone for the season and to help incorporate new members and increase cohesion), and specific outcomes and goals the team hoped to accomplish through the program (e.g., setting goals for the upcoming season and to develop more effective on-the-field communication skills) were gathered. With this information, the consultant/facilitator could then construct a meaningful, appropriate, and purposeful program. Without first gathering background information, the facilitator could only produce a "cookie-cutter" program based on assumptions and best-guesses. The more relevant a program is made to the client and the more their language and personal experiences are incorporated, the greater the effectiveness of the program. The overall strength of the program is very reliant on this initial process of getting to know a team, who they are, and what they want to become.

While the activities of a given teambuilding experience will vary according to the group or team involved, a distinct sequence of activities is often used based on the premise that various activities, and the timing of their presentation, will be received by and affect a group in different ways. The facilitator must use his/her knowledge of the group and the potential effects of the activities when selecting the challenges and their order of presentation for a given program. The schedule used for Titans was: (1) introduction of facilitators and expectations for the day; (2) ice breakers and energizers; (3) low initiatives; (4) high initiatives; and (5) final program debriefing. Each of these will be described below.

When the Titans arrived at Adventure Inc.'s outdoor experiential campus, the first concern of the facilitators was to make sure that the group became acclimated to the novel and potentially intimidating environment (many adventure education courses, especially ropes courses, are in secluded, wooded areas, unfamiliar to many participants). If this step had not been taken, the athletes may have been too overwhelmed and distracted by the surroundings of the program and may have missed the learning opportunities presented to them. The Titans also had to be acclimated to the staff of Adventure Inc. Without establishing a familiarity with the facilitators, a group will most likely not be primed to hand over the trust needed to fully engage in the teambuilding experience. For these reasons, teambuilding programs start out with minimally challenging and more play-like activities, so as not to push the team members too far out of their comfort zones. An activity used in this stage of the program with the Titans was a "get-to-know-you"-type game called "have you ever." The athletes linked hands in a circle, with one athlete alone in the center of the circle. In order for the center member to get out of the middle, she/he had to tell a true statement about her/himself (participants are often prompted to share something that their teammates most likely do not already know – e.g., places they have traveled, foods they dislike, secret talents they have). If the statement is also true about any of the other teammates, those individuals and the center member leave their places and find a new spot in the circle. The last athlete to join the circle is now the new middle member. After a few activities like this one, a discussion about goals and expectations for the day, as well as a review of a few ground rules, are carried out before the next stage of the teambuilding program begins. In this case we talked with the members of the Titans about the goals that Coach Johnson had mentioned previously during the information gathering session (e.g., to enhance communication skills), and solicited other goals from the athletes themselves (e.g., to have fun and to gain a sense of bonding). Safety precautions, integrity issues, and choice in participation were also discussed.

After the first two phases of the teambuilding program were completed, a series of low initiatives or challenges were carried out that did not require participants to be more than one to two feet off the ground. These activities focused on initiatives that call for the group to work as a whole unit and to utilize skills such as problem solving, effective communication, trust, and planning (goal setting). Through these activities, groups are given a clear picture of how they tend to approach challenges, the skills they already make use of, and the skills they need to improve. At first participants may see these activities as games, thus the facilitator is responsible for helping the individuals see that how they think, behave, and interact in the teambuilding program reflects how they think, behave, and interact out in the "real world." These insights are not intuitively apparent, however, so facilitators often use a four-part strategy designed by Kolb (1984) to set up and process each activity. The four parts of the strategy are: *the concrete experience, reflection, generalization,* and *application.* Before an activity begins, a facilitator provides the group with appropriate instructions as well as metaphors the activity in a way that it is meaningful to the team (e.g., labeling certain elements of the activity with terms commonly used in the group's environment, such as referring to a hole in a web of ropes as a team role that one of the athletes must fill). Then, Kolb's first stage is initiated when the group executes the activity. The focus of this stage is simply to provide the group with the *concrete experience* from which the group will later draw and assign deeper and transferable meanings. The assignment of meaning to the activity takes place when the facilitator aids the group in debriefing (Kolb's *reflection* stage) the activity and discussing what group processes were observed. Once the group identifies several elements that were at work in the activity (e.g., skills that were used, obstacles that arose, and interactions between team members that took place), a discussion takes place on what implications these factors have in the "real world" (e.g., on the court, field, etc.). Finally, the group discusses how these reflections might translate into actions or changes (*application* stage) in the sport/work/classroom setting.

An activity that the Titans participated in during this phase of the teambuilding program is known as the "bullring" activity. The goal and rules of the activity were explained to the group by the facilitators who metaphored the situation to a personally relevant situation of the Titans. More specifically, while the object of the challenge is to problem-solve a way to carry a tennis ball to a distant container using a metal ring with a dozen six-foot strings tied to it, while dropping the ball as few times as possible, the facilitator did not relay this information to the group using these terms. Instead, the facilitator stated that the group was about to go on a journey, similar to the one they would be experiencing as they go through their season. By transporting the ball from the starting point to the container, they would be achieving some team goal. The group was then given a few minutes to decide on a team goal for the season. The Titans committed to having perfect attendance at each practice, with only illness and academic conflict serving as exceptions. Each of the strings attached to the ring symbolized the individual role each team member plays in achieving the team goal (*frontloading*). As the activity progressed, the facilitator imposed certain demands on the groups' functioning (e.g., muting a certain team member or having the group carry the ball through a narrow space), and had the group describe what these obstacles (e.g., poor time management with homework) in the activity might represent in their efforts to reach their team goal in the real world (*experience*). Once the activity was finished, the group processed what sort of behaviors they observed among the members (interpersonal and individual actions) and how these behaviors positively or negatively affected the group's functioning (*reflection*). For example, a few of the athletes pointed out that they noticed when a team member was not "carrying his or her weight" during the activity, and when others would get frustrated and yell at the teammate. Participants then discussed where they saw these same behaviors taking place on their team (e.g., during games, when athletes would get frustrated with a teammate and would often find themselves arguing), and the repercussions on their functioning and performance (e.g., this arguing would lead to a loss of focus and a decrease in performance) in sport (*generalization*). Finally, the Titans talked about which behaviors they would like to focus on to help them achieve their goal in the future and the pitfalls they need to avoid to be more successful (*application*). In this case they said they would use the phrase "stay in the game" until a break in play when they could address the athlete in a more calm and constructive manner. During this stage of the teambuilding experience, several other challenges focusing on different outcomes Coach Johnson had designated as important were completed.

High initiatives in the team building program are activities similar in nature to the low initiatives, but have an inherent sense of risk because they are carried out anywhere from

10 to 30 feet off the ground. These activities tend to focus on individual or paired performances, but also highlight the importance of a strong sense of support from the entire team in order to be most successful. Members of the Titans were faced with the challenge of individually climbing a 20-foot pole to stand on a foot-wide disk before jumping off the pole in an attempt to touch a dangling rope. While one member was engaged in the challenge, the rest of the team members acted as the safety system by managing a set of ropes attached to the climber (i.e., belaying), so that if the climber were to fall or when jumping from the pole, he or she would be supported by the ropes and would not fall to the ground or otherwise become injured. Each activity in this phase was also conducted using Kolb's (1984) processes.

A final debriefing was then conducted at the end of the program, for several reasons. First, the Titans were given the opportunity to reflect on the program as a whole by choosing the elements that they felt were most important and by commenting on how their group performed throughout the day. For example, some comments were made about how teammates admired each others' persistence in the face of adversity and how important they felt remembering that their goal for attendance would apply throughout the season. Secondly, this discussion allowed the facilitator to aid the group's development of action plans for carrying out what they had learned on the field/court/etc.

So, how can one evaluate whether or not learning within the group has taken place? One indication of learning is the level of understanding and awareness the group displays during the debriefing of the activities. In this case, the Titans showed signs of learning when they discussed how some of their behaviors in the challenges reminded them of their on-the-field interactions, instead of simply focusing on if they thought they "won" or "lost" the challenge. Another indicator is the changes in strategies, behaviors, and interactions the groups make throughout the teambuilding program. If the group continues to engage in the same ineffective approaches to the challenges after those interactions and behaviors were identified as unproductive, learning most likely did not take place or the dedication to making changes was not successful. For instance, in the first few activities the Titans jumped into them quickly without planning, causing many mistakes to be made. As the day progressed, the Titans devoted more time to strategizing and were able to transfer learning from one activity to the next.

Even if positive outcomes are achieved, these changes are sometimes short-lived. Meyer and Wenger (1998) suggested videotaping the teambuilding program for future viewing and arranging follow-up sessions with the program facilitators as strategies that could enhance long-term transference of positive outcomes. Team leaders (e.g., coaches and captains) are also potential sources of transference of program outcomes to "real world" outcomes. It would be useful for these individuals to periodically refer back to the group's shared experiences, lessons learned, and commitment to change. Fortunately for the Titans, Coach Johnson was committed to carrying out the lessons learned in the teambuilding experience back in the practice and playing fields. Several conversations were held between Coach Johnson, team members, and the lead facilitator pertaining to the positive impact the program had on the team's initial bonding, as well as to some of the action plans that were still being implemented as the season was nearing completion.

## LESSONS LEARNED FROM
## APPLIED SPORT PSYCHOLOGY CONSULTATIONS

One of the most important elements of effective consulting is to reflect on and learn from one's work (Gould, 2001, 2002). Lessons learned can then be used to improve future programs and to avoid pitfalls that have occurred in the past. Below are a number of lessons learned from our consulting experiences.

- *Develop realistic expectations by realizing that you will not reach or be successful with all athletes.* It is important to recognize that even the best consultants do not reach all athletes or coaches. Some athletes and coaches will simply not be convinced that mental skills training is important. Similarly, there are times where you will run what should be an effective program, but will be unsuccessful. This might result from factors out of your control such as coaches or parents unknowingly counteracting your effects, a poor match between your personality (or consulting style) and the athlete's, or having to overcome too severe of a problem in the amount of time available. This does not mean you should be pessimistic—in fact, effective consultants are optimistic and try to reach even the most disinterested athlete (and they sometimes do). However, they realize that at times, despite their best efforts, they will not be successful. This hurts and can be hard on the ego, but comes with the territory of being an applied sport psychology consultant.
- *Do not be afraid to discuss mistakes with colleagues.* Becoming an effective consultant takes considerable experience, and similar to developing as an athlete, one will make mistakes and encounter setbacks. It is a natural reaction not to want to talk about these issues, but it has been our experience that it is essential to find a place where you can discuss your successes and failures with colleagues (of course while maintaining confidentiality) and obtain ideas and feedback for improvement.
- *Recognize that there are a number of effective consulting styles, and find the style that works best for you.* Having observed and interacted with numerous consultants, we have learned that while effective consultants follow certain general principles (e.g., gaining athlete trust, providing concrete recommendations in terms athletes can understand), each consultant is unique and must develop his or her own style. Some are charismatic and exhibit high energy, while others are quiet and laid back. Still, others use humor effectively, while others seldom tell a joke. However, while novice consultants can learn from more experienced practitioners, each consultant needs to develop his or her own style – one that best fits his or her personality. Consultants cannot be someone they are not, and it is a mistake to think there is only one effective consulting style or approach.
- *Recognize that athlete and coach trust takes time to develop.* As consultants, we are passionate about our work and anxious to help athletes and coaches develop psychologically. However, we have found that we need to learn to be patient, because maximum effectiveness does not occur until athletes and coaches develop trust in the consultant, which takes time.
- *Realize that mental skills training takes time to develop.* One fallacy of applied sport psychology is the notion that a mental training consultant can give some advice and the athlete who follows it will experience immediate success. Seldom is this the case, and experienced consultants have learned that it takes time and considerable practice for one to develop effective mental skills.

- *Integrate mental skills into on-the-field situations.* Many envision a sport psychology consultant as someone who sits in an office, meets with an athlete, and discusses psychological issues. The athlete then goes off and plays better. Our experience is that while sport psychology consultants certainly meet with athletes in office settings, many are now working with coaches and athletes on the field, helping athletes transfer mental skills learned and discussed in the office to actual performance situations. Other consultants are using activities like adventure programming as ways to teach their athletes psychological skills. For example, we have worked with athletes on how to incorporate relaxation techniques during actual performance situations, how to use imagery to correct mistakes on the court or field during practice, and ways to regulate self-talk during tough physical training sessions. In our opinion, taking mental training to the pool, court, or playing field is the wave of the future of applied sport psychology.
- *Do not unknowingly make interventions more complex than they need to be.* One common mistake of well-trained, knowledgeable sport psychology consultants is that they try to tell athletes or coaches more than they need to know and/or make things too complex. While it is important to know that many of the issues we discuss are complex and multivariate, a secret of effective consultants is that they recognize that they do not necessarily need to convey this to an athlete. Quite the opposite, they should develop the ability to keep things simple, focused, and easy to understand. Athletes respond well to this on-target, focused approach.
- *Learn from the athletes and coaches you work with.* While athletes and coaches do not want consultants who provide complex, jargon-filled explanations, it is a mistake to assume that these same consultants are not knowledgeable about psychological issues. In fact, we have found that there is much to learn about applied sport psychology from most athletes and coaches, and to fail to do so is a great mistake. The lesson, then, is to listen when you consult and not only impart information but learn from those with whom you work.

## SUMMARY AND CONCLUSIONS

Psychological preparation for individual athlete and team performance is critical for athletic success. While athletes and coaches are aware of this, 30 years of sport psychological research is helping us to better understand and identify the psychological preparation needed to achieve athletic success, as well as how mental preparation training programs can help in this regard. Combining this research with consulting experiences allows us to formulate psychological preparation programs that will help athletes of all ages and ability levels achieve their athletic goals. However, this can only happen with quality consultants and coaches leading these efforts. It is our hope that this chapter will help you develop your skills to better psychologically prepare athletes for success.

## REFERENCES

Bakker, F. C., & Kayser, C. S. (1994). Effect of a self-help mental training programme. *International Journal of Sport Psychology, 25,* 158-175.

Bronson, J., Gibson, S., Kichar, R., & Priest, S. (1992). Evaluation of team development in a corporate adventure training program. *The Journal of Experiential* Education, 15, 50-53.

Buckles, T. (1984). *The effects of visuo-motor, behavior rehearsal on competitive performance tasks, anxiety, and attentional style.* Unpublished doctoral dissertation, The University of Tennessee, Knoxville.

Burton, D. (1988). Do anxious swimmers swim slower? Reexamining the elusive anxiety-performance. *Journal of Sport and Exercise Psychology, 10,* 45-61.

Carron, A. V., & Hausenblas, H. A. (1998). *Group dynamics in sport* (2nd ed.). Morgantown, WV: Fitness Information Technology.

Cason, D., & Gillis, H. (1994). A meta-analysis of outdoor adventure programming with adolescents. *The Journal of Experiential Education, 17,* 40-47.

Danish, S. J., & Nellen, V. C. (1997). New roles for sport psychologists: Teaching life skills through sport to at risk-youth. *Quest, 49,* 100-113.

Elko, P., & Ostrow, A. (1991). Effects of a rational emotive program on heightened anxiety levels of female college gymnasts. *The Sport Psychologist, 5,* 235-255.

Goldenberg, M. A., Klenosky, D. B., O'Leary, J. T., & Templin, T. J. (2000). A means-end investigation of ropes course experiences. *Journal of Leisure Research, 32,* 208-224.

Goldman, K., & Priest, S. (1991). Risk taking transfer in development training. *Journal of Adventure Education and Outdoor Leadership, 7,* 43-87.

Gould, D. (2000). Performance enhancement consulting: Lessons, guidelines, and common problems. In B. A. Carlsson, U. Johnson, & F. Wetterstrand (Eds.), *Sport psychology conferences in the new millennium: A dynamic research-practice perspective:* Proceedings (pp. 43-54). Halmstad, Sweden: Centre for Sport Science/School of Social and Health Sciences.

Gould, D. (2001). Sport psychology and the Nagano Olympic Games: The case of the US freestyle ski team. In G. Tenenbaum (Ed.), *Reflections and experiences in sport and exercise psychology* (pp. 49-76). Morgantown, WV: Fitness Information Technology.

Gould, D. (2002). The psychology of Olympic excellence and its development. *Psychology, 9,* 531-546.

Gould, D., & Damarjian, N. (1998). Mental skills training in sport. In B. C. Elliot (Ed.), *Applied sport science: Training in sport. International Handbook of Sport Science:* Vol. 3. (pp. 69-116). Sussex, England: Wiley.

Gould, D., Damarjian, N., & Medbery, R. (1999). An examination of mental skills training in junior tennis coaches. *The Sport Psychologist, 13,* 127-143.

Gould, D., Dieffenbach, K., & Moffett, A. (2002). Psychological characteristics and their development in Olympic champions. *Journal of Applied Sport Psychology, 14,* 177-209.

Gould, D., Greenleaf, C., Chung, Y., & Guinan, D. (2002). A survey of U.S. Atlanta and Nagano Olympians: Factors influencing performance. *Research Quarterly for Sport and Exercise, 73*, 175-186.

Gould, D., Greenleaf, C., Guinan, D., & Chung, Y. (2002). A survey of U.S. Olympic coaches: Factors influencing athlete performances and coach effectiveness. *The Sport Psychologist, 16*, 229-250.

Gould, D., Greenleaf, C., Guinan, D., Dieffenbach, K., & McCann, S. (2001). Pursuing performance excellence: Lessons learned from Olympic athletes and coaches. *Journal of Performance Excellence, 4*, 21-43.

Gould, D., Greenleaf, C., & Krane, V. (2001). The anxiety athletic performance relationship: Current status and future directions. In T. Horn (Ed.), *Advances in sport psychology* (2nd ed., pp. 207-241). Champaign, IL: Human Kinetics.

Gould, D., Guinan, D., Greenleaf, C., Medbery, R., & Peterson, K. (1999). Factors affecting Olympic performance: Perceptions of athletes and coaches from more and less successful teams. *The Sport Psychologist, 13*, 371-395.

Gould, D., Medbery, R., Damarjian, N., & Lauer, L. (1999). A survey of mental skills training, knowledge, opinions, and practices of junior tennis coaches. *Journal of Applied Sport Psychology, 11*, 28-50.

Greenleaf, C., Gould, D., & Dieffenbach, K. (2001). Factors influencing Olympic performance: Interviews with Atlanta and Nagano U.S. Olympians. *Journal of Applied Sport Psychology, 13*, 154-184.

Hall, C., & Rodgers, W. (1989). Enhancing coach effectiveness in figure skating through a mental skills training program. *The Sport Psychologist, 3*, 142-154.

Hanrahan, S., & Gallois, C. (1993). Social interactions. In R. N Singer, M. Murphy, & L. K. Tennant (Eds.), *Handbook for sport psychology* (pp. 623-346). New York: Macmillan.

Hardy, L., & Jones, G. (1994). Current issues and future directions for performance-related research in sport psychology. *Journal of Sports Sciences, 12*, 61-92.

Hardy, L., Jones, J. G., & Gould, D. (1996). *Understanding psychological preparation for sport: Theory and practice of elite performers*. Sussex, UK: Wiley.

Hellison, D. (1995). *Teaching responsibility through physical activity*. Champaign, IL: Human Kinetics.

Ingham, A. G., Levinger, G., Graves, J., & Peckham, C. (1974). The Ringleman effect: Studies of group size and group performances. *Journal of Experimental Social Psychology, 10*, s.

Jones, G., Hanton, S., & Connaughton, D. (2002). What is this thing called mental toughness? *Journal of Applied Sport Psychology, 14*, 205-218.

Kadel, S. (1988). Executives grasp goals, teamwork in outdoors. *The Business Journal, 5*, 3.

Kolb, D. A. (1984). *Experiential learning: Experience as the source of learning and development*. Englewood Cliffs, NJ: Prentice Hall.

Mamassis, G., & Doganis, G. (2004). The effects of a mental training program on juniors pre-competitive anxiety, self-confidence, and tennis performance. *Journal of Applied Sport Psychology, 16*, 118-137.

McCaffrey, N., & Orlick, T. (1989). Mental factors related to excellence among top professional golfers. *International Journal of Psychology, 20*, 256-278.

Meyer, B. B., & Wenger, M. S. (1998). Athletes and adventure education: An empirical investigation. *International Journal of Sport Psychology, 29,* 243-266.

Nowicki, D. (1995). Using mental training during residential squad training in combat sports: A Polish experience. *The Sport Psychologist, 9,* 164-168.

Orlick, T., & McCaffrey, N. (1991). Mental training with children for sport and life. *The Sport Psychologist, 5,* 322-334.

Orlick, T., & Partington, J. (1987). The sport psychology consultant: Analysis of critical components as viewed by Canadian Olympic athletes. *The Sport Psychologist, 1,* 4-17.

Orlick, T., & Partington, J. (1988). Mental links to excellence. *The Sport Psychologist, 2,* 105-130.

Pain, M. A., & Harwood, C. G. (2004). Knowledge and perceptions of sport psychology within English soccer. *Journal of Sport Sciences, 22,* 813-826.

Patrick, T. D., & Hrycaiko, D. W. (1998). Effects of a mental training package in an endurance performance. *The Sport Psychologist, 12,* 283-299.

Ravizza, K. (1988). Gaining entry with athletic personnel for season-long consulting. *The Sport Psychologist, 2,* 243–254.

Savoy, C. (1993). A yearly mental training program for a college basketball player. *The Sport Psychologist, 7,* 173-190.

Savoy, C. (1997). Two individualized mental training programs for a team sport. *International Journal of Sport Psychology, 28,* 259-270.

Savoy, C., & Beitel, P. (1997). The relative effect of a group and group/individualized program on state anxiety and state self-confidence. *Journal of Sport Behavior, 20,* 364-376.

Thomas, P. R., Murphy, S. M., & Hardy, L. (1999). Test of performance strategies: Development and preliminary validation of a comprehensive measure of athletes' psychological skills. *Journal of Sport Sciences, 17,* 697-711.

Weinberg, R. S., & Gould, D. (2003). *Foundations of sport and exercise psychology.* (3rd ed.). Champaign, IL: Human Kinetics.

Williams, J. M., & Krane, V. (2001). Psychological characteristics of peak performance. In J. M. Williams (Ed.), *Applied sport psychology: Personal growth to peak performance* (4th ed., pp. 137-147). Mountain View, CA: Mayfield.

# CHAPTER 7

## PERIODIZATION AND PLANNING OF PSYCHOLOGICAL PREPARATION IN INDIVIDUAL AND TEAM SPORTS

RONNIE LIDOR, BORIS BLUMENSTEIN, AND GERSHON TENENBAUM

One of the main issues attracting the attention of both researchers and practitioners in the area of sport and exercise psychology is how to psychologically prepare an elite athlete or a team to achieve their best during the training program. Research (e.g., Cohn, Rotella, & Lloyd, 1990; Crocker, Alderman, & Smith, 1988; Elko & Ostrow, 1991; Hill & Borden, 1995) and applied (e.g., Gould, Eklund, & Jackson, 1992; May & Brown, 1989) articles have provided coaches and athletes with useful techniques, interventions, and experiences on how elite athletes in individual and team sports should prepare themselves mentally, cognitively, and emotionally for a practice, game, or competition. Psychological preparation has become a major foundation of any sport program that aims to train elite athletes and prepare them for the competitive event (Singer & Anshel, 2006a, b).

However, psychological preparation is only one aspect of the athlete's preparation. Training programs for the elite athlete are composed of other types of preparations, for example physical, technical, and tactical (Bompa, 1999; Matveyev, 1981; see also chapters 1 and 2 in this book). Therefore, in order to maximize the potential of an athlete or a team, an interrelationship should exist among all types of preparations. In addition, effective psychological preparation should also reflect the specific objectives of each phase, such as the preparation and competition phases, in the training program. For example, the objectives of the initial phase of the training program, the preparation phase, are not similar to the ones of the competition phase (Bompa, 1999). It follows that the psychological preparation given to the individual athlete or the team at an early phase is different than that provided at a more advanced phase of the training program.

The purpose of this chapter is to examine the use of psychological preparation, as it is combined with the physical, technical, and tactical preparations, in different phases of a training program. Our main argument is that the psychological preparation within the seasonal training program must also consider the physical, technical, and tactical preparations if maximal positive benefits are to be gained from the psychological preparation. These interrelationships are examined in individual and team sports.

The chapter is composed of four parts. The first part provides a short overview of the critical phases within an annual training program, as well as of the different preparations in each phase. The second part introduces five basic principles of the consultation approach the sport psychologist can use in his or her attempts to appropriately link all types of athletic preparations. The third part examines the use of psychological preparation in three different individual sports, and the fourth part for two team sports. All preparations presented in the third and fourth parts were conducted by the second author, who served as the official sport psychologist of the Israeli delegations in the 1996 (Atlanta), 2000

(Sydney), and 2004 (Athens) Olympic Games. He has also been appointed as the official sport psychologist of the Israeli delegation to the 2008 Olympic Games in Beijing.

## TRAINING PROGRAMS FOR THE ELITE ATHLETE: A MULTI-FACETED PROCESS

According to sport theorists, a typical training program for the elite athlete is composed of three phases: preparation, competition, and transition (see Bompa, 1999; Dick, 1980; Harre, 1982; Matveyev, 1981; Zatsiorsky, 1995). This structure is applicable to the needs of both individual (e.g., judo, gymnastics, and swimming) and team (e.g., basketball, soccer, and volleyball) sports. In each phase, four specific types of preparations are included: physical, technical, tactical, and psychological. Each phase makes a specific contribution to the athletes' success; however, the interaction among the four types of preparations is most likely the determining factor in the quality of the practice and its contribution to the athlete's and the team performance (Blumenstein, Lidor, & Tenenbaum, 2005; Lidor, Blumenstein, & Tenenbaum, manuscript submitted for publication; see also chapters 1, 2, and 10 in this book).

### THE THREE PHASES OF A TRAINING PROGRAM

The objectives and characteristics of the preparation, competition, and transition phases are presented briefly, as follows.

#### THE PREPARATION PHASE
During the preparation phase the athlete is readying him/herself physically, technically, tactically, and psychologically for the upcoming season. The length of the preparation phase varies according to the type of sport; it can last a few weeks, such as in basketball (Lidor at al., manuscript submitted for publication), or a few months, such as in judo (Blumenstein et al., 2005) or kayaking (Blumenstein & Lidor, 2004). A high volume of training, long-duration practice sessions, and moderate intensity are the main characteristics of the preparation phase in most sports (Bompa, 1999; Zatsiorsky, 1995). The athlete is engaged most of the time in practice sessions and a lesser amount of time is devoted to competitions or games. The main objective of practice in this phase is to strengthen the physical/technical/psychological foundations of the athlete. The tactical preparation will serve a major role later during the competition phase.

#### THE COMPETITION PHASE
In this phase the athlete is required to perform at his or her best against another skilled and motivated opponent. In most of the individual and team sporting events during the competition phase, the athlete or the team is required to reach a number of peaks. This means that the athletes have to "pull it all together" on various occasions during a period of a few months. In most sports the number of international competitions, championships, and tournaments has increased dramatically during the last two decades (Coakley, 1998). For example, ball players today play 40 (such as in soccer and team-handball) to 70 (such as in basketball) games per season, and athletes in individual sports may take part in more than ten competitive events during a season. Due to this expanded load, the athlete spends

less amount of time on practicing motor and physical skills, and more time on tactical and psychological preparations. In this phase, efforts are made to prevent athletes from incurring injuries and to encourage them to maintain a high level of motivation and attention-focusing.

### THE TRANSITION PHASE

The main objective of the transition phase is to assist the athlete in recovering from the competition phase, from both the physical and psychological perspectives, as well as to encourage him or her to maintain a low level of physical activity (Bompa, 1999). This phase is relatively short, lasting between 4 to 8 weeks depending on the type of sport. The athlete is typically engaged in recreational sports and spends time on activities other than sport. During this phase the athlete is asked to clear his or her mind, to relax, and to "charge batteries" for the upcoming preparation phase. In unique cases, the athlete engages in practice sessions in order to improve some technical skills.

Each of the training sessions is composed of four different preparations: physical, technical, tactical, and psychological.

## THE FOUR TYPES OF PREPARATIONS

The objectives and characteristics of the physical, technical, tactical, and psychological preparations are discussed briefly in the following section.

### THE PHYSICAL PREPARATION

There are two main objectives in the physical preparation: to increase the athlete's physiological potential and to develop a variety of physical abilities (Bompa, 1999; Matveyev, 1981). A typical physical preparation is composed of two parts: general preparation (GP) and specific preparation (SP). The objective of GP is to improve working capacity; namely, to enable the athlete to adapt to the physical and psychological demands of the training program. The objective of SP is to further develop the athlete's ability to adapt to the requirements of the specific sport, but in more challenging settings, which will assist him or her to be ready for the competition phase. In both GP and SP the athlete concentrates on improving physical abilities such as endurance, strength, speed, and coordination. The structure of SP and GP can be used in other types of preparation as well.

### THE TECHNICAL PREPARATION

The term "*technique*" encompasses "all the technical structures and elements in a precise and efficient movement through which the athlete performs an athletic task" (Bompa, 1999, p. 60). Therefore, the objective of the technical preparation is to enable the athlete to improve both the form and content of all sport tasks he or she is required to perform in a given sport. The athlete is asked to perfect an arsenal of motor skills to be used in real-life events, such as competitions and games. Biomechanics, kinesiology, motor learning, motor development, and sport pedagogy considerations are taken into account by the athlete and the coaching staff in the technical preparation.

### THE TACTICAL PREPARATION

The objective of the tactical preparation is to assist the athlete in developing *tactical knowledge* required for the specific sport event. The term tactical knowledge refers to the strategies which are used by the athlete during competitions and games (Bompa, 1999). In both individual and team sports performers are required to establish a general plan (e.g., a strategy) according to which they approach their opponents and perform specific maneuvers (e.g., tactics) which will help them to carry out the general plan. The objective of the tactical preparation is to provide the athlete with a variety of simulations that reflect the potential physical and psychological conditions to be faced during actual competitions and games (Tenenbaum & Lidor, 2005). Video simulations, external artificial distractions, and fatigued conditions are introduced on a regular basis to the athlete during the tactical preparation.

### THE PSYCHOLOGICAL PREPARATION

The objective of the psychological preparation is to provide the athlete with psychological techniques which can help him or her to overcome psychological barriers, such as a high level of anxiety, lack of motivation, lack of attention-focusing, or difficulty in recovering from injury (Bull, Albinson, & Shambrook, 1996; Clarkson, 1999; Hardy, Jones, & Gould, 1996; Moran, 2004). In addition, these learned techniques should help the athlete in setting realistic and attainable goals as well as to enable him or her to analyze their performance and its outcome. The athletes aim to master these techniques in such a way that he or she will be able to use them before, during, and after the actual competition or game.

## PRINCIPLES OF PSYCHOLOGICAL CONSULTATION DURING THE TRAINING PHASES

In order to establish an effective linkage among the four types of preparations in each phase of the training program, a consultation approach has been developed reflecting five principles which can be applied in both individual and team sports (Blumenstein, 2001; Henschen, 2001; Lidor & Henschen, 2003).

The five principles are as follows:

(1) The sport psychologist should be one of the members of the professional staff who works on a regular basis with the individual athlete or the team. Typically, a professional staff is composed of the head coach, assistant coaches, strength and conditioning coach, athletic trainer, sport medicine physician, and sport psychologist/sport consultant. Ideally, the sport psychologist should attend all staff meetings, practice sessions, and competitions/games.

(2) The sport psychologist should discuss his or her psychological plan with the coaching staff. Only after being given full agreement from the head coach and his or her assistants can the sport psychologist begin the consultation process.

(3) The sport psychologist should meet on a weekly basis with the coaching staff, the strength and conditioning coach, and the athletic trainer in order to exchange ideas, experiences, and knowledge on the actual contribution of the components of the training program to the progress of the individual athlete or the team. The sport psychologist will then be able to use the fruits of these discussions in his or her applied work with the athlete or the team.

(4) The psychological consultation should be given in three settings: (a) laboratory settings – the psychological techniques are taught in controlled and sterile conditions, (b) practice sessions – the psychological techniques are used during actual practice, and (c) home settings – the athlete practices the learned psychological techniques at home, in a quiet and relaxed atmosphere.

(5) The sport psychologist should be available to consider any request coming from the coaching staff, the individual athlete, or the team during the time he or she provides the consultation. The sport psychologist should maintain an "open door approach" in order to build professional and solid relationships with the coaching staff as well as with his or her major clients – the individual athlete and the team.

In the next section five cases are presented that reflect the periodization and planning process of psychological preparation during different phases of the training program. All cases took part in real life; they describe authentic psychological preparations that were conducted in different elite training programs during the past several years. Three cases represent individual sports and two represent team sports.

## PERIODIZATION AND PLANNING OF PSYCHOLOGICAL PREPARATION IN INDIVIDUAL SPORTS

The use of psychological preparation in three individual sports is presented. In each case the interrelationships between the psychological preparation and other types of preparations are described as well. The three sports are kayaking, judo, and rhythmic gymnastics. A sport-specific background, brief information on the individual athlete/s, and the uses of the psychological preparation are presented for each case.

### CASE 1: KAYAKING

#### SPORT-SPECIFIC BACKGROUND
The sport of kayaking involves high endurance and speed as well as the ability to make an explosive start and maintain high speed and tempo throughout the entire distance (Blumenstein & Lidor, 2004; Ford, 1995). It involves most of the muscle groups in the body, especially those of the back, shoulders, and arms. Physiological factors such as cardiorespiratory, anaerobic, and local muscular efficiency are required in order to achieve a high level of proficiency in kayaking (Richards, Wade, & Dear, 1981). Kayakers are required to perform numerous starts within a relatively short period of time. In addition, they have to cooperate with their crews under the demands and stress of competition. From a psychological point of view, it has been argued that mental control, mental toughness, and mental self-regulation are essential for achieving success at the higher levels of kayaking competition (Blumenstein & Bar-Eli, 2001; Crews, Lochbaum, & Karoly, 2001).

#### THE KAYAKERS
Psychological preparation is an integral part of a training program developed for Olympic kayakers. The kayakers are part of a group of individual athletes who are training for the

2008 Olympic Games. The group is sponsored by the Olympic Committee in Israel, and thus is provided with the required professional and scientific support during the training program. The psychological preparation presented in the next part reflects the involvement of the sport psychologist during one year of the training program. The sport psychologist has been working with the kayakers for several years and has joined them for major competitions.

## PSYCHOLOGICAL PREPARATION IN DIFFERENT PHASES OF THE TRAINING PROGRAM

Table 1 presents an annual training program for elite kayakers [2 males; ages = 24 and 28; group = K1 (individual); distances = 500 m and 1,000 m]. The main objective of this program is to prepare the kayakers for major competition events. The preparation phase

**Table 1** An Annual Training Plan for Kayaking (adapted from Blumenstein & Lidor, 2004)

| Month / Periodization | Physical Preparation | Technical Preparation | Tactical Preparation | Psychological Preparation | Calendar of Competitions |
|---|---|---|---|---|---|
| **Preparation Phase (GP)** | | | | | |
| October, 2005 | + + + + | | | + + + | |
| November, 2005 | + + + + | + + + | | + + | |
| December, 2005 | + + + + | + + + + | + + | + + + | |
| **(SP)** | | | | | |
| January, 2006 | + + + | + + + + | + + + | + + + | |
| February, 2006 | + + + + | + + + + | + + + + | + + | |
| March, 2006 | + + + | + + + + | + + + | + + + + | * |
| **Competition Phase (PC)** | | | | | |
| April, 2006 | + + + | + + + + | + + + + | + + | *** |
| May, 2006 | + + | + + + + | + + + + | + + | ** |
| June, 2006 | + + | + + + + | + + + + | + + + + | * |
| **(MC)** | | | | | |
| July, 2006 | + + + | + + + + | + + + + | + + + | • |
| August, 2006 | + + | + + + + | + + + + | + + + | • |
| **Transition Phase** | | | | | |
| September, 2006 | + | | | + | |

GP – general preparation     * – competition
SP – specific preparation     • – European and World Championships
PC – precompetition phase     + – weekly phase
MC – main competition

lasts about 19 weeks – 12 weeks for GP and 7 weeks for SP. In this period, the kayakers are involved in difficult and monotonous work, such as weight-lifting, interval running training, and distance running. In addition, during this period the kayakers focus on improving their individual style of paddling, developing strategies and race plans, and creating optimal tempo-rhythm while paddling.

In order for the kayakers to achieve progress during the preparation phase, appropriate psychological techniques should be taught by the sport psychologist. Among these techniques are relaxation, relaxation incorporated biofeedback (Blumenstein, Bar-Eli, & Tenenbaum, 1997), imagery (Hall, 2001), and self-talk. The psychological techniques are introduced to the kayakers in three different frameworks: (1) sterile laboratory settings, (2) training (practice sessions), and (3) home settings. The use of the psychological techniques administered to the kayakers in this phase of the training program has two objectives: first, to provide the kayakers with the fundamentals of imagery, relaxation-incorporated

**Table 2** Example of a Weekly Psychological Training Plan for the Preparation Phase in the Training Program for Kayaking (adapted from Blumenstein & Lidor, 2004)

| | Days of the Week | | | | | | |
|---|---|---|---|---|---|---|---|
| | Sunday | Monday | Tuesday | Wednesday | Thursday | Friday | Saturday |
| Relaxation 10-15 min. | | | H | | | T | |
| Relaxation 5-10 min. | | T | | | H | | |
| Relaxation 3-5 min. | L | | | L | | | |
| Imagery 5 min. | | T | | L | T | | |
| Attention-focusing 3 X 1 min. | L | | H | | T | T | |
| Biofeedback training 15 min. – EMG channel 5 X 30 sec. | L | | | L | | | |
| GSR channel 5 X 30 sec. | L | | | L | | | |
| Self-talk | L | T | | | | | |
| Tempo/rhythm exercises | L | | | L | T | | |

L – laboratory settings    T – training settings    H – home exercises biofeedback, and self-talk, so that they can use these techniques while acquiring and refining a variety of technical skills practiced during the preparation phase; and second, to teach them the fundamentals of a relaxation technique so they can use it to recover from practice sessions and workouts at early stages of the season. Table 2 presents various examples of the use of psychological techniques during the preparation phase.

During the competition phase, which lasts about 16 weeks, the volume of training is lower in comparison with the preparation phase; however, the intensity of training is increased (Bompa, 1999). The kayakers practice under training-simulated conditions which reflect actual competition settings. In these practices the focus is on developing a race strategy or a plan, and therefore special attention is given to actual environmental and situational factors such as the start of the race, the distance of the race, and the finish of the race (Blumenstein & Lidor, 2004). In addition, the kayakers are taught how to perform under different weather conditions.

**Table 3** Example of a Weekly Psychological Training Plan for the Competition Phase in the Training Program for Kayaking (adapted from Blumenstein & Lidor, 2004)

| | Days of the Week | | | | | | |
|---|---|---|---|---|---|---|---|
| | Sunday | Monday | Tuesday | Wednesday | Thursday | Friday | Saturday |
| Relaxation 5-10 min. | | T | H | L | | T | |
| Relaxation 1-3 min. | L | | | | T | | |
| Imagery 3 min. | L | | | L | T | | |
| Attention-focusing 3 X 30 sec. | | T | | L | T | T | |
| Biofeedback training with EMG channel 5 X 30 sec. | L | | | L | | | |
| GSR channel 5 X 30 sec. | L | | | L | | | |
| Biofeedback +VCR+TV | L | | | L | | | |
| Self-talk | | T | | | T | T | |
| Tempo/rhythm exercises | L | | | L | | | |

L – laboratory settings     T – training settings     H – home exercises

The same techniques that are used during the preparation phase, namely relaxation, relaxation-incorporated biofeedback, imagery, and self-talk, are also used during the competition phase (see Table 3). However, during the competition phase the focus is on how to use these techniques before, during, and after the competitive event. More specifically, the objective of the psychological support given to the kayakers during the competition phase is to assist them in handling pressure and coping with stress. In addition, the kayakers spend a considerable amount of time on improving their ability to maintain a high level of attention-focusing during competition. For example, while the kayaker develops a race plan, he is asked to use an imagery technique and to memorize it vividly and effectively. During the actual race, the kayaker is told to apply both attention-focusing and self-talk techniques in order to appropriately execute the plan of the race.

The transition phase is relatively short in kayaking (Blumenstein & Lidor, 2004). The kayakers are asked to stay active by engaging in different sport activities such as ball games, racquet activities, and swimming. The volume, length, and intensity of the physical activity performed in this phase are low. No psychological sessions are provided during the transition phase.

## CASE 2: JUDO

### SPORT-SPECIFIC BACKGROUND

Skills in judo have been classified as *open skills*, namely acts that are performed in unstable and unpredictable environmental settings (Schmidt & Lee, 2005; Schmidt & Wrisberg, 2004). The judoka performs in a dynamic situation which demands various uses of cognitive processes, such as perceiving the environment, anticipating the acts made by the opponent, making a decision, and executing the planned act (Williams, Davids, & Williams, 1999). These processes are applied within extremely short periods of time, namely 100 to 200 msec. The judoka competes with an opponent who has the same goal: to win the 5-min combat. Therefore, it is not an easy task for the judoka to simultaneously attack and defend while concealing his or her intentions from the opponent, and while in an extreme state of tension; it is challenging to make decisions under time pressure while facing aggressive opponents, and to decide on alternative tactical movements (i.e., attention flexibility) – all while striving to achieve the designated goals (Blumenstein, Bar-Eli, & Collins, 2002; Blumenstein et al., 2005; Pedro & Durbin, 2001). In summary, activities in judo require quick responses as well as high levels of attention, self-control, consistency, and will power (Pedro & Durbin, 2001; Pieter & Heijmans, 1997).

### THE JUDOKAS

Psychological preparation is part of a training program developed for elite judokas in Israel (males; n = 6; ages = 19 to 26 yrs.). One of the judokas was awarded a bronze medal in the 1992 Barcelona Olympic Games. Another judoka was awarded a bronze medal in the 2004 Athens Olympic Games, a silver medal in the 2001 World Championship, and won the European Championships in 2001 and 2003. Like the kayakers, the elite judokas are part of a group sponsored by the Olympic Committee in Israel, and thus are provided with the required professional and scientific support. The psychological preparation presented for the sport of judo also reflects the involvement of the sport psychologist during one year of the training program. The sport psychologist has been working with the elite judokas for a several years and joined them for all major competitions, such as the Olympic Games and the World and European Championships.

## Psychological Preparation in Different Phases of the Training Program

An annual training program for judo is presented in Table 4. The main objective of this program is to assist the judoka in reaching his or her best performance in major judo events. Among the events are the World Championship, the European Championship, and the National Championship. Therefore, the judokas are required to attain their best performance a number of times during the annual training program.

The preparation phase is composed of GP, which lasts about 15 weeks, and SP which lasts about 16 weeks. The main objective of GP is to improve the judoka's working capacity, strength, and endurance – all elements required for judo (Blumenstein et al., 2005). Emphasis is made on strength training in order to provide support for the exercises introduced to the judoka during the technical preparation. In this phase, as in the case of kayaking, a large number of exercises and repetitions with low intensity are given. The main objective of SP is to further develop the judoka's physical ability according to the unique physical and physiological demands of judo (Pedro & Durbin, 2001).

During the preparation phase the judokas perfect their technical skills by participating in 4 or 5 training sessions of a medium intensity level per week, each lasting 90-120 min. The judokas execute a variety of technical elements that help them improve their defensive and offensive combat skills. Different conditions and simulations are applied, and different opponents are used (Blumenstein et al., 2005). In addition, the judoka performs simulated combats according to the number and duration of combats that will be undertaken during a given day of a tournament.

Among the psychological techniques used during the preparation phase are relaxation, imagery incorporating biofeedback, and self-talk. As indicated in the previous part on kayaking, the psychological preparation is implemented in three settings: (a) laboratory sessions, (b) training sessions, and (c) home assignments given to the judoka to do in his or her free time. The objective of the psychological preparation during the preparation phase is to enable the judokas to realize the benefits they can gain from appropriate implementation of psychological readiness techniques. The psychological techniques are related especially to the physical and technical preparations of the judokas. The interventions practiced in this phase are conducted at different time intervals, such as at 5, 10, and 25 min. An example of a weekly psychological training plan reflecting the specific objectives of the preparation phase is presented in Table 5.

During the competition phase in judo, the intensity of practice increases; however, the number of the repeated acts substantially decreases. The judoka is exposed to a variety of actual environmental factors related to combat situations. In this respect, the psychological techniques are practiced within the 5-min time limitations of the combat. During this phase

**Table 4** A Training Plan for Judo (adapted from Blumenstein et al., 2005)

| Month / Periodization | Physical Preparation | Technical Preparation | Tactical Preparation | Psychological Preparation | Calendar of Competitions |
|---|---|---|---|---|---|
| Preparation Phase (GP) | | | | | |
| September, 2005 | + + + + | + + + + | + + | + + | |
| October, 2005 | + + + + | + + + + | + + + | + + + + | |
| (SP) | | | | | |
| November, 2005 | + + + | + + + + | + + + | + + + | * |
| December, 2005 | + + + | + + + + | + + + | + + + | |
| Competition Phase (PC) | | | | | |
| January, 2006 | + + + | + + + + | + + + | + + + | ** |
| February, 2006 | + + + | + + + | + + | + + + | *** |
| (MC) | | | | | |
| March, 2006 | + + + | + + + | + + + | + + + | ** |
| April, 2006 | + + + | + + + | + + + | + + + | ** |
| May, 2006 | + + + | + + + + | + + + | + + + | • |
| Transition Phase June, 2006 | + + | | | | |
| Preparation Phase (GP) | | | | | |
| July, 2006 | + + + + | + + | + + | + + + | * |
| (SP) | | | | | |
| August, 2006 | + + + | + + + | + + + | + + | * |
| Competition Phase (MC) | | | | | |
| September, 2006 | + + | + + + | + + + + | + + + | * |
| Transition Phase October, 2006 | + | | | | |

GP – general preparation
SP – specific preparation
PC – precompetition phase
MC – main competition

* – tournament "A" and Grand Prix
• – European and World Championships
+ – weekly phase

emphasis is made on the actual use of psychological techniques during combat-simulated sessions. The objectives of the use of the psychological techniques administered in this phase, such as relaxation, imagery, imagery incorporating biofeedback, and self-talk (as can be seen in Table 6), are not only to assist the judoka to prepare him/herself for the combat, but also in recovering effectively from combat. For example, the length of the

**Table 5** Example of a Weekly Psychological Consultation Plan for the Preparation Phase in the Training Program for Judo (adapted from Blumenstein et al., 2005)

| | Days of the Week | | | | | | |
|---|---|---|---|---|---|---|---|
| | Sunday | Monday | Tuesday | Wednesday | Thursday | Friday | Saturday |
| Relaxation 20-25 min. | | | | L | | | |
| Relaxation 10-15 min. | | | | | H | | |
| Relaxation 5 min. | | L | | | H | T | |
| Imagery 5 min. | T | L | T | L | | T | |
| Music 10-15 min. | | | | L | | | |
| Biofeedback 20 min. – EMG channel | | L | | L | | | |
| GSR channel | | L | | L | | | |
| Self-talk | T | | T | | | T | |
| Breathing exercises | T | | T | | H | | |
| Response exercises | | L | | L | | | |

L – laboratory settings      T – training settings      H – home exercises

relaxation techniques is varied from 1 to 10 min so that the judokas can use them during warm-up sessions before combats, as well as in break periods between combats. In addition, the judokas are taught to perform the relaxation procedure for about 5 min, so that it can match the time constraints of the combat. Video simulations of combats or fragments of combats are used in both laboratory and training conditions. The simulations are combined with psychological techniques such as imagery (e.g., imagining successful performances), attention-focusing on relevant cues (before and during the fights), and self-talk (before, during, and after the fights).

The transition phase in judo lasts about 4 weeks, and during this time the judoka is asked to maintain a low level of physical activity. Psychological recovery techniques are implemented, such as relaxation, listening to music (Blumenstein, 1992), and breathing exercises (Blumenstein et al., 2005), combined with medical treatments such as physiotherapy and message. The objective of the combined psychological and medical techniques is to assist the judoka in recovering after the effort made during the competition phase and in preparing him/herself for the following GP.

**Table 6** Example of a Weekly Psychological Training Plan in the Competition Phase in the Training Program for Judo (adapted from Blumenstein et al., 2005)

|  | Days of the Week | | | | | | |
|---|---|---|---|---|---|---|---|
|  | Sunday | Monday | Tuesday | Wednesday | Thursday | Friday | Saturday |
| Relaxation 10-15 min. |  | L |  | H |  | T |  |
| Relaxation 5 min. |  |  |  |  | T |  |  |
| Relaxation 1-3 min. | T |  | T | L |  | T |  |
| Imagery 3 min. | T |  | T | L | T | T |  |
| Imagery 1 min. | T |  | T |  | T | T |  |
| Biofeedback with EMG channels 5 min. |  | L |  |  |  |  |  |
| GSR channels 5 min. |  | L |  |  |  |  |  |
| Biofeedback +VCR+TV |  | L |  | L |  |  |  |
| Self-talk | T | L | T |  | T | T |  |
| Response exercises |  | L |  | L |  |  |  |

L – laboratory settings    T – training settings    H – home exercises

## CASE 3: RHYTHMIC GYMNASTICS

### SPORT-SPECIFIC BACKGROUND

In elite rhythmic gymnastics the female athlete is required to perform a 90-sec routine in which one of five apparatus is used: ball, clubs, hoop, ribbon, and rope (Jastrjembskaia & Titov, 1999). During the competition a panel of referees assesses the performance of the gymnasts. The assessment reflects the individual's ability to (1) coordinate the movements of the body, particularly the lower and upper body parts, (2) handle the apparatus while moving on the surface, and (3) demonstrate artistic and creative movements. Typically, the routine of the gymnast is based on a selected theme and is accompanied by music and unique choreography. In order to achieve a high level of proficiency in this individual sport the gymnast is required to demonstrate strength, balance, coordination, flexibility, and accuracy. The gymnast is also required to cope with the attendance of a "silent" audience and the "eye steering" of the referees – that is to say, to be able to cope with external stress. In addition, she should be able to focus attention effectively during the entire 90-sec routine as well as to demonstrate consistency in her performance.

## THE GYMNASTS

The gymnasts (females; mean age = 18.2 yrs.) were members of the Israeli rhythmic gymnastics national team. The team is sponsored by the national Olympic Committee, and therefore is provided with the required professional and scientific support. The psychological preparation is part of a 4-year training program aimed at preparing the gymnasts for the 2008 Olympic Games. As in the case of the judokas, the psychological preparation presented to the gymnasts reflects the involvement of the sport psychologist in one year of the training program. The sport psychologist has been working with the gymnast for several years and attended all their major competitions, such as the Olympic Games, European Championships, and National Championships.

## PSYCHOLOGICAL PREPARATION IN DIFFERENT PHASES OF THE TRAINING PROGRAM

In the preparation phase, the gymnast is involved mainly in physical and technical sessions. The objective of the physical sessions is to improve the physical fundamentals required for rhythmic gymnastics, such as coordination, balance, strength, and flexibility. The objective of the technical sessions is to improve the gymnastics skills necessary for developing the individual routine of the gymnast. The gymnast spends a great amount of time on repetitions of the specific movements which comprise her routine. These movements are typically performed accompanied by music.

In order to assist the gymnast in coping effectively with the "repetition-mode" atmosphere that exists during practice sessions at the early phase of the training program, each gymnast is provided with a thorough explanation about the importance and contribution of such repetitions to the development of her routine. Two psychological techniques are introduced during the preparation phase: goal setting (Burton, Naylor, & Holliday, 2001) and self-talk. These techniques are matched individually by taking into account the specific professional needs of each gymnast, and her physical and psychological states, as well as her motivational state. In both SP and GP the technique of goal setting is used mainly to increase motivation and self-confidence, and to improve attention-focusing. A goal setting session is applied almost on a daily basis before practice begins and during breaks within the practice. The sport psychologist attempts to establish a vivid link between the specific goal set by the gymnast and her coach at the beginning of the practice session and the actual process the gymnast goes through during practice, and also between the goals and the outcome of this process. For example, the gymnast learns not only to assess the quality of her performance (i.e., "I made a nice catch," "I failed to complete the motion," or "I did not make a good enough throw"), but also to provide an overall assessment of the performance (i.e., "poor," "adequate," or "good"). In essence, she learns to compare the "already set goals" with the outcomes of her performance.

During the preparation phase, a "map of goals" is established for each gymnast. Two stages are used to compose the map. In Stage 1, the map is composed of conceptual goals, such as "what do I want to achieve during the up-coming season?," as well as of practical goals, such as "how do I want to achieve this goal during the up-coming season?." In Stage 2, specific goals are set for the daily practices, the weekly program, and the monthly program, in order to carry out the conceptual goals set in Stage 1. An assessment on the effectiveness of the goals is given every two weeks by the coach, the gymnast, and the sport psychologist. The objective of this process is to assess the contribution of the goal setting technique to actual performances of the gymnast as well as to her motivation, self-confidence, and attention-focusing. Modifications in the use of the technique are made, if necessary.

The self-talk technique combined with imagery is also introduced to the gymnasts during the preparation phase. The objective of these psychological techniques is to help the gymnast feel in control when she prepares herself for the execution of the routine. The gymnast is taught how to use a number of key words that are connected to specific aspects of her routine. In order to do this, the gymnast is first asked to draw a sketch, segment by segment, of her routine. Second, she is directed to list key words that best reflect the way she views herself performing each segment of the routine. She is instructed to select and list words which are mainly related to those parts of her routine that she feels uncomfortable with; therefore, more time will be needed to improve these parts. For example, after sketching her routine, a 19-year old elite gymnast listed 19 key words related to a variety of segments of her ball routine. On the list were "keep ball," "fast flexibility," "stand," "keep balance," and "foot twist." The high number of items on the list reflected the gymnast's dissatisfaction with some segments of her routine. Therefore, the objective of the coach, after consulting with the sport psychologist, was to concentrate on those segments that according to the gymnast needed to be improved. Practically speaking, the selected words were used by the gymnast while working on her routine during practice. After a few weeks of practice the gymnast was once again asked to sketch her routine and make a new list of key words. This time the number of words decreased dramatically, since the gymnast felt comfortable with more segments of her routine.

The use of self-talk helped the gymnast to develop awareness and self-awareness of those elements that needed to be improved. A combined effort of the coach and the sport psychologist helped the gymnast to focus attention on those elements that needed more repetitions. After enhancing most of the elements of her routine, the *negative* words were eliminated from the list. The gymnast was taught to include other key words which helped her to feel better before performing her routine. Among these words were "smile," "confidence," and "be good." These are *positive* words which can help the gymnast increase her self-confidence, self-esteem, and self-satisfaction. Table 7 presents an example of a psychological session conducted during the preparation phase.

During the competition phase the gymnast takes part in major gymnastics events. The length of the practice sessions and the number of repetitions are decreased. Emphasis is made on refining the routine and "pulling together" all the elements. The use of psychological techniques during this phase – goal-setting, self-talk, and imagery – is directed toward the competition events. More specifically, the objectives of the

**Table 7** Example of One Psychological Training Session in the Preparation Phase for Rhythmic Gymnastics

| | |
|---|---|
| Place: Sport Psychology Laboratory<br>Day: Sunday<br>Time: 13:00-13:45 | |
| Introductory part: – reviewing the goals of the week – 5 min | |
| Main part: | – attention-focusing exercises using biofeedback – 5 X 30 sec<br>– imaging ball routine and analyzing performance – 5 times<br>– self-talk during routine (key words – examples for the ball routine) – 5 times |
| Final part: | – muscle relaxation accompanied by music – 10 min |

psychological techniques in the competition phase are to enable the gymnast to (1) pay attention to small details related to her routine, (2) be able to focus attention consistently during the 90-sec routine, coping with external (e.g., audience) and internal (e.g., negative thoughts) distractions, (3) demonstrate a relaxed behavior and mood, and (4) be able to smile before and during the performance of the routine.

While using imagery the gymnast is taught to imagine her routine for a 90-sec period of time, without being exposed to music. The gymnast practices the 90-sec imagery routine during weekly practice sessions and prior to actual competitions. During practices she uses a stopwatch while imaging; however, after a number of practice sessions she uses imagery

**Table 8** Example of One Psychological Training Session in the Competition Phase for Rhythmic Gymnastics

| | |
|---|---|
| Place: Gymnastics Hall<br>Day: Monday<br>Time: 10:00-13:00, during a practice session | |
| Warm-up: | – developing motivation and positive thinking (together with the coaching staff)<br>– attention-focusing exercises – 2-3 times X 10-20 sec |
| Main part: | – relaxation – 1-3 min<br>– imagery – between exercises and repetitions<br>– self-talk (establishing key words for specific segments)<br>– relaxation – 1 min<br>– imagining successful performances – 2-3 min<br>– relaxation – 1 min |
| Final part: | – muscle relaxation – 15-20 min |

without any aiding devices. It is assumed that the 90-sec imagery exercise enables the gymnast to facilitate the transfer of her routine from sterile conditions, namely practice sessions, to performance settings (e.g., an actual competition) (Moran, 1996).

During the preparation and competition phases the gymnast is also provided with guidance for relaxation. The relaxation technique helps the gymnast mentally recover from competitions, practice sessions, and traveling. At the end of GP and the very beginning of the competition phase the length of the relaxation session is about 20 to 25 min. After understanding the main fundamentals of the technique and performing it for a few weeks, the gymnast is able to practice relaxation for shorter periods of times, namely 5 to 10 min. At about the mid-point of the competition phase the gymnast practices relaxation also for 1 to 2 min in order to be able to use it before the actual competition. The variations of the time intervals used for relaxation enable the gymnast to utilize the technique for a relatively long period of time, such as between 15-to 20 min on the evening before the competition, as well as for a very short periods of time, such as 1 to 3 min, just prior to the beginning of the competition. Table 8 presents an example of a psychological session conducted during the competition phase.

## PERIODIZATION AND PLANNING OF PSYCHOLOGICAL PREPARATION IN TEAM SPORTS

Two cases of different uses of psychological preparation in team sports are described. The relationships between the psychological preparation and other preparations are described as well. The two sports are soccer and basketball. For each of these sports a sport-specific background, brief information on the teams, and the use of the psychological preparation are presented.

## CASE 1: SOCCER

### SPORT-SPECIFIC BACKGROUND
The game of soccer is composed of 11 players, each in a different position. The members of the team are required to play within a coordinated defensive and offensive structure (Gray & Drewitt, 1999). In order to do this, players are required to master individual defensive (e.g., positioning) and offensive (e.g., dribbling, kicking, and passing) skills, as well as team skills (e.g., defensive and offensive). The psychological preparation presented for soccer was part of a training program whose aim was to spend almost equal time on both individual and team skills. This instructional objective was taken into account by the sport psychologist in his practical work with the individual soccer players and with the whole team.

### THE TEAM
The team represented a medium-size club located in one of the largest cities in Israel. The team (males; mean age = 25 yrs.) played in Division 1 which is composed of 12 professional clubs and is the highest level in Israel. About 30 games are played by each club during the season.

PSYCHOLOGICAL PREPARATION IN DIFFERENT PHASES
OF THE TRAINING PROGRAM

The preparation phase was composed of two parts; the first part was composed of practice sessions which were conducted on a daily basis in the local team's stadium. The second part was devoted to a 21-day training camp which took place in Holland. The objective of the preparatory phase, particularly of GP, was to improve the physical conditioning of the players. More specifically, players were involved in endurance, strength, speed, and agility sessions. The physical workouts were performed with and without a ball. During SP, the players worked on their defensive and offensive skills as well as on the defensive and offensive team structure as established by the head coach.

During the daily practice sessions the sport psychologist met individually with the players, both the veterans and the newcomers, as well as with the head coach and his two assistants, the strength and conditioning coach, the athletic trainer, and the team managers. The objective of these meetings was to develop a framework for the psychology consultation. The sport psychologist met only once with the whole team. The objectives of this meeting were (1) to introduce the domain of sport psychology, its objectives, and potential contribution to the success of the whole team and the individual players, and (2) to present a multi-faceted program, namely the physical, technical, tactical, and psychological preparations, for the training camp.

During an early stage of the training camp the sport psychologist administered a few questionnaires [e.g., State-Trait Anxiety Inventory (STAI) (Spielberger, Gorsuch, & Lushene, 1970) and Sport Competition Anxiety Test (SCAT) (Martens, Vealey, & Burton, 1990)] to the players. In addition, he conducted a few reaction time (Blumenstein et al., 2005) and self-regulation (Blumenstein et al., 2002) tests. The knowledge obtained from these tests assisted the sport psychologist in planning his psychological consultation sessions with the players during the training camp as well as during the competition phase. During the 3-week camp each player was provided with four to five psychological sessions. In these sessions the players were taught the fundamentals of three psychological techniques: relaxation, imagery, and self-talk. Some of the players were already familiar with one or more of these techniques, so the sport psychologist focused on those techniques that were not in use by the players. In addition to the individual sessions conducted with the players, the sport psychologist held four team meetings in which different lectures on main topics in sport psychology were given. The topics of the lectures were: "Mental preparation for the game: warm-up and psych-up," "The use of self-talk during the game," "The link between individual and team goals", and "Concentration before and during the game." In order to link all four types of preparations (i.e., the physical, technical, tactical, and psychological), daily meetings between the sport psychologist and the coaching staff took place. Discussions on the progress of the team as well as of individual players were held and practical suggestions for the future were proposed.

During the training camp the team played three games against local teams competing in Division 1 in Holland. The sport psychologist used these games as psychological learning experiences for the players. More specifically, team psychological preparation sessions were conducted before the games and team relaxation sessions were performed after the games. At the end of the training camp a captain for the team was selected by the coaching staff. The sport psychologist took part in the selection process by providing the staff with concrete psychological reports on the candidates for the captaincy position.

During the competition phase, most of the preparation time was devoted to defensive and offensive tactical maneuvers. The team played one game per week, and for several weeks toward the end of the season the team played two games per week. The team practiced every day, and psychological consultations were part of the weekly program. Table 9 presents an example of a weekly psychological training program for the team during the competition phase. On the day of the game (Saturday), the sport psychologist conducted sessions with only selected players, according to the request of the coach. Among the players chosen were those who returned from injury, young players who were playing for the first time in the season, and players who were asked to play on a different position than they were used to playing. The objective of these meetings was to enhance positive thinking, attention-focusing (Moran, 2003), and self-confidence in the players. On the day of the game, a pre-game routine was maintained. The attitude adopted by the coaching staff and the sport psychologist was "not to unnecessarily disturb the players."

On the day following the game (Sunday), only the players who did not participate in the game on Saturday completed a full practice session. The players who did play in the game were provided with a relaxation session by the sport psychologist for about 20 to 30 min, as well as a light physical activity session conducted by the strength and conditioning coach for about 30 min. On Monday and Tuesday the sport psychologist conducted individual

**Table 9** Weekly Psychological Consultation Schedule in Soccer

| Days | Physical Preparation | Technical Preparation | Tactical Preparation | Psychological Preparation | Competition |
|------|---------------------|----------------------|---------------------|--------------------------|-------------|
| Saturday | | | | Individual session with select players | Official game in national league |
| Sunday | + | + | + | Team session | |
| Monday | + | + | | Individual session | |
| Tuesday | + | + | + | Individual session | |
| Wednesday | + | + | + | Individual & team session | |
| Thursday | | | + | Individual session | |
| Friday | | | + | Individual sessions (team sessions on rare occasions) | |

sessions with some of the players. The main objective of these meetings was to strengthen the attention-focusing of the players who "lost" attentional control during previous games. No psychological team meetings were undertaken.

The practice sessions of the team held on Wednesday and Thursday were devoted to tactical preparation toward the next game. Therefore, relaxation sessions were conducted by the sport psychologist in order to "clean the players' mind" and increase their attention. In addition, attention-focusing exercises were presented to the players combined with positive thinking and self-talk.

On Friday, the sport psychologist conducted individual meetings with selected players upon the request of the coaching staff. The objective of these meetings was to increase self-confidence in some of the players who were to take part in the game on the next day. Only rarely did psychological team meetings take place with the sport psychologist on the day before the game.

## Case 2: Basketball

### Sport-specific background

In basketball five players are required to perform against five opposing players in a rapid and changeable environment (Wooden, 1980). Each player has his or her own specific role on the team. The court in which the game is played is relatively small; therefore all actions must be performed fast and accurately by the individual player in effective cooperation with his or her teammates.

Basketball players are required to spend a great deal of time on improving physical abilities such as agility, speed, explosive power, and strength. Playing the game also requires the basketball player to perform a variety of open offensive skills such as dribbling, passing, and shooting. Together with performing these skills, the player should perceive information emerging from an on-going environment, anticipate his or her acts in advance, and make decisions (Tenenbaum, 2003; Williams et al., 1999). Cognitive processes such as anticipation and decision making are also applied in defensive maneuvers.

In addition to open skills, closed skills, such as free-throw shots, are also performed by the player. In these skills the player performs the same task under similar conditions and therefore is able to plan the act in advance (Schmidt & Wrisberg, 2004). In order to achieve success, basketball players aim at improving both open and closed skills by using physical and cognitive task-enhancement drills.

### The team

The Cadets national team of Israel was composed of 14 male players (mean age = 15.9). The players were selected by the coaching staff after a 1-year selection process which was conducted in different sport centers in the country. During the selection process, the players were observed, assessed, and interviewed by the coaching staff. At the end of the selection process, they invited 25 players to take part in three 2-day training camps. Following the third camp, 14 players were selected by the coaching staff to be on the Cadets national team.

The team met twice a month during one year of preparation. Two 2-day training camps were conducted each month during two weekends (Fridays and Saturdays, two weeks apart). Two practice sessions were given on Friday and two to three practice sessions were given on Saturday. Toward the end of the training program, the team played one game in each camp against semi-professional adult teams. During the weeks not at the camp, the players practiced and played for their local youth clubs. Most of them practiced on a daily basis and played one game per week in Division 1 (the highest one) for youth players.

The objective of the training camps was to build a team concept. Most of the time was devoted to developing offensive and defensive structures for the team, namely preparing the players tactically for the coming tournament. Not much time was spent on the physical and technical aspects of the game. The players worked on these aspects of the game during practice sessions conducted in their own clubs. The players were provided with psychological consultations in each training camp.

## PSYCHOLOGICAL PREPARATION DURING TRAINING CAMPS

The involvement of the sport psychologist with the team started about two weeks before the first training camp. The sport psychologist met with the coaching staff in order to set short- and long-term goals for the psychological preparation provided to the team during the camps. More specifically, the sport psychologist presented the background, objectives, and procedures for the psychological techniques he planned to introduce to individual players and to the whole team.

During the first five camps the sport psychologist conducted individual meetings with all players, in order to (1) collect basic information on the selected players, such as personal and family background, (2) administer a few questionnaires [e.g., the STAI (Spielberger et al., 1970) and the SCAT (Martens et al., 1990)], and (3) teach the players the fundamentals of psychological techniques such as imagery, self regulation accompanied by biofeedback, self-talk, and attention-focusing (Brown & Burke, 2003; Mikes, 1987). Each session lasted about 45 min; the sessions were conducted between practices and in the evenings.

After the fifth camp, the sport psychologist provided a report on each individual player to the coaching staff. He discussed the psychological strengths and weaknesses of all players. Based on this report, as well as on the feedback obtained from the coaching staff on this report, the sport psychologist planned the psychological preparation for the upcoming camps. Because the players were mainly involved in tactical preparation, the sport psychologist used imagery and self-talk techniques to help them develop the game plans and memorize offensive and defensive team maneuvers.

Special meetings were conducted with players according to the request of the coaching staff. The objective of these meetings was to assist some of the players in coping with mental barriers such as lack of motivation, over training, injuries, and lack of playing time in games played in their home clubs. In addition, a few lectures were given in front of the entire team on topics such as "Developing attention focusing in free-throw shots," "Mental preparation for the game," and "Self regulation during the game."

Upon the request of the coaching staff, the sport psychologist also met with some of the players between camps. Typically, the meetings were held in the sport psychologist's office and lasted about 45 min. In these meetings, the sport psychologist continued the consultation process in which the individual player was involved during the training camps. For example, if the player demonstrated difficulties in attention-focusing while performing free-throw shots, then the sport psychologist used a focusing-attention technique to help the player overcome this situation.

Towards the end of the training program the sport psychologist began to emphasize the importance of team cohesion, in both individual and team meetings (Henschen & Cook, 2003). He conducted a few group dynamics sessions in order to build leadership as well as a positive climate among the members of the team. In addition, he attempted to increase team motivation and the desire to win. Emphasis was made on the whole team conducting a relaxation technique at the end of each game, in order to maintain the "stay together approach" of the team – irregardless the final score of the game.

Our aim in this chapter was to demonstrate how psychological preparation can be integrated into other training preparations, such as physical, technical, and tactical, within the preparation, competition, and transition phases of individual and team sports. It is our belief that psychological preparation can be linked to other components of preparation within each of the three critical phases of the training program. In order to demonstrate this, we provided five examples of training programs in which psychological preparation was used to achieve the specific objectives of the phase of the training program.

# REFERENCES

Blumenstein, B. (1992). Music... before starting. *Fitness and Sports Review International,* April, 49-50.

Blumenstein, B. (2001). Sport psychology practice in two cultures: similarities and differences. In G. Tenenbaum (Ed.), *The practice of sport psychology* (pp. 231-240). Morgantown, WV: Fitness Information Technology.

Blumenstein, B., & Bar-Eli, M. (2001). A five-step approach for biofeedback in sport. *Sportwissenschaft,* 4, 412-424.

Blumenstein, B., Bar-Eli, M., & Collins, D. (2002). Biofeedback training in sport. In B. Blumenstein, M. Bar-Eli, & G. Tenenbaum (Eds.), *Brain and body in sport and exercise: Biofeedback applications in performance enhancement* (pp. 55-76). Chichester, UK: Wiley.

Blumenstein, B., Bar-Eli, M., & Tenenbaum, G. (1997). A five-step approach to mental training incorporating biofeedback. *The Sport Psychologist,* 11, 440-453.

Blumenstein, B., & Lidor, R. (2004). Psychological preparation in elite canoeing and kayaking sport programs: Periodization and planning. *Applied Research in Coaching and Athletics Annual,* 19, 24-34.

Blumenstein, B., Lidor, R., & Tenenbaum, G. (2005). Periodization and planning of psychological preparation in elite combat sport programs: The case of judo. *International Journal of Sport and Exercise Psychology,* 3, 7-25.

Bompa, T. (1999). *Periodization: The theory and methodology of training* (4th ed.). Champaign, IL: Human Kinetics.

Brown, D., & Burke, K. (2003). *Sport psychology library: Basketball.* Morgantown, WV: Fitness Information Technology.

Bull, S. J., Albinson, J. G., & Shambrook, C. J. (1996). *The mental game plan: Getting psyched for sport.* East Sussex, UK: Sports Dynamics.

Burton, D., Naylor, S., & Holliday, B. (2001). Goal setting in sport: Investigating the goal effectiveness paradox. In R. N. Singer, H. A. Hausenblas, & C. M. Janelle (Eds.), *Handbook of sport psychology* (2nd ed., pp. 497-528). New York: Wiley.

Coakley, J. (1998). *Sport in society: Issues and controversy* (6th ed.). New York: Mosby.

Clarkson, M. (1999). *Competitive fire: Insights to developing the warrior mentality of sports champions.* Champaign, IL: Human Kinetics.

Cohn, P. J., Rotella, R. J., & Lloyd, J. W. (1990). Effects of a cognitive-behavioral intervention on the preshot routine and performance in golf. *The Sport Psychologist,* 4, 33-47.

Crews, D. J., Lochbaum, M. R., & Karoly, P. (2001). Self-regulation: Concepts, methods, and strategies in sport and exercise. In R. N. Singer, H. A. Hausenblas, & C. M. Janelle (Eds.), *Handbook of sport psychology* (2nd ed., pp. 566-581). New York: Wiley.

Crocker, P. R. E., Alderman, R. B., & Smith, F. M. R. (1988). Cognitive-affective stress management training with high performance youth volleyball players: effects and affect. *Journal of Sport & Exercise Psychology,* 10, 448-460.

Dick, F. (1980). *Sport training principles.* London: Lepus Books.

Elko, P. K., & Ostrow, A. C. (1991). Effects of a rational-emotive education program on heightened anxiety levels of female collegiate gymnasts. *The Sport Psychologist, 5*, 235-255.

Ford, K. (1995). *Whitewater and sea kayaking.* Champaign, IL: Human Kinetics.

Gould, D., Eklund, R., & Jackson, S. (1992). 1988 U.S. Olympic wrestling excellence: I. Mental preparation, precompetition cognition, and effect. *The Sport Psychologist, 6*, 358-382.

Gray, A., & Drewett, J. (1999). *Flat back four – The tactical game.* London: Boxtree.

Hall, C. R. (2001). Imagery in sport and exercise. In R. N. Singer, H. A. Hausenblas, & C. M. Janelle (Eds.), *Handbook of sport psychology* (2nd ed., pp. 529-549). New York: Wiley.

Hardy, L., Jones, G., & Gould, D. (1996). *Understanding psychological preparation for sport: Theory and practice of elite performers.* Chichester, UK: Wiley.

Harre, D. (Ed.). (1982). *Principles of sports training: Introduction to theory and methods of training.* Berlin: Sportverlag.

Henschen, K. (2001). Lessons from sport psychology consulting. In G. Tenenbaum (Ed.), *The practice of sport psychology* (pp. 77-88). Morgantown, WV: Fitness Information Technology.

Henschen, K. P., & Cook, D. (2003). Working with professional basketball players. In R. Lidor & K. P. Henschen (Eds.), *The psychology of team sports* (pp. 143-160). Morgantown, WV: Fitness Information Technology.

Hill, K. L., & Borden, F. (1995). The effect of attentional cueing scripts on competitive bowling performance. *International Journal of Sport Psychology, 26*, 503-512.

Jastrjembskaia, N., & Titov, Y. (1999). *Rhythmic gymnastics – hoop, ball, clubs, ribbon, rope.* Champaign, IL: Human Kinetics.

Lidor, R., Blumenstein, B., & Tenenbaum, G. *Psychological aspects of elite training programs in European basketball: Conceptualization, periodization, and planning.* Manuscript submitted for publication.

Lidor, R., & Henschen, K. P. (2003). Working with team sports: Applying a holistic approach. In R. Lidor & K. P. Henschen (Eds.), *The psychology of team sports* (pp. 1-18). Morgantown, WV: Fitness Information Technology.

Martens, R., Vealey, R. S., & Burton, D. (1990). *Competitive anxiety in sport.* Champaign, IL: Human Kinetics.

Matveyev, L. (1981). *Fundamentals of sports training.* Moscow: Progress Publishers.

May, J., & Brown, L. (1989). Delivery of psychological services to the U.S. Alpine Ski team prior to and during the Olympics in Calgary. *The Sport Psychologist, 3*, 320-329.

Mikes, J. (1987). *Basketball fundamentals: A complete mental training guide.* Champaign, IL: Leisure Press.

Moran, A. P. (1996). *The psychology of concentration in sport performers: A cognitive analysis.* United Kingdom: Psychology Press.

Moran, A. P. (2003). Improving concentration skills in team-sport performers: Focusing techniques for soccer players. In R. Lidor & K. Henschen (Eds.), *The psychology of team sports* (pp. 161-189). Morgantown, WV: Fitness Information Technology.

Moran, A. P. (2004). *Sport and exercise psychology – A critical introduction*. London: Routledge.

Pedro, J., & Durbin, W. (2001). *Judo: Techniques and tactics*. Champaign, IL: Human Kinetics.

Pieter, W., & Heijmans, J. (1997). *Scientific coaching for Olympic taekwondo*. Germany: Meyer & Meyer Verlag.

Richards, G., Wade, P., & Dear, I. (1981). *The complete book of canoeing and kayaking*. London: B. T. Batsford.

Schmidt, R. A., & Lee, T. D. (2005). *Motor control and learning: A behavioral approach* (4th ed.). Champaign, IL: Human Kinetics.

Schmidt, R. A., & Wrisberg, C. A. (2004). *Motor learning and performance: A problem-based learning approach* (3rd ed.). Champaign, IL: Human Kinetics.

Singer, R. N., & Anshel, M. (2006a). An overview of interventions in sport. In J. Dosil (Ed.), *The sport psychologist handbook – A guide for sport-specific performance enhancement* (pp. 63-88). West Sussex, UK: John Wiley & Sons.

Singer, R. N., & Anshel, M. (2006b). Assessment, evaluation, and counseling in sport. In J. Dosil (Ed.), *The sport psychologist handbook – A guide for sport-specific performance enhancement* (pp. 89-117). West Sussex, UK: John Wiley & Sons.

Spielberger, C. D., Gorsuch, R. L., & Lushene, R. E. (1970). *Manual for the State-Trait Anxiety Inventory*. Palo Alto, CA: Consulting Psychological Press.

Tenenbaum, G. (2003). Expert athletes: An integrated approach to decision making. In J. L. Starkes & K. A. Ericsson (Eds.), *Expert performance in sports: Advances in research on sport expertise* (pp. 191-218). Champaign, IL: Human Kinetics.

Tenenbaum, G., & Lidor, R. (2005). Research on decision-making and the use of cognitive strategies in sport settings. In D. Hackfort, J. L. Duda, & R. Lidor (Eds.), *Handbook of research in applied sport and exercise psychology: International perspectives* (pp. 75-91). Morgantown, WV: Fitness Information Technology.

Williams, A. M., Davids, K., & Williams, J. G. (1999). *Visual perception and action in sport*. London: E & FN Spon.

Wooden, J. R. (1980). *Practical modern basketball* (2nd ed.). New York: Wiley.

Zatsiorsky, V. M. (1995). *Science and practice of strength training*. Champaign, IL: Human Kinetics.

# CHAPTER 8

# RECOVERY FOLLOWING TRAINING AND COMPETITION

ANNE-MARIE ELBE AND MICHAEL KELLMANN

"I was able to reach my personal best and win second place in the European Junior Championships because I felt fit and had enough time to recover from the training camp that took place before the championships."

This statement, made by a young high jumper, emphasizes the importance of recovery for peak performance. Recovery has been receiving more and more attention lately in competitive sports. Up to now much research has been performed in the field of stress and overtraining. However, knowledge about one of the key factors in preventing overtraining, namely recovery, is still fairly minimal.

After defining and illustrating the basics of the recovery process, as well as showing different methods of how to measure recovery, we will take a look at several phases in the training cycle of competitive athletes. The described phases are periods of highly intense training, taking place at training camps as well as during competitions. For each phase the relevant recovery aspects are illustrated and practical advice on how to integrate recovery activities into training are given. We show how athletes and coaches can apply these activities and integrate them into training and competitions. In the relevant places differentiations between recovery for individual athletes and for team athletes are made.

## DEFINITION OF RECOVERY

A clear and sufficient definition of recovery can rarely be found in the literature (see Kellmann, 2002a). When dealing with the topic of overtraining, especially in the field of sports medicine, authors often refer to recovery but do not provide detailed information on what physiological and psychological recovery really is. Whereas much of research about the relationship of stress and sport exists in the areas of sport medicine, general psychology, and sport psychology, there is little research about recovery. Currently, the main focus is on detecting activities that reduce stress rather than on the systematic enhancement of recovery. Therefore, only limited knowledge about systematic recovery enhancement and the assessment of recovery exists. One can also find different definitions of recovery. Allmer (1996), for example, points out that recovery definitions always imply over-demanding situations. Hacker and Richter (1984) emphasize that stress can be initiated by underdemanding circumstances as well, such as sleepiness, psychological stress, psychic saturation, or monotony, which also follow the above-defined recovery demands. This approach highlights that recovery results from a variety of causes, and not only from an increase in activity.

The definitions described above are all quite general, and consider recovery as a counterpart to the disturbance in an initial state or a deficit condition of the organism, which enables the individual to perform. Kellmann and Kallus (1999, 2000) claim that recovery encompasses active processes of re-establishing psychological and physiological resources and states which allow an individual to tax these resources again. This definition explains the complex issue of recovery more precisely, but it is still not sufficient to define recovery merely as an elimination of fatigue or a system restart. Only a differentiated and longitudinal observation can explain the complex individual recovery process.

There are different concepts of how recovery functions (Kellmann, 2002a). Kenttä and Hassmén (2002), for example, describe universal methods of optimizing total quality recovery, namely by clearly defining the stress in order to find the most efficient recovery strategy. Psychological and emotional stressors need to be eliminated, and training for increased stress tolerance needs to take place. Hanin (2002), on the other hand, does not agree with these universal recovery strategies. He describes a very individual way of achieving recovery, namely by using individual emotional profiling to identify optimal states. These optimal states need to be achieved in order for recovery to occur.

In the following, a detailed overview will be given of the different aspects of recovery and the factors that influence it.

## RECOVERY: THE BASICS

Kallus and Kellmann (2000) have established a list of general recovery features. The most important aspects are summarized in the following.

### RECOVERY DEPENDS ON A REDUCTION OF, A CHANGE OF, OR A BREAK FROM STRESS

There are three conditions under which recovery can take place. While reduction of stress and breaks from stress seem to be the obvious ones, a change of stress may need more explanation. Following Löhr and Preiser's (1974) claim that recovery does not always have to be relaxation but occasionally can also be tension, recovery can be initiated by activity changes which, for example, take place during changes in action types. According to Selye (1974), these single stressful activities can be eu-stress (positive stress) related. By alternating physiological and psychological stress, it is possible to optimize recovery. The body can relax while one is reading a book or watching a film. On the other hand, the psychological system can recover during physiological activity. The underlying mechanism is that one system can rest while another is active. For example, an overall task such as house cleaning is not as physically stressful if the required activities can be alternated as soon as one specific body part gets tired. In sports, this approach is used systematically in circuit training. While one muscle group is trained, the others can rest. Alternating exercises systematically can enhance the total training time. However, it should be mentioned that during circuit training the whole body is stressed to a certain extent, due to the all-round exercise activity.

While the first author was working with a group of top-level track and field athletes she noticed a continual decline in the recovery rates of one of the athletes. This decrease could not be explained by the training schedule, since no significant changes or increases in the training load or frequency had occurred during that time. When the athlete, who was a physical education major, was questioned, she revealed the following: The athlete described that her recovery was hindered because she was unable to attend her regular university classes. The university had gone on strike, and all classes were cancelled for a period of four weeks. During this period of intensive training she missed not being able to alternate training with the activities of school, and could not recover from training properly without having this counter-activity. After the strike ended, however, her recovery state improved. In summary, recovery takes place through an enhancement of activity (e.g., physical exercise), reduction of activity (e.g., sleep) or a change of activity (e.g., circuit training).

## RECOVERY IS INDIVIDUAL-SPECIFIC AND DEPENDS ON INDIVIDUAL APPRAISALS

When ten people are asked to name their "personal number-one recovery strategy," seven or eight different answers will probably be given. An exercise with a group of athletes demonstrates this quite well. Each individual is asked to write down his or her "personal number-one recovery strategy," and afterwards the paper is passed on to the next person. In almost all cases the personal favorite of one athlete does not match the choice of his or her neighbor. The recovery strategy "going shopping for a new pair of shoes" might be relaxing for one person but could describe an extremely stressful situation for another. In the sport context this means that athletes have different recovery strategies and needs, and that the recovery activity selected by the coach does not necessarily lead to the desired result. After the same activity, one athlete is highly relaxed, whereas another does not feel that he or she has recovered at all. For example, some athletes feel uncomfortable in a sauna. They perceive the intense sweating and heat as stressors and consequently, for them, a sauna is not relaxing at all.

Recovery needs to be applied individually, and it is recommended that each person have more than one available strategy. Sometimes the first choice cannot be used or does not work, due to external or internal circumstances. For example, the recovery strategy "getting a massage" works perfectly in the home training environment. However, during training camps or out-of-town competitions, it may not be possible to obtain this same recovery activity "getting a massage" when, for example, there are only a limited number of physical therapists available for a whole team. This shows that a second, third, or fourth "backup" recovery strategy should be available and applied, depending on current individual and situational factors.

## RECOVERY IS A PROCESS IN TIME
## AND DEPENDS ON THE TYPE AND DURATION OF STRESS

Recovery takes time and cannot be realized in the same way as switching a light on and off. The total recovery time depends on the previous activities and the duration of stress.

## PASSIVE, ACTIVE, AND PROACTIVE RECOVERY

Recovery can be divided into three types – passive, active, and proactive. Several studies have shown that recovery is faster when subjects exercise moderately instead of resting passively (Ahmaidi et al., 1996; Taoutaou et al., 1996; Thiriet et al., 1993; Wilmore &

Costill, 1988). In sports, the term for moderate exercise during the recovery process is *active recovery*, and the term for sitting and lying quietly is *passive recovery* (Hollmann & Hettinger, 2000; Maglischo, 1993). Passive recovery also includes treatments like massages, hot and cold baths, steam baths, and sauna, all of which initiate physiological reactions through physiological stimuli (heat, cold, pressure) affecting blood flow, respiration rate, and muscle tone (Weineck, 1994). In summary, passive recovery includes automatic psychological and biological processes to restore the initial state. Unfortunately, activities referred to as passive recovery often are the only ones that are applied systematically.

Recovery, however, is also a proactive self-initiated process for re-establishing psychological and physiological resources. Active recovery such as cool-downs, muscle relaxation, and stretching after practice and competition are known as cool-down activities. The purpose of these exercises is to eliminate effects of fatigue through targeted physical activity. During cool-down, increased blood circulation in the muscles results in a state of high metabolism. For example, because lactic acid does not have a chance to build up in the muscles, the blood gases can sink to a normal level more quickly. Light exercise is preferable to rest during recovery periods because a faster rate of blood flow is maintained. Thus, more lactic acid can be removed from muscles in less time. At lower levels of effort, including complete rest, the rate of removal is slower. If the effort is too high, however, additional lactic acid will be produced (Maglischo, 1993).

What makes sense regarding the physiological systems also applies to the general life of humans. When recovery includes a purposeful action, it can be defined as proactive recovery. A person is responsible for his or her own activities, and can actively initiate the process. For example, going to a movie, visiting close friends, and going for a run can be self-initiated, and proactively put a person in charge.

## RECOVERY IS CLOSELY TIED TO SITUATIONAL CONDITIONS AND IS A SELF-DETERMINED PROCESS

Sometimes it is as simple as it sounds: "If my roommate in the training camp snores, I don't get any sleep." The impact of situational conditions which affect recovery (e.g., amount of sleep, quality of a bed, partner contact) is obvious.

It is also important to consider how individuals appraise the obvious situational conditions. For example, if an athlete's accommodation is close to a noisy street, his or her rest may be disturbed day and night. However, if an athlete is used to living in a loud neighborhood, he or she may have no problem sleeping through loud noises, and instead might be irritated by an absolutely quiet environment. The sensitivity of individuals to disturbing events depends on their own experiences.

Coaches have to be aware of these circumstances and should encourage athletes to communicate about disturbances in their surroundings. The coach is not in the same room when the traffic noise is too loud or when the roommate snores. Situational circumstances can often be easily changed if the coach/staff receives the necessary information soon enough (Kellmann, Kallus, Günther, Lormes, & Steinacker, 1997). Therefore, awareness and communication are the key elements in preventing underrecovery due to situational conditions (see also Botterill & Wilson, 2002).

In addition to the criteria described by Kallus (1995) and Kallus and Kellmann (2000), recovery is a self-determined process, as pointed out by Botterill and Wilson (2002). A dramatic change occurs when individual perception and self-awareness are altered. Suddenly, the supposed recovery strategy may have an opposite effect. Taking a short nap, or "power nap," between two training sessions is a common recovery strategy among athletes and is described in the literature as a valuable recovery method (see Glasser, 1984). However, the athlete has to stay in control of the power nap. If he or she does not force him- or herself to awaken and get up after the alotted time, the power nap turns into a longer nap. After a long nap in the middle of the day, many athletes describe themselves as feeling even more tired and much weaker. They do not feel they have recovered at all. According to Maas (1998), the optimal length of a power nap is 20 min. After the athlete realizes that the nap has gone on too long, the supposed recovering effect turns into disturbed recovery. This highlights how important control is in recovery.

## MEASURING RECOVERY

Understanding what recovery is, and which factors have an influence on it, is very important. The central question for sport psychology practice and intervention is: "How can recovery be assessed?" Which instruments can be applied to determine if an athlete is, for example, underrecovered or overexerted? This is extremely important, since so far physiological measures have not been very successful in diagnosing overtraining and/or are very elaborate (Steinacker & Lehmann, 2002). Differentiating normal from abnormal modifications in response to overtraining is complex, since various physiological characteristics alter when the shift from standard to intense training is made (Hooper, Mackinnon, Howard, Gordon, & Bachmann, 1995). Kuipers (1998) summarizes that no specific, simple, and reliable parameters are known for diagnosing overtraining at the earliest stage. However, studies to establish decisive factors of overtraining have demonstrated that psychological indicators seem to be more sensitive and consistent than others (Kellmann, 2002b; Kenttä & Hassmén, 1998; Raglin, 1993). The great advantage of psychometric instruments is the quick availability of information they provide. While common blood analysis and/or specific medical/physiological diagnostics may take hours or days (and even sometimes weeks), psychological data are available within minutes.

## RECOVERY-STRESS QUESTIONNAIRE FOR ATHLETES

One widely applied instrument in measuring recovery and stress is the Recovery-Stress Questionnaire for Athletes (RESTQ-Sport; Kellmann & Kallus, 2000, 2001). The questionnaire, made up of 76 items, can be completed by the athletes in about 8 to 10 min. Evaluation is simple using the computer program accompanying the questionnaire. The theory behind the questionnaire is that an accretion of stress in life, coupled with weak recovery potential, will cause a variation in the general psychophysical state. The specific characteristics of the RESTQ-Sport measure appraise events, states, and activities regarding their frequency in a direct and systematic manner, together with consideration of stress and recovery processes. A scale measures to what extent the respondent took part in different activities within the past three days/nights. A Likert-type scale is used with values ranging from 0 (never) to 6 (always) indicating how often the respondent participated in various activities during the past three days/nights. The RESTQ-Sport includes a precise subjective appraisal of events in the assessment of, and an accurate focus on, the frequency of behavior. This objective was attained by focusing on frequencies of events, activities, and states in the previous three days/nights, using statements such as "*I had a good time with friends*" instead of "*I met some friends.*" Based on these items specific interventions can be suggested.

The RESTQ-Sport consists of twelve general stress and recovery scales, as well as seven sport-specific stress and recovery scales. The first seven scales deal with different aspects of *General Stress, Emotional Stress,* and *Social Stress,* as well as resulting consequences. The scales *Conflicts/Pressure, Fatigue,* and *Lack of Energy* are concerned with performance aspects, whereas *Physical Complaints* addresses the physiological aspects of stress. *Success* is the only recovery-oriented scale concerned with performance in general and not in a sport-specific context. *Social Relaxation, Physical Relaxation,* and *General Well-being* are the basic scales of the recovery area, with an additional scale assessing *Sleep Quality.*

The sport-specific scale *Disturbed Breaks* is sensitive to deficiencies of recovery and interrupted recovery during periods of rest (e.g., half-times, time-outs). *Emotional Exhaustion* is characterized by the component of wanting to give up or lack of persistence. This relates to any disappointments in the context of sport that might lead to quitting the sport. *Injury* consists of any statements dealing with injuries, vulnerability to injuries, or an impairment of physical strength. *Being in Shape* assesses subjective feelings about performance ability and competence, one's perceived fitness, and vitality. *Personal Accomplishment* primarily asks about appreciation and empathy within the team and the realization of personal goals in sports. *Self-Efficacy* measures the level of expectation and competence regarding optimal performance preparation in practice. *Self-Regulation* refers to the availability and use of psychological skills when preparing for performance (e.g., goal setting, mental training, motivation).

The RESTQ-Sport has proven to be a psychometrically validated instrument. Validated versions of the RESTQ-Sport are available in German (Kellmann & Kallus, 2000), English (Kellmann & Kallus, 2001), Latvian (Jürimäe, Mäestu, Purge, Jürimäe, & Sööt, 2002), and Portuguese (Samulski, Costa, & Kellmann, 2003). French and Spanish versions are in the validation process.

## THE RECOVERY-CUE

Another instrument that can be applied to measure individual recovery is the Recovery-Cue. Knowing that time is always an issue for athletes as well as coaches, Kellmann,

Patrick, Botterill, and Wilson (2002) developed the Recovery-Cue. The Recovery-Cue is a recovery protocol consisting of the following seven items:

1) How much effort was required to complete my workout last week?
2) How recovered did I feel before my workouts last week?
3) How successful was I at rest and recovery activities last week?
4) How well did I recover physically last week?
5) How satisfied and relaxed was I as I fell asleep in the last week?
6) How much fun did I have last week?
7) How convinced was I that I could achieve my goals during performance last week?

Three items were developed in reference to this concept by Kenttä and Hassmén (1998), focusing on perceived exertion, perceived recovery, and recovery efforts; four items represent the areas of the RESTQ-Sport which have been detected as being crucial for recovery processes (Physical Recovery, Sleep Quality, Social Recovery, and Self-Regulation). Being aware of the problems with one-item assessments, the researchers' goal was to develop a practical tool for athletes and coaches that could be completed during training and that provided immediate feedback.

Athletes are requested to consistently fill in the items on the Recovery-Cue before, during, or after their training session, on the same day and at the same time from week to week. In addition, it is important to determine whether the coach, athlete, or support staff wants to receive information about the recovery effects of the past weekend (therefore the Recovery-Cue would be completed on Mondays, for example), or whether they want to determine the impact that training had over the current week (therefore it should be completed on Friday or Saturday).

The advantage of the RESTQ-Sport and the Recovery-Cue is that they measure stress and recovery multi-dimensionally.

## FURTHER INSTRUMENTS

Three other instruments which measure singular aspects of stress and recovery can be used as well. Borg's Rating of Perceived Exertion (RPE; Borg, 1975, 1998) is used in sport research to measure the level of perceived exertion of an individual. Morgan (1994) pointed out that RPE is usually accurate in estimating the intensity of an exercise stimulus. RPE is an accurate indicator of training adaptation in exercise programs involving cardiac and hypertensive patients as well as clinically normal patients (Noble & Robertson, 1996). The Profile of Mood States (POMS; McNair, Lorr, & Droppleman, 1971, 1992) is a self-assessment tool for mood and affective states. The POMS is a 65-item Likert format questionnaire which rates on a scale of 1 to 4, from "not at all" to "extremely." Shorter versions have also been discussed in the literature (for an overview see LeUnes & Burger, 2000). The POMS provides a measure of total mood disturbances and six mood states (Tension, Depression, Anger, Vigor, Fatigue, and Confusion). Kenttä and Hassmén (2002) describe case studies using the POMS to monitor training.

Both the RPE and the POMS have shown results that overlap with actual exercise performance; however, these two instruments only assess singular aspects of stress and/or recovery and are not constructed in a multidimensional fashion.

Elbe, Schimanke, and Wenhold (2003) developed the 30 item Acute Stress Measure (ASM), which assesses emotional, mental, and physical stress within the previous half-hour. The measure, which has shown good reliability and validity, is currently being used in recovery experiments in which several physiological measures are assessed simultaneously. It is intended to apply this questionnaire in the future in the sport setting.

However, Kellmann et al. (2002) point out that these instruments should not be used as a replacement for effective communication. Instead, they should be seen as important, proactive tools that can aid in the creation of a more dynamic and responsive training environment. Finally, it is worth mentioning that the monitoring of both recovery and stress should remain the responsibility of the athletes themselves, who should use the tools in a manner that facilitates improved levels of both self-awareness and personal responsibility.

## INTEGRATING RECOVERY INTO THE TRAINING SCHEDULE

Knowing about recovery and how to measure it enables the laying of groundwork for its integration into the training schedule. During the course of a training year an athlete completes different training phases, e.g., the preparatory training phase, competition phase, and transformation phase. An annual training periodization which reflects the long term periodization is necessary in order to achieve peak performance (Bompa, 1999). The training schedule should be divided into smaller cycles, allowing for better control over the training process. The length and specific content of each cycle depends on different factors, for example, the stage of long-term development, the type of sport, and the individual athlete. Recovery plays a different role in each of these phases of the training cycle. Furthermore, recovery in team and individual sports can be different.

## RECOVERY ASPECTS OF TEAM AND INDIVIDUAL SPORTS

As already stated above, recovery is very individual. The name already suggests that individual recovery is easier to achieve in individual sports than in team sports. However, this is an area in which little research has been performed. The results of the research project "Personality and Achievement Development of Young Elite Athletes in Potsdam" (Beckmann, Elbe, Szymanski, & Ehrlenspiel, in preparation) reveal aspects relevant to recovery in individual and team sports. In this project, which was funded by the German Institute for Sport Science and the Brandenburg Ministry for Education, Youth, and Sport, the recovery-stress state of young elite athletes was monitored over the course of three years using the RESTQ-Sport. The students tested in this project attended a special school, namely a high school exclusively for young elite athletes. Thirty-eight of these schools exist in Germany at present. In order to be admitted to such a school, the young athletes must undergo a strict selection procedure, including several tests of sport performance. They must also have a recommendation from the state sport organization. Once they are admitted to the school, they train on a daily basis and frequently take part in training camps and competitions. Many of the students live in the on-campus boarding school. The aim of these schools is to optimally enhance athletic development. The evaluation of the individual training loads in this study showed that the team sport athletes in general had a lighter training load than the individual athletes. A look at the stress rates of the team athletes, however, showed that those of the team athletes were significantly higher than those of the individual athletes at two measuring points. Before Easter vacation in grade 11, the scale "Fatigue" ($p < 0.05$) and after Easter vacation the scale "Lack of Energy" ($p < 0.05$) were significantly higher in the team athletes. These results indicate that additional attention needs to be paid to the recovery of team athletes, and that a lower training load does not automatically lead to less stress.

The following describes recovery aspects that are relevant for different phases of the training process as well as for competitions. If relevant, differentiations are made for individual and team athletes, respectively.

## ASPECTS OF RECOVERY IN TRAINING

Peak performance is achievable only if athletes optimally balance training stress and adequate recovery (Kuipers, 1998; Rowbottom, Keast, & Morton, 1998). This is especially true in phases of highly intense training, for example, in the preparatory phase at the beginning of a season, where the foundation for the upcoming season (e.g., endurance training) is laid.

When intensity and volume are increased during training, the subjective assessment of athletes turns out to be very important, because a long-term imbalance of stress (including training, competition, and non training-stress factors) and recovery can lead to performance deficits and a state of overtraining (Budgett, 1998; Kellmann, 2002b; Lehmann, Foster, Gastmann, Keizer, & Steinacker, 1999). Therefore, it is recommended that stress and recovery be continuously monitored during the training process (see Berglund & Säfström, 1994; Hooper, Mackinnon, & Howard, 1999; Kellmann, Altenburg, Lormes, & Steinacker, 2001). The RESTQ-Sport as well as the Recovery Cue are very useful instruments for accomplishing this objective. The RESTQ-Sport, for example, identifies athletes whose *recovery-stress states* during training do not correspond with changes in the training schedule. In addition, with the RESTQ-Sport one can compare individuals with the group during the season, at training camps, and over the course of many years. Based on this information, training can be individually adapted (i.e., decreased or increased).

The RESTQ-Sport monitors and evaluates effects of training. An increase in stress values, for example, is not a problem. This can occur when training is intense, and athletes are supposed to approach their limits. It is important, however, for athletes to be given adequate space and time to recover after an intense training load. For example, before resuming training, the recovery state should be examined.

It is important to keep in mind that recovery processes involve various organismic sub-systems that monitor the body and have important functions before, during, and after physical exercise. Different sub-systems, such as the cardiovascular, hormonal, endocrine, and muscular sub-systems, are involved during and, of course, after exercise (Lehmann et al., 1997; Norris & Smith, 2002; Smith & Norris, 2000). For example, during exercise, mainly the muscular and cardiovascular sub-systems are stressed, whereas some parameters of the endocrine sub-system peak during night sleep. If night sleep, especially when delta brain waves occur, is disturbed, the restoration and rejuvenation of the body are affected (Savis, 1994). Growth hormones and cell division are at their peak during delta sleep; metabolic rate, respiration, core temperature, and heart rate are at their circadian lowest. According to Savis, delta sleep has been described as an "agent of recovery relative to the metabolic activity and energy expended by an individual" (p. 115), which underlines the importance of sufficient and good quality sleep.

As indicated, the organismic sub-processes of recovery can be dissociated – the amount of time necessary for recovery from the stress of training may vary within and between the different organismic systems of the human body (see Gabriel, Urhausen, Valet, Heidelbach, & Kindermann, 1998; Steinacker, et al., 2000; Urhausen, Gabriel, & Kindermann, 1995). Viru and Viru (1999) pointed out that the variability of hormonal responses is frequently caused by the combined influence of factors such as temperature, hypoxia, biorhythm, diet, fatigue, and the initial hormone level. Incorrect evaluation of hormonal responses can be avoided if these determinants and modulators are appropriately considered.

## UNDERRECOVERY AND OVERTRAINING

If insufficient attention is paid to recovery, problems can occur. One of these problems is the state of underrecovery. Underrecovery is a key component in the development of overtraining and burnout (Kellmann, 2002b). The main assumption is that a constant lack of recovery or disturbed recovery turns into overtraining or burnout. Even being slightly underrecovered over a long period of time can result in underperformance. Overtraining is caused by a long-term imbalance between stress and recovery, meaning too much stress combined with too little regeneration. Overtraining can lead to burnout, the symptoms of which Maslach and Jackson (1986) describe as emotional exhaustion, depersonalization, and lack of personal fulfillment. Burnout is the psychological, physical, and emotional withdrawal from a formerly enjoyable and motivating activity, resulting from prolonged or chronic stress. Burnout can lead to a decrease in performance as well as dropout from sports.

Underrecovery, as one important precursor of burnout, can be caused by many different circumstances, one of which is not paying enough attention to adequate recovery. It is important to note that underrecovery can also be brought about by training mistakes such as (a) having a monotonous training program, (b) having more than three hours training per day, (c) having more than a 30% increase in training load each week, (d) ignoring the training principle of alternating hard and easy training days or by alternating two hard days followed by an easy training day, (e) having no training periodization and respective regeneration micro-cycles after two or three weeks of training, or (f) having no rest days (Gastmann, Petersen, Böcker, & Lehmann, 1998; Norris & Smith, 2002).

In highly intense training phases or cycles, there is little opportunity for physical and psychological recovery. In addition, many athletes and coaches focus on the amount and intensity of the training loads rather than on recovery (Hanin, 2002). There is often an overemphasis on quantity rather than on the quality of the training. Sometimes the athletes become part of a vicious circle. Demanding training and lack of recovery decreases their performance. Instead of taking a break, their underperformance is then countered with even more training, leading to more underrecovery and even poorer performance.

To prevent overtraining, physiological and psychological recovery should be an integral part of the training plan (Hooper & Mackinnon, 1995; Kellmann, 2002b).

In general, if practice is completed in a high training volume phase, recovery time usually takes longer compared to that of a taper phase (see, for example, Hooper & Mackinnon, 1995, 1999; Raglin, 1993).

## RECOVERY ACTIVITIES IN TRAINING

The question is how can recovery activities be integrated into the training process in order to enable recovery in all organismic subsystems and to prevent underrecovery, overtraining and burnout. Kallus and Kellmann (2000) have discussed the different levels on which recovery can be described (e.g., physiological, psychological, behavioral, social, environmental). On a physiological level, recovery takes place by restoring resources such as the body's need for nutrition, for example by the ingestion of food, water, and minerals (Kenttä & Hassmén, 1998, 2002; Norris & Smith, 2002). The re-establishment of physiological fitness after injury or of the hormonal and biological processes during sleep indicate other, more biological processes of recovery (Hollmann & Hettinger, 2000; Savis, 1994). Sleep affects psychological aspects as well. The feeling of relaxation and the re-establishment of well-being and a positive mood demonstrate the psychological aspects of recovery. Behavioral aspects of recovery support the biological processes, and result in recovery by changing the activity from one stressor to another or in the planning of leisure activities. Social aspects of recovery take place, for example, when people get together for the weekend for social events such as having dinner, throwing parties, or just having fun together. Interpersonal relationships such as those with a friend or partner demonstrate more private and intimate aspects of social recovery.

The first step towards integrating recovery into the training process is that the coach and athlete realize the importance of recovery and understand that it is an individual process. A helpful tool in developing this understanding is the application of the RESTQ-Sport. With the help of the RESTQ-Sport the athlete's subjective perception, which can differ from the coach's, can be assessed. In addition, it provides a picture of the athlete's condition from a different point of view and from which concrete solutions can be derived. If the value on the scale Physical Complaints, for example, is too high, certain activities to lower this scale value can be performed.

There are many recovery methods that can enhance the physiological well-being of athletes and can replenish resources that were depleted during training. Drinking (hydration) restores fluids lost during the sport activity. Adequate nutrition, including receiving enough minerals and vitamins, refuels energy resources. To enhance recovery of the muscles, procedures such as massages, warm baths, or saunas can be applied. Examples of other more active recovery activities are stretching or moderate jogging. Getting the right amount of sleep is also an important aspect of physical recovery. Loehr (1994) describes too little as well as too much sleep as problematic for the recovery process. According to Glasser (1984), power naps are a helpful tool in enhancing recovery.

It must be kept in mind, however, that performing some of these recovery strategies may not have the desired effect in a team sport. Often team coaches, because of organizational reasons or facility constraints, prefer or demand a common recovery strategy for the entire team. However, the coach's demand for a common recovery strategy after training may not be relaxing for all of the team members. In team sports, coaches often tell the team members to do 15 to 30 min of light jogging after training. However, many athletes perceive this as an additional training element and sometimes even turn it into a competition, showing the other team members how fast they can run. For them, because this light jogging is not relaxing at all, the recovery effect is not achieved.

An effective tool for physiological as well as psychological recovery is the use of relaxation techniques. For successful learning of relaxation techniques, practice should start at the beginning of the new season and be continued during the entire preparation period. Relaxation techniques can be used effectively for individual as well as team athletes. Research has shown that even young children can effectively learn and apply relaxation techniques (Petermann, 1996), and these techniques can be a useful tool for training groups of all ages. According to Kellmann and Beckmann (2004), relaxation techniques fulfill three very important purposes for athletes: They enhance recovery by furthering personal growth, they speed up regeneration, and they can be used as a strategy of self-regulation. The first two points are of great relevance for the training phase, whereas self-regulation competence is especially important in a competition situation.

Relaxation procedures can further the personality development of athletes if they are embedded in regular training and practiced on a regular and long-term basis. In time the athletes learn to confront problems in a focused but relaxed manner; this resulting competence simultaneously furthers personality development. During this learning process the athletes learn to pay attention to tension and relaxation, thus developing a better sense of their own body and the generated movement taking place in it. The ability to relax is closely tied to the ability to self regulate one's own physical and psychological condition. At the same time the psyche develops more "coolness", which allows individuals to more easily accept unexpected and/or unfavorable circumstances.

Furthermore, a systematized relaxation technique optimizes the limited time resources competitive athletes have available for recovery. If relaxation techniques are applied after training or within short training breaks, the somatotropic and psychotropic effects of relaxation can enhance and speed up recovery. Relaxation techniques applied between training units cause an acceleration of the natural recovery process and make more intensive and increased training loads possible. Allmer (1996) states that the physical recovery after training loads takes place faster with support from relaxation procedures than via passive recovery.

Due to their effectiveness, relaxation techniques can also be helpful in preventing overtraining. An important indicator of overtraining is stagnation in performance and/or a performance decrease not intended in the training plan. In addition, a main characteristic of the overtraining condition is problems falling asleep or sleeping through the night. Another characteristic is thoughts circling around a certain topic (usually the decreased performance), which makes falling asleep difficult and consequently leads to decreased recovery which negatively affects performance (Kellmann, 2002b). This situation is frequently the beginning of a vicious circle. However, by consciously forcing relaxation, the thought circles are interrupted, giving the thoughts a focused procedural instruction. Many athletes fall asleep during the relaxation training, which is the first step in interrupting the vicious cycle and ending the athlete's overtired state.

There are several relaxation techniques that can be learned. In the following, breathing, progressive muscle relaxation, and autogenic training are described. It is often easiest to begin with a breathing technique (Kellmann & Beckmann, 2004). According to Lindemann (1984), relaxing breathing is characterized by exhalation that is markedly prolonged in comparison to inhalation. After exhalation there is a short break until inhalation continues automatically.

In a second step, the relaxation technique called *progressive muscle relaxation* can be introduced into the training process. This is a procedure that can be learned quite quickly by athletes. The technique of progressive muscle relaxation, described by Edmund Jacobson in the 1930s (Jacobson, 1934), is based on the premise that mental relaxation should naturally result from physical relaxation. In progressive muscle relaxation the tensing or tightening of one muscle group at a time is followed by a release of the tension. The muscle groups are tightened and relaxed one at a time in a specific order, generally commencing with the lower extremities and ending with the face, abdomen, and chest. The individual muscle groups are tightened for 5 to 8 sec and the tension is then released. While releasing the tension, athletes are asked to focus on the changes they feel when the muscle group is relaxed.

A relaxation technique that is more difficult to master is autogenic training, a century-old European method for achieving relaxation based upon passive concentration and body awareness of specific sensations. The German psychiatrist and neurologist Johannes Schultz was the first to describe this technique (Schultz, 1932).

As with other meditative or relaxation techniques, effective practice of autogenic training results in a reduction in heart rate, blood pressure, respiratory rate, and tension, all of which can have long-ranging health benefits. Autogenic training can be practiced anywhere, at any time. Schultz (1932) described six autogenic "formulae" or "states," as follows:

1. focus on heaviness in the arms and legs
2. focus on warmth in the arms and legs
3. focus on warmth and heaviness in the heart area
4. focus on breathing
5. focus on warmth in the abdomen
6. focus on coolness in the forehead.

The first two formulae are often broken down to focus first upon the dominant arm, followed by the other arm or the legs. For each formula, one repeats a phrase, or formula, such as "my arm feels heavy," silently with closed eyes. Breathing is paced slowly and the phrase is repeated five to seven times before opening the eyes and stretching.

Concerning emotional and psychological well-being, Botterill and Wilson (2002) describe emotional management as another very important recovery tool. Because one's inability to manage emotions can lead to performance and health problems, it can also hinder recovery. It is important to learn to be prepared for emotions, to accept and share strong emotions, to bring emotions into perspective through the help of others, and to channel the energy created by these emotions (Botterill & Wilson, 2002). Simple techniques like picturing a stop sign can be helpful in regulating emotions or stopping negative thoughts.

Botteril and Brown (2001) emphasize that emotional management is very important in team sports. Team emotional dynamics can be very powerful, and the impact of emotions can increase. Teams, therefore, should work on creating efficient team dynamics (Werthner & Botterill, 2000) in order to optimize recovery. Robertson (2000) claims that recovery can be enhanced if there is a high level of trust, respect, and support among the team. This is the prerequisite so that emotions don't escalate or be a distraction to what is important. If emotional management is not practiced in a team, emotions can dominate and thus hinder recovery. Therefore, it is advisable that exercises to improve team cohesion be performed at the beginning of the season, to lay the basis for sufficient recovery. Exercises aimed at building teams and improving cohesion can be found, for example, in Janssen (1999).

Further important recovery activities are of a social nature. Spending time with friends, for example, is generally beneficial for recovery. Being with friends from the team as well as with non-sport related friends can be helpful, depending on what kind of recovery is intended. Receiving positive feedback and encouragement from teammates can also help the recovery process. In other situations, one might want to get one's mind off the intensive training or an unsuccessful performance and prefer to discuss other, non-sport related topics. In this case, meeting with friends outside the sport domain might be better. A whole range of social activities can be performed with friends that can have a relaxing effect, for example going to the movies, dancing, going to parties, or playing a board game.

## ASPECTS OF RECOVERY DURING TRAINING CAMPS

Special training elements are training camps. Training camps take place in different phases of the training periodization, for example to lay the endurance groundwork during the preparatory phase (the beginning of the training cycle) or as immediate preparation for a big competition, namely towards the end of yearly training cycle.

Regardless of what kind of a training camp the athletes attend, paying attention to adequate recovery is essential. During training camps, athletes are taken out of their normal surroundings, such as their home environment, and experience a different one.

Furthermore, they become very close to their coach and teammates and are confronted with new surroundings (e.g., training facilities, bed, etc.) and an increase in frequency and/or load of daily training. All of these factors can affect the recovery state. Athletes who normally can recover quickly may experience an impaired recovery in the training camp situation. Simple things, like a bed that is too small, a teammate that snores, or homesickness, can impair sleep and lead to underrecovery. Also, being unable to apply the usual recovery strategies, such as going to the movies or spending time with friends who are not on the team, can cause underrecovery. Coaches need to be aware that because training camps can influence the amount of recovery needed, athletes might not recover as quickly there as in their home environment.

In order to prevent underrecovery in training camps, it is helpful to continually assess the recovery-stress state. First of all, it is important to measure the recovery-stress state at the beginning of the training camp. If there is an imbalance in recovery and stress already at the beginning of the training camp, not much performance improvement can be expected over the course of the training camp if adequate space for recovery is not given.

At the beginning of a training camp for cyclists, the following profile of an athlete was found (Katschemba, 2003). The data collection during the training camp was performed merely for research and not for intervention purposes, and was not evaluated until after the camp.

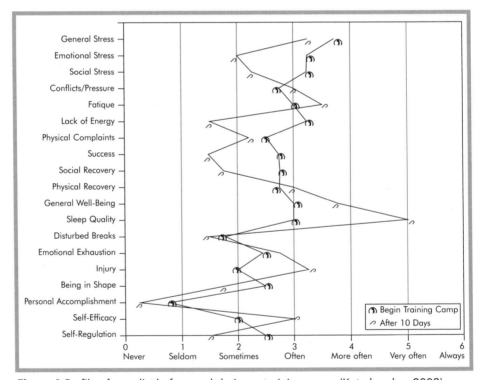

**Figure 1** Profile of a cyclist before and during a training camp (Katschemba, 2003).

Figure 1 clearly shows that the athlete is underrecovered at the beginning of the training camp. Generally speaking, recovery values above four and stress values under the value of two indicate a sufficient recovery-stress state. This athlete's recovery values were below four in all of the recovery scales. In addition, almost all the stress values were above the value of two. The coach could not be made aware of the athlete's underrecovered state, because the data were not evaluated until after the training camp. He therefore did not make any adjustments for this athlete in the training schedule. Over the course of the training camp some of the values deteriorated even further.

The second line of Figure 1 shows that the recovery rates improved slightly in some scales over the course of the training camp, for example, concerning "Sleep", "Success", and "General Well-Being." However, many of the stress rates increased. Needless to say, the continual decrease in recovery and increase in stress values can also lead to a decline in performance. The intention of the training camp, namely to improve performance, may not have been achieved for this athlete.

However, assessing the recovery state only at the beginning of the training camp is insufficient. It is important that monitoring occurs over the entire duration of the training camp. Underrecovery can occur after a period of time or even towards the end of a training camp. In addition, other factors such as conflicts in the team, which develop because the team members are so close together for such a long period of time, can cause underrecovery. If recovery is not continually monitered, the goal of the training camp, namely to enhance the performance (for example in preparation for an upcoming important competition), may not be achieved due to the increasing underrecovery of the athletes.

## RECOVERY ACTIVITIES DURING TRAINING CAMPS

It is important that athletes and coaches have alternative recovery activities they can apply in the training camp situation, since it may not be possible to perform the regular recovery activities. Kellmann (2002c) describes a toolbox for planning rest days, illustrating many activities and their implications for recovery. It is important for the coach to remember that recovery is a very individual process and that not every activity has the same effect on each athlete. There are important considerations to make if new recovery activities are experimented with in a training camp situation. If, for example, a new athletic activity such as inline skating or mountain climbing is tried out, it might cause muscle pain or additionally tire the athletes. Also, going out for a drink or dancing might be a socially valuable recovery activity during the training camp, but one needs to keep in mind that dancing until three a.m. may not allow enough time for physiological recovery if one has training at eight o'clock the next morning. All in all, additional considerations need to be made to allow for good recovery in training camps.

## ASPECTS OF RECOVERY BEFORE, DURING, AND AFTER COMPETITIONS

Probably the most important part of competitive sports is competitions. Recovery plays an important role here as well. To achieve peak performance athletes have to be recovered before the competition, and have to be able to quickly recover during competition.

Furthermore, recovery has to follow the competition in preparation for the following competition. To illustrate this, several examples are given from different types of sports.

At the 2002 Soccer World Championships in Japan and Korea, some teams who were favored to win the World Cup, such as France and Portugal, did not survive the first round in the tournament. During and shortly after the World Cup, some journalists and officials of the World Soccer Association (FIFA) had a discussion about why these teams were not able to perform at their expected level. The connection to underrecovery, due to the game schedule of the players during the season, was quickly made. Athletes from clubs playing successfully in international competitions like the Champion League or the UEFA-Cup in Europe have a very tight competition schedule and are especially vulnerable. For example, Hertha BSC played more games than any of the other German professional soccer teams in the first half of the 1999/2000 season – 29 games within 18 weeks, an average of one game in 4.3 days including travel time. And, it is not only the large number of games but also the fact that travel time is not recovery time. This is especially true when players have to overcome a time change. By mid-season, the players described themselves as physically and mentally drained. These examples from soccer show that, due to organizational constraints, the players often do not have enough time to recover from one game to another.

Optimal performance is achievable only if athletes recover after competition and optimally balance training stress and adequate recovery (Kuipers, 1998; Rowbottom et al., 1998). Therefore, coaches and athletes need to regularly evaluate the relationship between training load and performance. Recovery, an essential component of athletic training and the opposite of training and non-training stress, is too often overlooked.

Recovery for individual athletes might be easier, since they have slightly more freedom in determining which competitions they want to take part in. If they do not compete it does not have negative consequences for a whole team.

According to the Associated Press (1999), Tiger Woods' only preparation for Part III of the PGA Tour in 1999 was not to touch a club for 10 days. He reported that he just "hung out" with friends and got away from the game. He had played four major tournaments and felt really burned out. After getting away from golf for several days and doing what he liked, he was fresh and relaxed at the next tournament.

A top-level long jumper the first author was working with described her elaborate recovery ritual before each important competition. She said that if she did not spend the day before a competition "grooming" herself intensively, she did not feel adequately relaxed for the upcoming competition. On the day before the meet she had to take a long bath, shave her legs, color her hair, do a manicure and pedicure, and apply a facial mask to feel optimally prepared for the event.

However, to achieve peak performance, athletes not only have to be adequately recovered before the competition, but they also have to be able to recover during the course of the competition. Decathletes, for example, have to compete in 10 disciplines over the course of two days in order to complete a decathlon. In the throwing and jumping events they have to perform three trials. For them it is essential to be able to recover in-between the individual disciplines and trials. Knowing how to apply relaxation techniques, as well as techniques to deal with unsuccessful trials, is essential. Even simple strategies like listening to one's favorite music in between two events can be very helpful.

In addition, recovering after a competition is also essential. However, here again it might be more difficult in a team sport. For some athletes it is important to be able to relax after an important match. In a small locker room, however, it is difficult to find a quiet space or to get away from the other team members. This is especially true when other athletes on the team prefer to celebrate after a successful game by being loud, screaming, jumping around, and listening to music. They want everyone to take part in the celebration and have little understanding for players who need time away from the team.

## RECOVERY ACTIVITIES BEFORE, DURING, AND AFTER COMPETITIONS

There are several effective methods for enhancing recovery during the competition phase. An effective recovery activity before and sometimes even during competitions is the already described relaxation techniques. As mentioned above, relaxation techniques enhance self-regulation, which is especially important before important matches or competitions (Kellmann & Beckmann, 2004). Many athletes report that they do not sleep well the night before a competition or suffer from insomnia. This decreased sleep quality and quantity can affect recovery in two ways. First of all, it is physically performance-reducing. Secondly, it has a psychological effect because the athletes develop a sense of uncertainty towards their effectiveness and strength. Relaxation techniques can help the athlete eliminate disturbing and diverting thoughts and can help him or her improve sleep behavior. In the beginning, the relaxation techniques can aid the athlete in falling asleep. During the day of the competition athletes experience different activation levels, depending on their experience and their self-control ability. Generally speaking, an adequate level of activation and tension is necessary for good performance. Therefore, it is often recommended that no relaxation training be performed on the day of the competition, so that necessary tension is not lost. However, some athletes complain of being "over-activated" or too nervous on the day of the competition, which impairs their performance. It is useful for these athletes to perform relaxation techniques, as well as for those athletes who are very experienced in regulating their level of activation. For some athletes relaxation is a strategy, and an essential condition for developing the concentration necessary for the match or game.

A strategy that can be applied during the competition is the positive psychological reaction (Loehr, 1994). It keeps negative thoughts from intruding and helps optimize recovery during short breaks, e.g., between two sets in tennis or in between trials and disciplines in the decathlon. Loehr describes top athletes who learned to apply this behavior even when they had just lost a point. By staying positive and smiling, for example, they could keep stress from accumulating during the match.

Following an important competition there is a strong need to discuss the outcome – especially if the outcome was unexpected. A win or a loss can cause strong emotions. A technique to channel these emotions in a constructive way is the method of debriefing

(Hogg, 2002; Hogg & Kellmann, 2002), which can enhance mental and emotional recovery. With the tool of debriefing, the event can come to a conclusion mentally, and recovery can follow.

## CONCLUSIONS

All in all, this chapter has covered multiple aspects of recovery in the hope of helping athletes enhance their recovery and prevent underrecovery and burnout. The chapter has illustrated different phases of training periodization and has discussed the relevant recovery aspects, as well as shown activities that positively influence the recovery process. The main focus of this chapter is on top-level competitive sports. However, recovery is relevant to many other sport settings, like adapted physical activity (Kellmann, Fritzenberg, & Beckmann, 2000), senior/masters sports, and youth sport. The results of the research project "Personality and Achievement Development of Young Elite Athletes in Potsdam" (Elbe, Beckmann, & Szymanski, 2002) reveal that even young athletes can show an imbalance in their recovery-stress state, which can, in the worst case, lead to dropout from youth sports and can negatively influence the role of sport in their entire lifespan. It is the authors' intention to raise awareness in athletes and coaches of the importance of recovery.

Although a substantial amount of knowledge exists about the topic of recovery, it is the authors' hope that in the future even more research will be preformed to further the understanding of this important aspect of competitive sports.

# REFERENCES

Ahmaidi, S., Granier, P., Taoutaou, Z., Mercier, B., Dubouchaud, H., & Prefaut, C. (1996). Lactate kinetics during passive and active recovery in endurance and print athletes. *European Medicine and Science in Sports and Exercise, 28*, 450-456.

Allmer, H. (1996). *Erholung und Gesundheit: Grundlagen, Ergebnisse und Maßnahmen* [Recovery and health: Basics, results and interventions]. Göttingen: Hogrefe.

Associated Press (1999). *http://cbs.sportsline.com/u/ce/multi/0,1329,1025913_64,00. html* (May 12, 2001).

Beckmann, J., Elbe, A.-M., Szymanski, B., & Ehrlenspiel, F. (in preparation). Chancen und Risiken vom Leben im Verbundsystem von Schule und Leistungssport – Psychologische, soziologische und Leistungsaspekte [Chances and risks of life in a school system for young elite athletes – psychological, sociological and achievement aspects]. Köln: Sport und Buch Strauß.

Berglund, B., & Säfström, H. (1994). Psychological monitoring and modulation of training load of world-class canoeists. *Medicine and Science in Sports and Exercise, 26*, 1036-1040.

Bompa, T. O. (1999). *Periodization – Theory and methodology of training*. Champaign, IL: Human Kinetics.

Borg, G. (1975). Perceived exertion as an indicator of somatic stress. *Scandinavian Journal of Rehabilitational Medicine, 2*, 92-98.

Borg, G. (1998). *Borg's Perceived Exertion and Pain Rating Scales*. Champaign, IL: Human Kinetics.

Botteril, C., & Brown, M. (2001). Emotion perspective in sport. *International Journal of Sport Psychology, 32*, 352-374.

Botterill, C., & Wilson, C. (2002). Overtraining: Emotional and interdisciplinary dimensions. In M. Kellmann (Ed.), *Enhancing recovery: Preventing underperformance in athletes* (pp. 143-159). Champaign, IL: Human Kinetics.

Budgett, R. (1998). Fatigue and underperformance in athletes: The overtraining syndrome. *British Journal of Sport and Medicine, 32*, 107-110.

Elbe, A-M., Beckmann, J., & Szymanski, B. (2002). Der Erholungs- und Belastungszustand von SportinternatsschülerInnen [The recovery stress state of young elite athletes]. In E. van der Meer, H. Hagendorf, R. Beyer, F. Krüger, A. Nuthmann, & S. Schulz (Eds.), *43. Kongress der deutschen Gesellschaft für Psychologie* (p. 420). Lengerich: Pabst Science Publishers.

Elbe, A.-M., Schimanke, K., & Wenhold, F. (2003). *Maß aktueller Beanspruchung.* [Acute Stress Measure]. Unpublished questionnaire, University of Potsdam, Germany.

Gabriel, H. H. W., Urhausen, A., Valet, G., Heidelbach, U., & Kindermann, W. (1998). Training and overtraining: An introduction. *Medicine and Science in Sports and Exercise, 30*, 1151-1157.

Gastmann, U., Petersen, K. G., Böcker, J., & Lehmann, M. (1998). Monitoring intensive endurance training at moderate energetic demands using resting laboratory markers failed to recognize an early overtraining stage. *Journal of Sports Medicine and Physical Fitness, 38*, 188-193.

Glasser, W. (1984). *Control theory*. New York: Harper and Row.

Hacker, W., & Richter, P. (1984). *Psychische Fehlbeanspruchung* [Psychological over- and understrain]. Berlin: Springer.

Hanin, Y. (2002). Individually optimal recovery in sports: An application of the IZOF Model. In M. Kellmann (Ed.), *Enhancing recovery: Preventing underperformance in athletes* (pp. 199-218). Champaign, IL: Human Kinetics.

Hogg, J. M. (2002). Debriefing: A means to increasing recovery and subsequent performance. In M. Kellmann (Ed.), *Enhancing recovery: Preventing underperformance in athletes* (pp. 181-198). Champaign, IL: Human Kinetics.

Hogg, J., & Kellmann, M. (2002). Debriefing im Leistungssport [Debriefing in competitive sports]. *Psychologie und Sport, 9*, 90-96.

Hollmann, W., & Hettinger, T. (2000). *Sportmedizin* [Sports medicine]. Stuttgart: Schlattauer.

Hooper, S. L., & Mackinnon, L. T. (1995). Monitoring overtraining in athletes. *Sports Medicine, 20*, 321-327.

Hooper, S.L., & Mackinnon, L. T. (1999). Monitoring regeneration in elite swimmers. In M. Lehmann, C. Foster, U. Gastmann, H. Keizer, & J. M. Steinacker (Eds.), *Overload, fatigue, performance incompetence, and regeneration in sport* (pp. 139-148). New York: Plenum.

Hooper, S. L., Mackinnon, L. T., & Howard, A. (1999). Physiological and psychometric variables for monitoring recovery during tapering for major competition. *Medicine and Science in Sports and Exercise, 31*, 1205-1210.

Hooper, S. L., Mackinnon, L. T., Howard, A., Gordon, R. D., & Bachmann, A. W. (1995). Markers for monitoring overtraining and recovery. *Medicine and Science in Sports and Exercise, 27*, 106-112.

Jacobson, E. (1934). *You must relax.* New York: McGraw Hill.

Janssen, J. (1999). *Championship team building.* Tucson, AZ: Winning the Mental Game.

Jürimäe, J., Mäestu, J., Purge, P., Jürimäe, T., & Sööt, T. (2002). Relations among heavy training stress, mood state, and performance for male junior rowers. *Perceptual and Motor Skills, 95*, 520-526.

Kallus, K. W. (1995). *Der Erholungs-Belastungs-Fragebogen* [The Recovery-Stress Questionnaire]. Frankfurt: Swets & Zeitlinger.

Kallus, K. W., & Kellmann, M. (2000). Burnout in athletes and coaches. In Y. L. Hanin (Ed.), *Emotions in sport* (pp. 209-230). Champaign, IL: Human Kinetics.

Katschemba, S. (2003). Erholungs- und Beanspruchungsprozesse Wissenschaftliche Grundlagen und beispielhafte Anwendung des Erholungs- und Belastungsfragebogen für Sportler im Radsport [Recovery and stress processes: Theoretical basis and application of the recovery-stress questionnaire for athletes in cycling]. Unpublished thesis, University of Potsdam, Germany.

Kellmann, M. (Ed.). (2002a). *Enhancing recovery: Preventing underperformance in athletes.* Champaign, IL: Human Kinetics.

Kellmann, M. (2002b). Underrecovery and overtraining: Different concepts – similar impact? In M. Kellmann (Ed.), *Enhancing recovery: Preventing underperformance in athletes* (pp. 3-24). Champaign, IL: Human Kinetics.

Kellmann, M. (2002c). Current status and directions of recovery research. In M. Kellmann (Ed.), *Enhancing recovery: Preventing underperformance in athletes* (pp. 301-311). Champaign, IL: Human Kinetics.

Kellmann, M., Altenburg, D., Lormes, W., & Steinacker, J. M. (2001). Assessing stress and recovery during preparation for the World Championships in rowing. *The Sport Psychologist*, 15, 151-167.

Kellmann, M., & Beckmann, J. (2004). Sport und Entspannungsverfahren [Sport and relaxation techniques]. In D. Vaitel & F. Petermann (Eds.), *Handbuch der Entspannungsverfahren* (pp. 320-331). Weinheim: Beltz.

Kellmann, M., Fritzenberg, M., & Beckmann, J. (2000). Erfassung von Belastung und Erholung im Behindertensport [Assessing stress and recovery in adapted physical activity]. *Psychologie und Sport*, 7, 141-152.

Kellmann, M., & Kallus, K. W. (1999). Mood, recovery-stress state, and regeneration. In M. Lehmann, C. Foster, U. Gastmann, H. Keizer, & J. M. Steinacker (Eds.), *Overload, fatigue, performance incompetence, and regeneration in sport* (pp. 101-117). New York: Plenum.

Kellmann, M., & Kallus, K. W. (2000). *Der Erholungs-Belastungs-Fragebogen für Sportler; Handanweisung* [The Recovery-Stress Questionnaire for Athletes; manual]. Frankfurt: Swets Test Services.

Kellmann, M., & Kallus, K. W. (2001). *Recovery-Stress Questionnaire for Athletes – User Manual*. Champaign, IL: Human Kinetics.

Kellmann, M., Kallus, K. W., Günther, K.-D., Lormes, W., & Steinacker, J. M. (1997). Psychologische Betreuung der Junioren-Nationalmannschaft des Deutschen Ruderverbandes [Psychological consultation of the German Junior National Rowing Team]. *Psychologie und Sport*, 4, 123-134.

Kellmann, M., Patrick, T., Botterill, C., & Wilson, C. (2002). The recovery-cue and its use in applied settings: Practical suggestions regarding assessment and monitoring of recovery. In M. Kellmann (Ed.), *Enhancing recovery: Preventing underperformance in athletes* (pp. 301-311). Champaign, IL: Human Kinetics.

Kenttä, G., & Hassmén, P. (1998). Overtraining and recovery. *Sports Medicine*, 26, 1-16.

Kenttä, G., & Hassmén, P. (2002). Underrecovery and overtraining: A conceptual model. In M. Kellmann (Ed.), *Enhancing recovery: Preventing underperformance in athletes* (pp. 57-80). Champaign, IL: Human Kinetics.

Kuipers, H. (1998). Training and overtraining: An introduction. *Medicine and Science in Sports and Exercise*, 30, 1137-1139.

Lehmann, M., Lormes, W., Opitz-Gress, A., Steinacker, J. M., Netzer, N., Foster, C., & Gastmann, U. (1997). Training and overtraining: An overview and experimental results in endurance sports. *Journal of Sports Medicine and Physical Fitness*, 37, 7-17.

Lehmann, M., Foster, C., Gastmann, U., Keizer, H. A., & Steinacker, J. M. (1999). Definition, types, symptoms, findings, underlying mechanisms, and frequency of overtraining and overtraining syndrome. In M. Lehmann, C. Foster, U. Gastmann, H. Keizer, & J. M. Steinacker (Eds.), *Overload, fatigue, performance incompetence, and regeneration in sport* (pp. 1-6). New York: Plenum.

LeUnes, A., & Burger, J. (2000). The profile of mood states research in sport and exercise psychology: Past, present and future. *Journal of Applied Sport Psychology*, 12, 5-15.

Lindemann, H. (1984). *Einfach entspannen* [Relax easily]. Psychohygiene-Training. München: Heyne.

Loehr, J. E. (1994). *The new toughness for sports.* New York: Penguin Books.

Löhr, G., & Preiser, S. (1974). Regression und Recreation - Ein Beitrag zum Problem Streß und Erholung [Regression and recreation - A paper dealing with stress and recovery]. *Zeitschrift für experimentelle und angewandte Psychologie, 21,* 575-591.

Maas, J. B. (1998). *Power sleep.* New York: Villard/Random House.

Maglischo, E. W. (1993). *Swimming even faster.* Mountain View, CA: Mayfield.

Maslach, C., & Jackson, S. E. (1986). *Maslach Burnout Inventory.* Palo Alto, CA: Consulting Psychologists Press.

McNair, D., Lorr, M., & Droppleman, L. F. (1971). *Profile of Mood States Manual.* San Diego, CA: Educational and Industrial Testing Service.

McNair, D., Lorr, M., & Droppleman, L. F. (1992). *Profile of Mood States Manual.* San Diego, CA: Educational and Industrial Testing Service.

Morgan, W.P. (1994). Psychological components of effort sense. *Medicine and Science in Sports and Exercise, 26,* 1071-1077.

Noble, B. J., & Robertson R. J. (1996). *Perceived exertion.* Champaign, IL: Human Kinetics.

Norris, S. R., & Smith, D. J (2002). Planning, periodization, and sequencing of training and competition: The rationale for a competently planned, optimally executed training and competition program, supported by a multidisciplinary team. In M. Kellmann (Ed.), *Enhancing recovery: Preventing underperformance in athletes* (pp. 121-141). Champaign, IL: Human Kinetics.

Petermann, U. (1996). *Entspannungstechniken für Kinder und Jugendliche.* Weinheim: Beltz.

Raglin, J. S. (1993). Overtraining and staleness: Psychometric monitoring of endurance athletes. In R. N. Singer, M. Murphey, & L. K. Tennant (Eds.), *Handbook of research on sport psychology* (pp. 840-850). New York: Macmillan.

Robertson, S. (2000). Creating an Olympic success story. *Coaches Report, 6,* 9-13.

Rowbottom, D. G., Keast, D., & Morton, A. R. (1998). Monitoring and preventing of overreaching and overtraining in endurance athletes. In R. B. Kreider, A. C. Fry, & M. L. O'Toole (Eds.), *Overtraining in sport* (pp. 47-66). Champaign, IL: Human Kinetics.

Samulski, D., Costa, L., & Kellmann, M. (2003). Validation process of the recovery stress questionnaire for athletes (RESTQ-Sport) in Portuguese language. *Proceedings of the 8th Annual Congress of the European College of Sport Science,* 9-12 July, 2003, Salzburg, p. 109.

Savis, J. C. (1994). Sleep and athletic performance: Overview and implications for sport psychology. *The Sport Psychologist, 8,* 111-125.

Schultz, J. (1932). Das autogene Training [Autogenic training]. Stuttgart: Thieme.

Selye, H. (1974). *Stress without distress.* Philadelphia: Lippincott.

Smith, D. J., & Norris, S. R. (2000). Changes in glutamine and glutamate concentrations for tracking training tolerance in elite athletes. *Medicine and Science in Sports and Exercise, 32,* 684-689.

Steinacker, J. M., & Lehmann, M. (2002). Clinical findings and mechanisms of stress and recovery in athletes. In M. Kellmann (Ed.), *Enhancing recovery: Preventing underperformance in athletes* (pp. 103-120). Champaign, IL: Human Kinetics.

Steinacker, J. M., Lormes, W., Kellmann, M., Liu, Y., Reißnecker, S., Opitz-Gress, A., et al. (2000). Training of junior rowers before World Championships. Effects on performance, mood state and selected hormonal and metabolic responses. *Journal of Sports Medicine and Physical Fitness, 40,* 327-335.

Taoutaou, Z., Granier, P. Mercier, B., Mercier, J., Ahmaidi, S., & Prefaut, C. (1996). Lactate kinetics during passive and active recovery in endurance and print athletes. *European Journal of Applied Physiology, 73,* 465-470.

Thiriet, P., Gozal, D., Wouassi, D., Oumarou, T., Gelas, H., & Lacour, J. R. (1993). The effect of various recovery modalities on subsequent performance, in consecutive supramaximal exercise. *Journal of Sports Medicine and Physical Fitness, 33,* 118-129.

Urhausen, A., Gabriel, H., & Kindermann, W. (1995). Blood hormones as markers of training stress and overtraining. *Sports Medicine, 20,* 251-276.

Viru, A., & Viru, M. (1999). Evaluation of endocrine activities and hormonal metabolic control in training and overtraining. In M. Lehmann, C. Foster, U. Gastmann, H. Keizer, & J. M. Steinacker (Eds.), *Overload, fatigue, performance incompetence, and regeneration in sport* (pp. 53-70). New York: Plenum.

Werthner, P., & Botterill, C. (2000). On sport psychology. *Coaches Report, 6,* 28-29.

Weineck, J. (1994). *Optimales Training* [Optimal training]. Erlangen: Perimed.

Wilmore, J. H., & Costill, D. L. (1988). *Training for sport and activity: The physiological basis of the conditioning process.* Dubuque, IA: Wm. C. Brown.

# Chapter 9

# Sport Injury: A Psychological Perspective

David Pargman

Injury is undoubtedly the bane of any and all athletes. Whether it occurs on the field of play, on the court, in the pool, or in the arena, it undermines the quality of sport behavior and diminishes the intensity and joy of participation. Injury interferes with the achievement of both short and long term competitive goals and redirects the athlete's goal setting focus away from competitive success to rehabilitative objectives. The injured athlete concentrates on repair, rejuvenation, and return to practice and play rather than winning and scoring. Therefore, injury dramatically alters an athlete's life.

At a later point in this chapter I will suggest that positive outcomes may occasionally accrue from sport injury. However, if and when they do, such benefits pale in comparison to injury's negative consequences. Sport injury is an impediment to competitive performance and skill improvement, and therefore athletes as well as coaches dread its occurrence. Moreover, injury to key players on a team certainly influences the performance of the entire team detrimentally.

Despite the established, time honored mind-body connection (Ray, 2004), many coaches and sport leaders are woefully unprepared to minister to injured athletes from psychological perspectives. They offer expressions of sympathy and wishes for a speedy rehabilitation, but soon turn their attention to the structurally sound and able athletes. Many injured participants become disenfranchised and are forced to exit the mainstream of team activity. Thus, they become prime candidates for membership in the inglorious sub-culture of the hurt, incapable, and useless. These wounded warriors are deserving of guidance, empathy, and assistance beyond that which is typically provided by medical personnel, namely physicians, physical therapists, and athletic trainers. Injured athletes require psychological intervention and support.

If a single indisputable assertion about the sport experience exists, and if it is therefore possible to make a sweeping comment about athletic participation, it is this: *Active participation in sport virtually assures the eventual occurrence of injury.* When injury does take place, deprivation of some kind is inevitable. This is true regardless of the athlete's age or skill level. While occurring infrequently, death itself is known to victimize sport participants with disturbing regularity. Physical injury occurs frequently in sport because of both the inherent and exaggerated loco-motor activity as well as the extraordinary expressions of strength and power demanded of athletes. The compulsion to compete in high-risk sports which offer opportunities to satisfy inordinately high thrill and adventure seeking needs for many participants may also contribute to the frequency of athletic fatalities. For decades, injury was considered to be an essentially physical phenomenon involving organic and structural damage. Now, however, it is being approached from psychological perspectives as well.

Duhlberg (1988) estimated that 8 out of 10 athletes would be injured at some point in their career annually and therefore be unable to participate in practice and competition for a minimum of 3 weeks. His prediction was offered some 15 years ago, and took into account only athletes in the United States. However, his estimate suggests that globally, millions upon millions of men, women, and children pursuing beneficial outcomes through the sport experience (including fun, excitement, entertainment, and improved self-image) may be in store for serious negative consequences. Despite a significant amount of technological improvement in the design of athletic equipment and facility construction, the incidence of injury has actually increased during the past 15-20 years. This paradox may be attributed to a number of factors, among them: (1) Leisure time availability in many parts of the world (certainly European and North American communities) has increased significantly and more people are therefore involved in recreational activities than ever before; (2) More people may be involved in sport activities due to encouragement by the medical community for people to exercise regularly for health reasons. In many contemporary western nations, overweight and obesity are considered to be major risk factors to health. Participation in regular, rigorous physical activity (particularly of the aerobic kind) is therefore advocated as a strategy for regulating the overweight condition. Sport is a form of exercise and the ranks of participants have grown enormously; (3) Today, professional athletes throughout the world are receiving unprecedented remuneration for their services, thus creating models for young aspirants to pursue with heightened enthusiasm and vigor. In other words, youth athletes are pushing themselves and being pushed by eager parents and adult coaches to take greater physical risks in their quest for athletic scholarships at American colleges and universities. Lucrative professional contracts are also incentives that inspire risk-taking behavior. In a similar vein, those who have already achieved elite status are highly motivated to sustain their careers at any cost. They understand that eager subordinates clamor to displace them and thus they do not hesitate to place themselves in harm's way. In order to remain on top of their game, they are inspired to pursue dangerous sport behavior; (4) Lastly, it may be speculated that the rise in sport injury is linked to the increased use of artificial surfaces that enable speedier locomotion than on natural surfaces such as grass (Orchard & Powell, 2003). Unfortunately, these surfaces increase the probability of various forms of athletic injuries.

Today athletes are heavier and stronger than they were decades ago, due to innovations in resistance training. Unfortunately, in all too many cases, the inappropriate use of anabolic steroids also contributes to the greater muscular strength and explosive power of many athletes today. Other chemical exogenous agents also allegedly contribute to relatively superior performance, but they place the athlete at increased risk of mental or physical harm. As Sokolove (2004) suggests, these dramatic changes in strength and explosive power among players in certain sports (notably elite level basketball competition) have changed the way the game is played. Whereas up until two decades ago basketball was a game of geometry and strategy formed around passing angles, it has become a venue for expressing power and aggression, now quintessential to success, especially when playing "under the boards." Although as a rule contact sport athletes, such as those in basketball and American football, are currently stronger and larger than their counterparts of previous years, their skeletal frameworks have not been altered. No amount of physical training (or for that matter, no chemical agent) is capable of altering the dimensions of the skeletal framework. Therefore, the torques and stresses exerted upon the athletes' long bones and joints are more formidable than in earlier times, thus rendering them more vulnerable to performance-related injury.

## Defining the Term "Sport Injury"

Scholars and researchers incorporate different emphases when interpreting the term "injury." For instance, Quinn and Fallon (1999) characterize sport injury as a "traumatic life event with physical and psychological ramifications" (p. 210). Gould, Udry, Bridges, and Beck (1997a) also incorporate "major negative life change events" in their definition. On the other hand, Brewer, Anderson, and Van Raalte (2002) understand sport injury as "an event or process involving physical damage that can lead to the initiation of rehabilitation" (p. 48). Thus, the athlete's need for rehabilitation is included in their definition.

The term sport injury is often defined with an eye toward duration of the inability to participate in practice or competition after injury. Accordingly, a particular researcher may limit his or her definition of injury to a minimum threshold of a one, two, or three day period of incapacitation. Therefore, based on the researcher's definition, an athlete who is able to return to participation one day after trauma may not be considered injured. Medical diagnosis is often necessary in order to confirm injury, and to this end X-ray and magnetic resonance imagery (MRI) may be used as part of the process of defining injury. This diversity in operational definitions tends to account for research findings that have low external validity.

A definition commonly utilized in sport science research is offered by the National Athletic Injury Registration Systems (Lysens, Weerdt, & Nieuwboer, 1991): "A sports injury is one which occurs as a result of participation in sports and limits athletic participation for a day after onset" (p. 281). I offer a simple and straightforward definition of the term sport injury: Debilitation resulting in the inability to function as competently as before the occurrence of physical trauma during sport participation.

## Causes of Sport Injury

Sport injury is usually attributable to non-psychological factors. On occasion, an athlete may be injured because of inappropriately prescribed training assignments. That is, the athlete is required to execute movements for which his or her personal resources are inadequate. With this in mind, training exercises and assignments should be consistent with the athlete's level of readiness (fitness), and adequate opportunities for rest should be provided. Frequency of training, if too high, may also be related to injury, particularly in children and older athletes. On the other hand, training that is too infrequent or not rigorous enough may fail to induce desired levels of readiness for competition, thereby creating a vulnerability to injury. The physical fitness level of athletes has been shown to correlate with injury frequency (Arnason et al., 2004).

Psychological factors may also be causally related to injury. An example would be the inappropriate execution of movements. In this case, the athlete has not succeeded in acquiring the correct biomechanical actions that a particular skilled behavior requires (i.e., he or she has not adequately learned the necessary task). Consequently, the movement is done incorrectly and the performer's susceptibility to injury is high. Because the execution of motor skill is contingent upon learning, and learning involves efficiency in information-processing and various other perceptual cognitive functions, as well as the ability to model correct movements, it may be concluded that psychological function is indeed very much involved in the onset of injury. Improper information processing may result in incorrect behavior, since knowledge relevant to proper and safe action, in the form of memory, may not be accessible.

In the early days of sport psychology research, considerable attention was directed toward personality traits in athletes. To date, it remains unclear whether athletes of different skill levels possess like or dissimilar personality profiles. It is also doubtful that personality traits may be reliably indicted as causal factors in sport injury. Some traits, however, have been identified as important factors in injury rehabilitation (Brewer, Van Raalte, & Linder, 1991; Gordon, Milios, & Grove, 1991; Wiese, Weiss, & Yukelson, 1991).

A third category of injury causality is that of environmental or exogenous factors. By exogenous, I mean factors that are external to the control of the athlete. The athlete is incapable of regulating barometric pressure, ambient temperature, precipitation, or the presence and velocity of prevailing wind. These factors affect optimal performance and contribute to injury vulnerability. Orchard and Powell (2003) discuss weather variability and playing surface (natural grass versus artificial) in terms of knee and ankle injury in American football. One of their conclusions is that injury is less likely when temperatures are cooler.

## PSYCHOLOGY AND INJURY: A GENERAL PERSPECTIVE

The psychology of injury has been the focus of considerable attention for decades, and relevant variables continue to be investigated by scholars in special interest areas. For instance, industrial psychologists have studied psychological factors linked to accidents in the work place (Cellar, Nelson, York, & Bauer 2001). Automobile and pedestrian accidents have also been investigated from psychological perspectives (Lajunen, 2001; Trimpop & Kirkcaldy, 1997). The military has expressed interest in psychological variables believed to be associated with accidents not necessarily related to enemy fire (such as friendly fire incidents, falls, vehicular accidents, and the misuse of equipment) (Pegula, 2005). Educators have studied factors alleged to be causally involved in injury in the school setting (Manheimer & Mellinger, 1967; Vollrath, Landolt, & Ribi, 2003).

In all of these areas of inquiry, connections have been sought between numerous psychological variables and injury. Among these variables are: personality traits such as optimism-pessimism, risk-taking tendencies, extraversion-introversion, and aggression; various perceptual abilities; gender; locus of control; attentional style; life stress; self-perception; mood states; social support (in terms of injury rehabilitation); and the phenomenon known as accident-proneness. Results from these studies have varied in terms of their statistical significance, meaningfulness, and applicability to other subjects and contexts (Grove & Bianco, 1999). It seems that domain, gender, and age specificity determine the usefulness and reliability of many of these findings.

## INJURY IN THE SPORT DOMAIN

One specific area of injury research that attempts to incorporate psychological theory is sport. I became interested in this topic decades ago, and accordingly published three early papers (Pargman, 1976; Pargman & Lunt, 1989; Pargman, Sachs, & Deshaies, 1976). In the first two, my interest focused upon the gestalt notion of visual disembedding (a cognitive style), as developed by the late Herman Witkin (Witkin, Dyk, Fattuson, Goodenough, & Karp, 1962). Witkin's work established that reliance upon information from the visual field in order to make judgements and solve problems is variable among individuals. Some persons require substantial information and have great difficulty in resolving mental challenges without environmental input. Others operate quite independently of the visual field. Witkin's assessment procedures, for example his Hidden Figures Test, yield values for what he termed *field dependence-independence*. Although Witkin prolifically explored possible connections between field dependence-independence and a host of variables, I believe I was the first to attempt to link this perceptual-cognitive ability to sport injury.It appeared appropriate to determine if sport behavior involving physical trauma is related to visual perception. I was able to report a significant difference in disembedding ability between injured and non-injured football athletes. Uninjured athletes demonstrated higher mean Hidden Figures Test scores, which suggests that they are better able to disembed. Football athletes who are better able to visually identify and process critical stimuli in the competitive environment may therefore be less vulnerable to injury.

In 1989, Pargman and Lunt reported a positive correlation between locus of control (as assessed by Rotter's Internal-External Locus of Control Scale; Rotter, 1954) and injury severity, and a negative correlation between self-concept and injury severity (as assessed by the Tennessee Self-Concept Scale; Fitts, 1965) in freshman football players. Despite their high potential for success, freshman football athletes in large American universities with well developed athletic programs are likely to be placed in the lower tier or bottom of the depth roster, until they earn a higher ranking. This is done so that they may acquire the skills and knowledge necessary to earn a "starting" role on the team. Their adjustment to university life, and the sport and academic demands to which they are exposed, is often problematic. Since many of these young men have come from very successful high school athletic experiences, their self-concept may thus be jeopardized by this change. Discouragement and disillusionment may follow, which in turn may increase vulnerability to sport-related injury. Yaffee (1978) was among the first to suggest that the psychological impact of injury (not necessarily sport injury) can be better understood by exploring self-concept. Lamb (1986) found a significant inverse relationship between self-concept and injury frequency in sport. Results also showed that athletes with a comparatively low self-concept tended to be injured on the day prior to competition. Lamb concluded that this reflects a desire to avoid competitive participation, because the established team goal or performance expectations may be perceived as unattainable by an athlete with a low self-concept.

Perceptions about the body are first developed very early in life, earlier than are speech and verbal comprehension (Harter, 1986; Hattie, 1992). These self-views of the body are believed to reside in the psychological core and are not easily dislodged or modified. Youth athletes who have early, unpleasant, or negative sport experiences may develop a body image that influences their eventual participation in physical activity. Body image is likely to correlate positively with sport self-confidence and perceptions about the ability to satisfy specific task demands in sport (Ferron, Narring, Cauderay, & Michaud, 1999). An athlete with low efficacy for a particular physical challenge who does not withdraw from tasks requiring high levels of skill in combination with high risk, may be destined for injury.

Soon others began to study linkages between various psychological variables and injury. Ultimately, however, many of us working in this area reached the conclusion that most of the shared variance in sport injury was not primarily or directly due to psychological causes per se, but rather to factors that may have some tangential psychological bases or connections. For example, overuse is likely to be a major contributor to sport injury, and overuse itself may very well be predicated upon a foundation that is psychological in nature. Why is the athlete resorting to abusive overtraining? What motivates the person prescribing the training to assign a regimen that is improper in frequency and intensity? Is it pure naiveté that underlies an incorrect prescription or is something more *psychological* involved? Victimization of the injured athlete by teammates or opponents and poor decision-making during competition by the coach, team physician, or trainer may also account for injury. Although factors such as these may be causally related to injury and have psychological affiliates, they do not originate or reside within the athlete.

## ERRORS IN DECISION-MAKING: A CAUSAL FACTOR IN SPORT INJURY

During the course of sport-related behavior, athletes are involved, to varying degrees, in cognitive functions. The so-called "mental side of the game" is a reality duly recognized by coaches and athletes alike. Even sport tasks comprised predominantly of gross motor activity have elements of problem solving and judgement-making. While performing athletically, the distance swimmer, weight lifter, and wrestler all think. As limbs flail and bodies hurl through space, athletes are also intellectually active. In some sports, such as golf and basketball, cognitive prowess is held at a premium. Those who are not good situational thinkers and problem solvers do not succeed in these sports, or at best are limited to mediocre achievement. At elite levels of competition considerable homogeneity prevails with regard to physical attributes and capacities. For example, a large number of soccer goalies are tall, move well laterally, and leap with great explosive power. In American football, at the highest level of achievement (within the National Football League) the quarterbacks appear to be cut from the same mold, physically speaking (a few inches above 6 feet in height, etc.). Not surprisingly, it is the "mental" aspect of performance that distinguishes the better goalkeeper and superior quarterback from their mediocre counterparts.

Some sports require deeper cognitive involvement than others, and athletes who process information efficiently and have access to useful memories, models, and schemes from central nervous system depositories are well prepared to make appropriate and timely performance oriented decisions. I propose that, to a meaningful extent, sport injury may be related to faulty information processing, the consequence of which is compromised decision-making. A result of this is susceptibility to motor error and, therefore, increased vulnerability to injury.

Athletes, like other learners, must either receive or construct knowledge that enables correct skill execution. This information must be stored and accessed upon demand in order for efficient and safe play to proceed. A depiction of the Computer Information Processing Model (Atkinson & Shiffrin, 1968; Leahey & Harris, 1997; Parsons, Hinson, & Sardo-Brown, 2001) is presented in Figure 1, which details the process of knowledge acquisition. Its use here implies that knowledgeable athletes are poised to make good and safe choices. When the model's components operate incorrectly or incompletely, knowledge may be improperly acquired or stored problematically, with the resultant probability of injury due to poor readiness to execute skills. Choice or decision-making is a function of cognition, and poor choices set the stage for injury.

## THE INFORMATION PROCESSING MODEL

Environmental stimuli are received by highly specialized organs of sensation, such as the ears, eyes, nose, etc. "Stimuli" may be understood as *perceptible changes in the environment*. A loud noise, such as the starting signal in a foot race, is an auditory

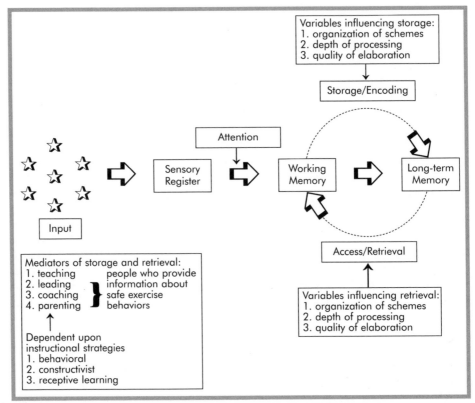

***Figure 1*** Computer Information Processing Model (Berger, Pargman, & Weinberg, 2002).

stimulus. The tennis ball moving over the net exemplifies a visual stimulus. In sport, some organs of sensation and their neurological pathways and operations are of little importance, while the functions of others are absolutely critical. Vision is very important in the execution of most sport tasks, whereas smell and taste are not. A wrestler or equestrian athlete may have a severe hearing handicap and still succeed at a very high competitive level, and so may a gymnast. Conversely, a yachtsman or sailor may be at a marked disadvantage if he or she is unable to hear the commands from his onboard teammates. Visual disability makes archery competition a serious challenge, whereas a faulty sense of smell does not. When kinesthetic senses such as various forms of balance or body-in-space awareness are compromised, high levels of success in sports such as diving and figure skating are improbable.

In Figure 1, the stars on the left side of the model represent environmental stimuli. The numbers on the basketball shot clock, to which the players anxiously attend, are visual environmental stimuli. The baseball catcher's digital signals create a change in the visual environment of the pitcher and also exemplify visual stimuli. Inspirational crowd cheering and foot stomping are further examples of auditory environmental stimuli.

According to the Computer Information Processing Model, the first of three centers in the brain hypothesized to receive information is the *sensory register*. Here, entering stimuli are sorted and roughly interpreted. They remain in the sensory register for no more than 2 or 3 sec before they make their way to the *working memory*. Broader and deeper processing and attachment of meaning to the stimuli occurs in this second brain center. Previous experiences are now brought to bear upon the entering material, which is sorted, categorized, and culled. That is, some of the information being processed is discarded because it is deemed irrelevant. Appropriate focusing upon pertinent stimuli (attentional focus) is believed to facilitate movement of material from the sensory register to working memory. It is speculated that information remains in the working memory for approximately 20 sec before it is transferred to *long-term memory*. A finite amount of information can be treated in short-term (working) memory during this time frame. However, practice, repetition, and mnemonic devices may extend this amount of time or increase the intensity and efficiency of the processing in this brain center.

Upon entering the long-term memory system, the information finds permanent residence. It is filed away in perpetuity, to be retrieved when it is needed for problem solving. Athletes with comparatively greater supplies of task-related experiences or memories installed in their long-term memory are well-prepared to meet action demands.However, some available research provides reason for doubting this assertion (Schwartz & Reisberg, 1991).

Short and long-term memory centers engage in an ongoing interaction, wherein information from one is directed to the other. Known as *encoding*, this process involves retrieval (sometimes conscious, sometimes not) of information from storage (long-term memory) that is selectively and strategically directed to working memory for purposes of problem-solving.After contributing to the problem's resolution, the information is returned from working memory to long-term memory. But when re-deposited, it is fuller and richer than before, since it is now complemented by the momentary problem-solving experience and all that it subsumes. However, on occasion, any number of factors may impede the material's circulation. Sometimes new stimuli entering the information processing system interfere with passage of information from long- to short-term memory; sometimes old memories surface unwittingly from long-term storage and interact with vital new stimuli, whose processing is accordingly slowed.

Effective coaching and teaching of sport skills and sport-related behaviors should facilitate information processing and eliminate its barriers. Coaches should be alert to developmental issues that may limit the processing capabilities of their athletes. Young children process and construct knowledge differently than adults, and athletes of all age categories process in idiosyncratic manners. Such differences not withstanding, those who deposit packets of information (schemes) in long-term memory with elaboration, logic, and order are likely to succeed in locating, accessing, and redirecting such material to working memory. Efficient information processing provides a necessary basis for good decision making and problem resolution. Once again, good decision-making in sport should reduce the likelihood of injury.

A second model is presented in Figure 2. This model illustrates the link between decision-making and sport injury. It is the right hand side of the model upon which the above discussion is predicated.

## ANDERSEN AND WILLIAMS' STRESS/INJURY MODEL

Andersen and Williams (1998) have proposed a model that incorporates psychosocial factors hypothesized to be predictors of sport injury (see Figure 3). The model incorporates cognitive, physiological, attentional, behavioral, intrapersonal, social, and stress history

| No Control | Much Control |
|---|---|
| (Involves Accidents: Little Decision-Making Prerogatives) | (Involves Choices: Decision-Making) |
| * Basketball court is wet and athlete slips on a wet spot | * Basketball player is in incorrect position on court, collides with teammate |
| * Standing by the dugout, a softball player is struck by the bat escaping the batter's grip | * Softball players slides incorrectly into 2nd base and fractures ankle |
| MEDIATING VARIABLES • Risk taking tendency • Level of cognitive development | |
| Accidents are dependent to a large extent upon happenstance: | Choices are dependent upon cognitive factors: |
| * Equipment failure * External causes (other people) | * Judgments * Decisions * Thought processes |

*Figure 2* The link between decision-making and sport injury.

variables. Quintessential are the athlete's stress-coping resources and stress responses. Implicit in the model is the notion that athletes who either manage stressful situations well or interpret environmental (sport) stimuli as non-stressful are likely to avoid athletic trauma. Referred to as a cognitive appraisal model of injury prediction, it places a premium upon what athletes are thinking during practice and competition. According to this model, those involved in thoughts about stress and injury are likely to have relatively greater vulnerability to on-the-field physical trauma. The relationship of stress to sport injury is based upon the assertion that stress build-up takes a toll on an athlete's ability to cope, which results in an increased susceptibility to fatigue, illness, or injury (Smith, Smoll, & Ptacek, 1990). High levels of sport-related anxiety would thus encourage appraisal of environmental stimuli as stressful. Since injury itself may be viewed as a source of stress, resultant anxiety may be responsible for additional injury.

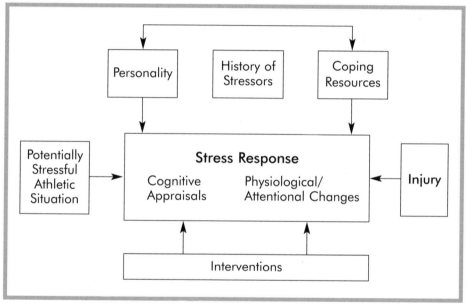

**Figure 3** Andersen and Williams Stress/Injury Model (Andersen & Williams, 1998, revised; the original model did not have the bi-directional arrows between personality, history of stressors, and coping resources).

Fletcher and Hanton (2003) suggest that this sport stress need not pertain exclusively to factors such as being cut from the team, losing a game or match, or not playing well, but also to "organizational concerns." They identify four main categories of concerns: environmental issues, personal issues, leadership issues, and team issues. Included in the above categories are specific stressors, such as team funding concerns, the training environment, accommodations while traveling, the competition environment, leadership issues, and coaching style. To say the least, sport is replete with a formidable array of stressors, and Andersen and Williams (1998) argue that the manner in which athletes interpret, integrate, and respond to these stressors is indicative of the frequency with which they will encounter injury.

## PAIN

Injury entails trauma to the body's many physiological systems and to its skeletal framework. Especially in contact and combative sports, trauma typically affects the skeletal, muscular, or nervous systems. However, connective tissue and various aspects of the vascular, digestive, and integumentary (skin) systems may also be victimized. Skin discoloration, swelling, and inhibition of mobility are common by-products of injury.

Located in proximity to organs within these systems is a multitude of specialized nerve endings that inform various brain centers about the sequela of injury. Thus we become aware of functional disruption of organs, fractured bones, tissue laceration and other compromising consequences. Accompanying the transmission of this information about damage and malfunction are pain messages. Pain receptors stationed throughout the body relay knowledge about acute physical discomfort to the brain via the spinal cord.

One common result of tissue damage is on-site collection and retention of bodily fluids, such as blood and lymphatic material. This build up causes pressure upon local pain receptors, which, in turn, forward electrochemical signals via the peripheral nervous system and spinal cord to appropriate brain centers. There they are processed in the *nociceptive system*. Since pain receptors are widely distributed throughout the body and vary in their anatomical construction, distance to the spinal cord, and rapidity of their transmissions, the time necessary for messages to reach the nociceptive system also varies. Certain injuries, therefore, "hurt more and sooner than others."

Nociception refers to the processing of sensory communications, as well as the attachment of meaning to them. The athlete interprets the sensation as something highly problematic and serious, as excruciatingly painful, or as insignificant and "nothing to worry about." Loeser's (1982) representation of this sequence of events is depicted in Figure 4 and provides for four steps.

| Step 1 | – The receptors forward sensations (sensing) to the nociceptive system. ("Something is not right here.") |
| Step 2 | – The sensation is interpreted (perception) in an attempt to gauge the pain's importance. ("This really hurts.") |
| Step 3 | – Significance (meaning) is attached to the perception of pain. ("Uh, oh, I'm in deep trouble.") |
| Step 4 | – The injured athlete signals the coach that he must leave the field. He then solicits and receives medical attention (action). |

**Figure 4** Loeser's (1982) four-step model.

Pain may be understood as a perceptual-cognitive phenomenon and, therefore, as basically a psychological concept. Past experiences assist in the interpretation of the stimuli captured and shunted by the body's pain receptors. Athletes who have previously known physical trauma with varying degrees of intensity, frequency, and consequence integrate the sensations differently than inexperienced athletes. Some athletes may act (step 4) to conceal or deny the pain, if its recognition (to self or others) may result in disgrace (Kotarba, 1983), embarrassment (Pike & Macguire, 2003), or a view of the athlete by others as being incompetent (Goffman, 1972). In this way, *attitude* about injury and pain contributes to both the interpretation of pain and the subsequent action taken. Dissociation from the sensation of pain is also a coping mechanism that athletes may attempt to implement.

## GENDER ISSUES

Some reported research findings suggest that males and females may be socialized to interpret pain differently, and therefore do not respond to the sensations associated with agony in the same way (Meyers, Bourgeois, & LeUnes, 2001). Injury and pain are often a consequence of engagement in risk-taking behavior, a topic expounded upon in a 1992 paper by Nixon (Nixon, 1992). Nixon speaks of the *culture of risk* and suggests that injury and pain are its integral components. Needless to say, few experiences other than sport are as fertile in terms of risk and injury. As Bendelow (1996) has put it, an athletic career has become a "pain career" (p. 271).

Messner (1992) discusses risk-taking behavior in sport in terms of gender, and proposes that such tendencies are associated with a masculine identity. However, in their work with female rowers, Pike and Maguire (2003) report that subjects responded to pain stimuli in ways that did not differ from those of males. Likewise, Theberge (2000) and Young and White (1995) observed similar risk-taking tendencies in men's and women's sport. It therefore seems likely that level of competition (elite, novice, etc.) rather than gender determines the manner in which pain is perceived and acted upon.

A second factor that might influence the manner in which males and females respond to pain and either enter into or avoid high risk-taking sports is the culture of a particular sport itself. Some sports encourage and emphasize precaution more than others.

## GATE CONTROL THEORY OF PAIN

Since prolonged involvement in sport, particularly at elite levels, is invariably associated with some sort of physical trauma, professionals engaged in the preparation of athletes for competition are obliged to understand as many ramifications of pain as possible. A grasp of the theoretical bases of pain is the initial step in securing this understanding. Wall and Melzack (1986) have proposed a theory that purports to clarify the variability in pain perception. According to their *Gate Control Theory*, checkpoints or gates are situated along the spinal column and open or close to permit or prevent the flow of pain messages to the brain. Physiological and psychological factors regulate the unblocked or blocked condition of these gates. Neurotransmitters such as the endorphins (the body's very own endogenously produced opiates) supposedly influence the gate's open-closed status (endorphins are associated with closed gates, i.e., not feeling pain). Messages that are blocked and consequently fail to reach the brain for processing obviously do not result in the perception of pain. A culling mechanism operates, whereby gate function determines whether or not an athlete responds painfully to trauma.

Spinal gating is also affected by memories and cognitions involving the athlete's past experiences, as well as his or her momentary emotional condition. A highly anxious athlete would thus have heightened susceptibility to pain, since muscle tension (a concomitant of anxiety) is likely to increase excitation of the muscles' pain receptors. When pain stimuli are sustained over an extended period of time, the term *chronic pain* is applied. This typically carries a negative connotation and may indicate a serious and harmful situation. The manner in which pain sensations are integrated into neurological function, interpreted by the relatively higher brain centers (cognitive function) and influenced by moods and emotions poignantly indicates the *mind-body connection*, a popularly discussed relationship so familiar to athletes and their mentors.

## MANAGING PAIN

Pain is unsettling and may inhibit efficient athletic behavior, since it tends to distract from task relevant cues. However, the intensity of pain does not correlate well with injury severity or seriousness. Sometimes, moderate pain is indicative of very significant tissue damage while acute discomfort may reflect moderate trauma. Modifying the intensity of pain by disengaging (dissociation) from a burdensome attentional focus, and thus being able to concentrate on relevant task demands is a vital management goal for the injured athlete.

Heil and Fine (1999) enumerate four factors that explain the level of *pain tolerance*. In this context, the term "tolerance" refers to the ability to deal with, or become used to, pain over time. It does not connote the application of strategies (cognitive, chemical, etc.) designed to modify or eliminate it. The four factors offered by Heil and Fine are (1) the expectation that pain can and will be tolerated, (2) a strong goal orientation, (3) absorption in the work in progress, and (4) the assumption of limited pain duration.

In factor number one, anticipation of pain because "It's part of the game" enables the injured athlete to abide by his or her lot. "That's the way it is, if you play rugby you have to expect to be hurt." Heil and Fine's second factor suggests that pain is a price you must pay to achieve success. "If you want to play professional Australian Rules Football (Footie) you have to pay your dues, and if it means being hurt, it's worth it." The third factor suggests that fixation on practice and environmental stimuli is so strong that other sensations are subordinated and mostly ignored. The athlete then pays little attention to pain, since he or she is intently focused on situational stimuli. Lastly, Heil and Fine argue that certain sport- or training related-pain is anticipated, but believed to be short-lived. For instance, runners may believe that "You always hurt after running a marathon, but after two or three days the aches subside and you're OK."

## TOLERANCE VERSUS COPING

*Coping* suggests the application of strategies utilized to alleviate pain. In other words, the athlete pursues a plan or procedure designed to reduce pain and discomfort. Such strategies may incorporate cognitive skills or behavioral techniques. On the other hand, when discomfort is *tolerated* it is simply endured with the expectation that "I'll get used to it." Coping techniques may emphasize cognitive as well as behavioral processes. Athletes often take chemical agents to relieve pain, and such interventions undoubtedly qualify as coping strategies. Tricker (2000) observed that of 563 elite collegiate athletes he interviewed, 29% reported that they felt there is nothing wrong with using painkilling drugs on the day of competition (when injured). Pain killings chemical agents do not fall within the purview of this chapter, and are therefore not addressed here. Suffice it to say, the use of such agents is potentially dangerous, in that obliteration of stimuli that signal pain may result in the athlete having reduced, or having no awareness of, significant pathology or compromised systemic function. Therefore, further and more serious injury may occur.

Acute pain may develop into chronic pain when *catastrophizing* (defined as an exaggerated negative orientation toward pain; Sullivan, Bishop, & Pivik, 1995) and fear of movement or (re)injury are prevalent (Severeijns, Vlaeyen, van den Hout, & Picavet, 2004). Anxiety about "protecting the bad knee" may result in preoccupation with injury repetition to the extent that it precipitates psychological depression and distress, as well as chronic pain (Crombez, Eccleston, Baeyens, & Eelen, 1998).

## ADJUSTMENT TO SPORT INJURY AND RETURN TO COMPETITION

Assertions about the frequency and seriousness of athletic injury were offered at the outset of this chapter. Some athletes do not return to competition after injury; however, many succeed in their rehabilitative efforts to the extent that they reenter the sport environment. Sometimes this return is fraught with trepidation and markedly reduced confidence and abilities. Often, despite heroic efforts, returning athletes are unable to reclaim their previous status or prowess. What psychological events do they endure upon learning of the extent of their injury and the need to desist from participation for prolonged periods of time? What mechanisms account for the differential manner in which they experience rehabilitation? What are their thoughts and feelings upon returning to the field of play and the demanding sport culture? These are the issues I will address in this portion of the chapter.

## STAGE MODELS

A number of researchers have inquired into the helpfulness of *stage models* as explicators of reaction to injury. Stage theories assume a stereotypic progression through distinctly identifiable phases. Thus, all injured athletes would experience stages one, two, three, etc., as they deal with the realization of their trauma, incapacitation, and necessary absence from practice and competition. Despite a number of attempts to support the efficacy of stage models, empirical evidence remains unavailable (Lynch, 1988; Pedersen, 1986; Rotella, 1985; Rotella & Heyman, 1993).

In order to clarify psychological responses to sport injury, the allegedly predictable sequences of responses such as that proposed by Kubler-Ross (1969) and Brown and Stoudemire (1983) have been examined in various research designs. However, evidence of a set of discrete phases through which injured athletes progress has not been forthcoming. This is not to say that seriously injured athletes do not experience dramatic emotional reactions to trauma, or that these changes do not tend to diminish with the passage of time. Smith, Scott, O'Fallon, and Young (1990) attempted to apply the five-stage Kubler-Ross model to athletic injury but were unable to find supportive evidence. Sport psychologists adapted the Kubler-Ross grief model to hypothesize that injured athletes proceed through (1) denial, (2) anger, (3) bargaining, (4) depression, and (5) acceptance. Evidence does exist that negative affective responses to injury do indeed decrease as rehabilitation proceeds, but evidently not in an anticipated progressive manner as stage models would predict. Also, McGowan (1991) observed that despite a significant passage of time (three weeks), injured athletes in his study never regained scores on self-concept evinced prior to injury, thus indicating that the Kubler-Ross fifth stage of "acceptance" had not been achieved. It appears that athletes respond variably to injury, and although many experience some of the emotions delineated in stage models (notably that of Kubler-Ross), they do so differentially and non-sequentially.

## IMPORTANCE OF THE SPORT EXPERIENCE, INJURY PROGNOSIS, AND RECOVERY PROGRESS

Athletes respond to injury with varying degrees of emotionality and a wide variety of cognitions. Rehabilitative success is contingent upon their attitude and affect. Tracey (2003) identifies feelings of loss, decreased self-esteem, frustration, and anger as consequences of injury. She suggests that such responses may fluctuate in positive directions in response to effective interventions that emphasize injury as a challenge, as well as to increased understanding about the self. The effects of injury and the athlete's reaction to these effects are subject to intervention and modification.

One factor that may be associated with adjustment to sport injury is its importance in the life of the participant. Meyers, Sterling, Calvo, Marley, and Duhon (1991) reported that competitive athletes experienced stronger negative moods after injury followed by orthopedic surgery than did recreational athletes. It may be that when sport is foundational to an athlete's self-concept and self-worth, a relatively greater sense of deprivation follows injury. It is therefore beneficial for those counseling injured athletes to determine their client's perception of sport significance in their lives. Athletes with deep, comprehensive, and extremely meaningful attachments to sport that are quintessential to their mental health are likely to be faced with greater adjustment challenges than those whose involvement is superficial and cavalier.

The concept of *importance* assumes another dimension in regard to emotional response to injury. The point in time during the competitive season (pre, mid, end, post) at which the injury occurs may also be associated with the athlete's emotional response. In their work with collegiate basketball players, Gayman and Crosman (2003) observed that timing of injury onset relates to interpretation of injury significance, and hence the emotional reaction of injured participants. Collinson (2003) also elaborates upon the criticality of different kinds of time (linear, cyclical, inner, and biographical) in relation to pain tolerance and management.

Another factor with possible connections to emotional and cognitive response to injury is the medical prognosis and assessment of long-range injury effects (Albert, McShane, Gordin, & Dobson, 1988). An athlete's emotional response to injury is influenced by his or her beliefs about the probabilities of successful rehabilitative outcome.Simply put, good news from the physician relative to what the future holds, and the assurance of a strong and speedy recovery, is uplifting and likely to minimize affective responses such as depression and anxiety. On the other hand, bad news about probable injury consequences is likely to elicit negative cognitive and emotional responses. Additionally, McDonald and Hardy (1990) were able to report that recovery progress as perceived by the injured participant influences his or her emotional adjustment processes. This suggests that personal assessment of rehabilitative success influences the athlete's psychological adjustment to injury.

## REHABILITATION OF THE INJURED ATHLETE

Having addressed sport injury issues such as its prevalence, the perceptual cognitive experiences that typically accompany injury (namely pain), and the cognitive/affective responses that follow injury, I now turn to the matter of *rehabilitation*. This term brings to mind a host of experiences designed to enable and facilitate the disabled athlete's return to the field of play. Paramount here is the emphasis upon psychological factors involved in rehabilitation, rather than protocols that exclusively address biomechanical and/or organic and structural issues.Of course, cognizance is taken of the inexorable connection between *mind* and *body*. As put so tersely by Ray in his essay "How the Mind Hurts and Heals the Body" (Ray, 2004), "The mind – a manifest functioning of the brain – and the other body systems interact in ways critical for health, illness, and well-being" (p. 29).

Rest, in the form of disengagement from practice and competition, is frequently the immediate remedial strategy in dealing with sport injury. Medical consultants (physicians, physical therapists, trainers, etc.) are instrumental in determining whether rest alone is a sufficient remedial response. Safai (2003) discusses the sometimes arbitrary, intuitive, and unreliable decisions made by such experts, who occasionally operate under the influence and wishes of team management and ownership at professional levels. She does point out that a prevailing *culture of precaution* adopted by most clinicians accounts for athlete protection. However, as I mentioned previously, the sport environment is accepting of injury. It countenances pain, and views participants who deal with it stoically as strong and heroic.

Elaborate interventions, sometimes transpiring over extended periods of time, are often indicated in the advent of serious injury. It is the psychological aspect of these treatments, and in some cases the exclusively psychological approach itself, that I now discuss.

Not surprisingly, it is during the initial phases of injury that the greatest mood disturbances are observed (Leddy, Lambert, & Ogles, 1994). For this reason, it is advisable to begin psychological assessment and intervention as close to the injury's onset as possible. Anxiety, fear, anger, and doubt are common reactions to injury and these feelings are understandably strong immediately after trauma. Participants in a study conducted by Tracey (2003) on male and female collegiate athletes described experiencing a "roller coaster" of emotions. Not only are emotions particularly potent at this time, but they are also in flux and highly variable. According to a number of researchers who have worked with injured athletes, it is best at this time to lead injured athletes to an internal locus of control, whereby they take responsibility for their recovery (Brewer, Linder, & Phelps, 1995; Gould et al., 1997a; Udry, 1996). Athletes who take control of their rehabilitation are more invested in the process, which can at times be extended over significant lengths of time.


## SOCIAL SUPPORT

Modalities for assisting injured athlete rehabilitation are numerous, but none enjoys a more prominent status than *social support*. In very simple terms and in the context of this chapter, social support refers to an athlete's transcending personal resources in order to cope with the stress of sport injury and the accompanying disability, absence from participation, pain and discomfort, and exigencies associated with rehabilitation. Sport trauma often exerts various and unusually powerful forms of stress upon its victims—to the extent that some actually contemplate suicide (Henderson, 1999). In the athlete's effort to countermand these effects, his or her depository of available psychological skills may be depleted. The athlete then turns to others in his or her environment for assistance, and as Hobfoll and Stokes (1988) suggest, extends his or her resource pool.

As is the case with all worthy psychological constructs, various theoretical bases underlie social support. Scholars disagree about some of its aspects; however, currently most are in agreement as to its multidimensional nature. Four elements comprise the social support process: (1) support provider, (2) support recipient, (3) the transaction between the provider and the recipient, and (4) the outcomes of the transaction (Hardy, Burke, & Crace, 1999). Support may be emotional, informational, or tangible (offer of transportation or money, etc.). It may also take the form of listening, reality confirmation (expression of empathy), or task challenge (encouraging the injured, for example, to broaden his or her way of thinking about the injury and resultant disability). It should be emphasized that recipients of social support have vital responsibilities to perform, if it is to yield meaningful outcomes. Such responsibilities entail identification of social support sources, making contact, and communicating with them.

Hardy et al. (1999) provide a lengthy list of research findings that argues favorably for the helpfulness of social support strategies in coping with an array of life crises that includes the rigors of childbirth, unemployment, bereavement, loneliness, and burnout. Generally speaking, recipients of social support evince relatively higher levels of mental and physical health than do unsupported persons. The published findings of Rees, Smith, and Sparkes (2003), Wallston, Alagna, DeVellis, and DeVellis (1983), Ievleva and Orlick (1991), Gordon and Lindgren (1990), Silva and Hardy (1991), and Weiss and Troxel (1986) testify to the efficacy of social support in the recovery from athletic injury.


## SOCIAL SUPPORT FOR THE INJURED ATHLETE

Who are the social support providers for injured athletes? Among the available supporters are *teammates, coaches, parents, family, friends, athletic trainers*, and *physical therapists. Counseling* and *sport psychologists* may also be considered as social supporters.

TEAMMATES

Isolation from the team should be assiduously avoided by encouraging the injured athlete to be present at as many team functions as possible. By their behavior and overt expressions of a supportive attitude, teammates can prevent the isolation of an incapacitated athlete. Friendships should be sustained, and the injured athlete should be encouraged to attend off the field social and recreational activities (Silva & Hardy, 1991).

Injured athletes may become disenfranchised from the team and experience conflict about their personal identity as "athletes." If unable to participate in practice or competition for weeks or months on end, the disabled athlete may doubt his or her claim to the encomium "athlete." Teammates have the ability to confirm and maintain this athletic identity throughout the course of injury rehabilitation. They are able to provide *listening support* (listening without being judgmental and without giving advice), *emotional support* (showing concern and providing comfort), *challenge support* (encouragement of the recipient to evaluate attitudes, values, and feelings), *reality confirmation support* (confirmation of the injured athlete's perspectives of the situation), *task appreciation support* (acknowledgement of the injured athlete's efforts at rehabilitation), *tangible support* (providing the recipient with financial assistance, transportation, or helpful products, and with personal assistance – providing time, knowledge, and expertise to the recipient) (Richman, Rosenfeld, & Hardy, 1993).

Hardy, Richman, and Rosenfeld (1991) offer a *buffering hypothesis* to suggest that social support has a direct impact on perceived stress and improves the coping abilities of injured athletes. In a similar vein, Sarason, Sarason, and Pierce (1990) propose that perceptions of support will encourage the development of coping strategies in advance of a stressful situation. Teammates are capable of providing such support and thereby enhancing the well-being of the disabled athlete. Teammates may also provide models for rehabilitation to be emulated by the injured athlete: "I've been there. I had the very same injury, and I've come back. You can do it."

COACHES

Men and women who coach represent another source of social support. Viewed by their subordinates as leaders, experts, and authorities, coaches should acknowledge the importance of paying attention to injured athletes. All too often coaches do not know what to say to injured athletes and feel awkward around them (Wiese-Bjornstal & Smith, 1999). Demonstrating an attitude of caring and concern should be an objective of coaches who have injured athletes on their team. Coaches would do well to monitor the rehabilitative progress of their athletes, reinforce their gains, and provide as much positive feedback as possible. The disabled athlete can be assigned officiating or time keeping responsibilities during practice sessions, or be asked to keep score during scrimmages. Record keeping or timing teammates in the pool or on the track are additional responsibilities that may provide a sense of belonging to the disabled athlete.

## Parents, Family, and Friends

Parents are extremely influential support providers for youth athletes, and in the case of very young children, perhaps the most influential of all. Parental emotional investment in the athlete, the intensity of their concern, and their availability exceeds that of other potential support providers. Parents transport their children, provide for their physical comfort at home, and are their primary caregivers. They preside over the rehabilitative regimens of their children, administer medication prescribed by medical personnel, and provide succor and comfort when anxiety and depression are heightened and self-esteem reduced. Children of different developmental stages are likely to respond to sport injury in variable psychological fashion (Brewer, 2003). Thus, it is important for parents to identify their children's stage of cognitive and psychosocial development in order to serve them appropriately.

Friends who are not team members, or for that matter, not athletes, may also contribute to the injured athlete's rehabilitation. Their availability as supportive, interested persons is invaluable to the recovery process. Many injured athletes contemplate return to competition and thus grapple with fear of re-injury and formidable therapeutic regimens. Their anxieties and insecurities may be somewhat alleviated by encouragement from friends and relatives. Such persons might even serve the athlete well by raising issues that argue against return. When it is clear that return to sport imposes the risk of permanent injury and is therefore not an appropriate option, trusted friends and relatives might possess the power of persuasion for which the athlete may eventually be grateful.

## Physical Therapists

Physical therapists typically meet regularly with injured athletes. They are therefore in an excellent position to establish relationships with them that permit education and clarification about the disability. They are also well positioned to provide motivation for adherence to the rehabilitation program. Physical therapists are not usually trained in counseling or "listening" skills; however, many develop adequacies in these areas through years of experience. They have at their disposal unusual opportunities to attend to the athlete's feelings, attitudes, and insights about the injury. They may interpret the physician's diagnosis and prognosis and explain various details of the trauma that are invaluable to the athlete's motivation for rehabilitation. And perhaps most important of all, physical therapists assist in the establishment and pursuit of realistic therapeutic goals.

## Imagery

The so-called mind-body relationship is well established in the scientific literature, and an argument for its existence need not be made here. What I wish to suggest, however, is that this mental activity has a meaningful role in sport injury rehabilitation. Imagery training, usually conducted in tandem with relaxation therapy, may be incorporated in various ways in order to assist injured athletes in their recuperative efforts. Mental imagery may produce physiological change associated with beneficial or therapeutic psychological response (Fiore, 1988; Hanley & Chinn, 1989; May & Johnson, 1973). As Green (1999) so aptly concludes: "From a sport psychology perspective, it appears that there is, at the very least, a logical step from the relationship of imagery and sport performance to the impact of imagery on the healing process of injuries" (pp. 235-251).

What exactly is mental imagery? It is a process whereby an individual creates in his or her mind visual, kinesthetic, auditory, taste, tactile, or any of a number of other sensations to which the body's physiologic systems respond authentically. These sensations do not occur actually, but virtually. In using imagery an athlete employs an interface between mental and physical healing potentialities. The athlete uses symbolic representations of the healing process in order to believe that he or she is indeed recovering.Green (1999) writes about three essential imagery applications during rehabilitation from sport injury:

PREINJURY
Here the athlete utilizes imagery to attain a level of relaxation that is conducive to safe and realistic skill execution and the pursuit and achievement of relevant competitive goals. In this application of imagery, stress and anxiety levels preceding performance are addressed. Green refers to this function as *preventive medicine*.

IMMEDIATELY SUBSEQUENT TO INJURY
Here rehabilitation protocols are imagined, and attitudes about adherence to therapeutic regimens established. Elements of the rehabilitative program are also imagined. Green calls this function *developing awareness*.

DURING REHABILITATION
In this application of imagery counterproductive thoughts are eliminated and pain coping is emphasized. Here an attempt is also made to bring closure to the injury; that is, the athlete understands and accepts the consequences of his or her trauma and resolves to rehabilitate. Green refers to this function as *creating the mind-set for recovery*. Affirmation imagery, in which the athlete imagines positive scenarios involving successful attempts at rehabilitative therapy, is an example of this mental skill.

## MODELING

Modeling has been shown to be an extremely efficacious strategy for motivating learners to pursue desirable behaviors, skills, and attitudes. In modeling, the observer watches the model and encodes in memory the symbolic representation of the behavior. Observation of a model who is similar to the learner with regard to a host of relevant variables, such as level of skill, age, gender, physical characteristics, etc., provides for the strongest effects. Because the observer identifies with the model, he or she is therefore likely to attend to and emulate what is observed. The research of Bandura (1986) and other social-cognitive psychologists have clearly established modeling as a preferred approach to the teaching of cognitive skills. Others (McCullagh, Weiss, & Ross, 1989; Weiss & Klint, 1987) have demonstrated its effectiveness in acquisition of motor skills in particular. However, observational learning or vicarious learning (synonyms for modeling) has only infrequently been applied to the psychological rehabilitation of sport injury. Flint's (1999) work has been innovative in this regard.

Flint (1999) has utilized rehabilitated athletes as models in her research protocols by videotaping their behaviors with which recently injured athletes, embarking upon a program of rehabilitation, can identify. Observers thus emulate attitudes about effort, positive beliefs about recovery, as well as the correct mechanics of rehabilitative exercises and regimens. Flint has been able to demonstrate the comparative superiority of the modeling interventions over other interventions she employed, such as "He did it; he came back after knee surgery, then so can I."

Observational learning is a powerful tool, however it may also inadvertently incorporate inappropriate models that enable acquisition of undesirable, counterproductive attitudes and behaviors. For this reason models should be selected carefully and wisely. Trainers and physical therapists should be alert to locker and training room statements, conversations, and behaviors that might provide negative models for injured athletes.

## ADHERENCE TO REHABILITATIVE REGIMENS

Medical interventions are prescribed to facilitate healing and rehabilitation in injured athletes. The more serious and traumatic the injury the more intense and prolonged the rehabilitation therapy. Adherence to these programs is often a challenge to both athlete as well as those responsible for the regimen's delivery and administration. Regular and rigorous compliance with assigned exercises executed in correct form is essential to positive recuperative outcomes. Yet, despite their acknowledgment of the importance of regular participation, many athletes do not adhere. Sport psychology researchers have therefore attempted to investigate causes of low adherence in injured athletes, and also to identify theories that might clarify such negligence and its underlying attitudes (Brewer et al., 2002).

Quinn and Fallon (1999) have observed that the injured athlete's emotional state is likely to change throughout the recovery process, and that therefore there is a fluctuation in resultant cognitive and behavioral outcomes. Many injured athletes must cope with cognitions that emphasize trauma denial, anger, depression, and irritability, and must also confront debilitating states such as insomnia and fatigue (Nideffer, 1989; Rose, 1991; Suinn, 1967). Motivation for adherence should therefore be monitored throughout the recovery process. With this in mind, a number of psychological variables have been studied in research frameworks in an effort to establish links with adherence. Among the variables reported to correlate with adherence to rehabilitation programs in injured athletes are: personality (Grove & Bianco, 1999), self-motivation and social support, (Duda, Smart, & Tappe, 1989; Fisher, Domm & Weust, 1988)), athletic identification (Brewer et al., 2000), and type of coping strategy (Brewer, 1994; Gould, Udry, Bridges, & Beck, 1997b; Grove & Bianco, 1999).

Among the prominent correlates of adherence to rehabilitative programs is the dimension of *causal attributions*. Causal attributions (or causal ascriptions) refer to the reasons individuals give for event outcomes in which they have been involved. For example, a tennis player who was defeated in a match might indict the court's poor surface for his loss and claim that slippery footing hampered his game. Or, he might attribute his failure to his having been ill the night before the match. These attributions would be examples of external, unstable, non-controllable causes. On the other hand, had he attributed his loss to lack of preparation (he didn't attend practice during the week because he was lazy), the ascription would be internal and controllable. Grove, Stewart, and Gordon (1990) observed that athletes who were recovering rapidly from injury attributed their recovery to more stable, internal and controllable factors than those who felt they were recovering slowly. Brewer et al. (2000) reported that rapid recovery from injury is linked to stable and personally controllable outcomes. In this case, the attribution is associated with the perception that the athlete has the prerogative to influence the outcome of the experience, and indeed he or she adheres to and does well in the rehabilitation program.

Other psychological factors are also linked to rehabilitation adherence in athletes. For instance, in a study with injured Olympic skiers, Gould et al. (1997b) found that those who could identify at least one positive outcome of their injury did better in adherence and rehabilitation. It may be speculated that these findings are supportive of the work reported by Scheier and Carver (1992) and Scheier, Weintraub, and Carver (1986), who investigated dispositional optimism in relation to coping style, and concluded that optimists tend to accept adverse situations and try to view their predicament in a positive manner. In other words, optimists strive to make the best out of a difficult situation and may therefore adhere well. Compared to non adherers, those who adhere believed they worked harder during rehabilitation, were more self-motivated, perceived greater support from others, reported a higher level of pain tolerance, and were less affected by environmental conditions and scheduling of rehabilitation sessions (Fisher, Domm, & Wuest, 1988). And lastly, a number of studies have concluded that injured athletes receiving various kinds of social support (discussed earlier in this chapter) are relatively strong on adherence to rehabilitative regimens (Bianco & Eklund, 2001; Udry, 1996).

## POSITIVE OUTCOMES OF INJURY

In the opening paragraphs of this chapter I urged readers to accept that sport injury generates mostly negative outcomes; that it is associated with undesirable and uncomfortable consequences such as depression, irritability, unhappiness, confusion, and anger. Athletes most certainly strive to avoid injury, and to be sure, a considerable number of references cited herein give credence to this assertion. Despite my making a definitive reference to injury as "the bane of all athletes," I promised to return to this matter with the implication that I would have more to say on the subject. At this point I wish to acknowledge the speculation offered by others that some good can actually accrue from sport-related injury. In deference to such a perspective I offer the following.

Udry (1999) and Udry, Gould, Bridges, and Beck (1997) are among the few who have written about how some athletes may come to consider their injuries in a positive light.

Udry et al. interviewed 21 elite athletes (members of the United States Olympic ski team) and observed that approximately 95% of their subjects were able to identify one or more positive consequences from their injury. The athletes' comments were grouped into three general categories: personal growth, psychologically based performance enhancements, and physical-technical developments. In the first, the athletes felt that their injury taught them how to be better persons since they learned to be more empathetic towards other athletes who also had experienced injury. Such empathic responses may also have inspired the development of new and profitable social relationships. In addition, athletes whose responses placed them in the first category felt that their injury and necessary temporary withdrawal from sport encouraged them to seek out skills and interests other than skiing, which had heretofore dominated their lives. In the second category (performance based enhancements) the athletes referred to the mental toughness they acquired as well as the work ethic they learned during rehabilitation efforts. These, they felt, would enhance the manner in which they confronted the rigorous training protocols to be encountered upon their return to the team. And finally, with regard to the last category (physical-technical developments), 48% of the athletes felt that their injury taught them about their bodies' functions, responses to physical stress, and about how hard they could push themselves during exercise. In a subsequent discussion of the earlier Udry et al. work, Udry (1999) discusses the potential positive consequences of sport injury, and concludes with the speculation that those with certain psychological dispositions might be more inclined to adapt such perspectives. She cites optimism, hardiness, and internal locus of control as examples of such tendencies.

It is appropriate to encourage counselors, physicians, physical therapists, and others who interact professionally with injured athletes to prompt them to find positive consequences of their trauma. This might not be easy to accomplish, and some athletes may resist. In addition, identification of positive injury outcomes might not be forthcoming until a substantial period of time has elapsed. Athletes should not be encouraged to confront this issue immediately after their injury. Athletes who have come to terms with their injury and its consequences, and who are able to focus upon its positive aspects, are likely to undertake rehabilitation with enthusiasm and high levels of adherence.

## SUMMARY AND CONCLUSIONS

In this chapter I have attempted to establish a connection between sport injury and selected psychological factors. Two dimensions of this connection are addressed: psychological factors with causal linkages to injury, and psychological implications for rehabilitation from sport injury.

The chapter begins with a discussion of injury's prevalence in sport and the serious mental health issues with which it is associated. Injury is related to cognitive processes in that athletes are constantly making choices and decisions – before, during, and after performance. Faulty information processing may lead to failure in knowledge retrieval or encoding that are essential to appropriate and correctly executed competitive behavior. This, in turn, may predispose the athlete to error on the field of play and subsequent injury.

The Andersen and Williams (1998) model is next presented to indicate the hypothesized association of stress appraisal, effectiveness of the athlete's stress-coping capabilities, and injury. Additional factors included in the model, such as history of past stressors and available social support mechanisms, are also discussed.

Next, the perceptual cognitive experience known as pain is clarified in terms of Wall and Melzack's (1986) *Gate Theory*, and discussed as a common correlate of injury.Terms such as *pain tolerance, pain coping,* and *chronic pain* are defined and discussed.

The chapter then turns to matters related to return to competition and adjustment to injury. Within this section, stage models are discussed as explicators of the return process. However, it is suggested that the research literature includes little support for such.

Social support is next presented as an important ingredient in rehabilitation programs. Various kinds of support and different kinds of social supporters are identified and elaborated upon. A considerable body of literature testifies to the effectiveness of social support from teammates, coaches, friends, parents, and medical professionals.

Imaginal experiences utilizing all senses (vision, hearing, smell, etc.) are next discussed in terms of their contribution to injury rehabilitation. Imagery is presented as a helpful adjunct to other rehabilitative strategies, and its effectiveness is clarified in terms of available theoretical understandings. Modeling and the seminal work of Bandura (1986) are also described as a valuable approach to the recovery process. Flint's (1999) applications of modeling strategies through the use of video taping of athletes who have successfully recovered from sport injury are also presented.

Since adherence to the rehabilitative regimen is essential to injury recovery, a section of this chapter is devoted to psychological variables that bear upon the athlete's ability to engage in medically prescribed therapy on a regular basis. Motivational factors related to adherence are discussed and recommendations made.

The chapter concludes with a review of alleged positive outcomes associated with sport injury. Udry's (1999) argument that personal growth and improvement may be a consequence of sport injury is taken up. She argues that those who work with athletes in efforts to diagnose their trauma's nature, prescribe rehabilitative protocols, and monitor recovery progress, should be alert to opportunities for positive psychological change in their clients.

In closing, let me once again emphasize the prevalence of injury in sport and the vital need for sport scientists and sport counselors to recognize the potential contributions of various psychological factors associated with injury causation and rehabilitation.

ACKNOWLEDGEMENTS
Thanks are extended to my graduate assistants, Kimberlee Bethany and Teresa Johnson, for their assistance in the preparation of this chapter.

# REFERENCES

Albert, N. J., McShane, D., Gordin, R., & Dobson, W. (1988, September). *The emotional effects of injury on female collegiate gymnasts.* Paper presented at the Seoul Olympic Scientific Congress, Seoul, South Korea.

Andersen, M. B., & Williams, J. M. (1998). Psychosocial antecedents of sport injury. Review and critique of the stress injury model. *Journal of Applied Sport Psychology,* 10, 5-25.

Arnason, A., Sigurdsson, S., Gudmundsson, A., Holme, I., Engebretsen, L., & Bahr, R. (2004). Physical fitness, injuries, and team performance in soccer. *Medicine and Science in Sports and Exercise,* 36, 278-285.

Atkinson, R. C., & Shiffrin, R. M. (1968). Human memory: A proposed system and its control processes. In K. W. Spence & J. T. Spence (Eds.), *The psychology of learning and motivation: Advances in research and theory* (Vol. 2, pp. 84-105). San Diego, CA: Academic Press.

Bandura, A. (1986). *Social foundations of thought and action: A social cognitive theory.* Englewood Cliffs, NJ: Prentice-Hall.

Bendelow, G. A. (1996). A "failure" of modern medicine? Lay perspectives on a pain relief clinic. In S. Williams & M. Calnan (Eds.), *Modern medicine: Lay perspective and experiences* (pp. 167-185). London: UCL Press.

Berger, B. G., Pargman, D., & Weinberg, R. S. (2002). *Foundations of exercise psychology.* Morgantown, WV: Fitness Information Technology.

Bianco, T., & Eklund, R. C. (2001). Conceptual considerations for social support research in sport and exercise settings: The case of sport injury. *Journal of Sport and Exercise Psychology,* 23, 85-107.

Brewer, B. W. (1994). Review and critique of models of psychological adjustment to athletic injury. *Journal of Applied Sport Psychology,* 6, 87-100.

Brewer, B. W. (2003). Developmental differences in psychological aspects of sport-injury rehabilitation. *Journal of Athletic Training,* 38, 152-153.

Brewer, B. W., Anderson, M. B., & Van Raalte, J. L. (2002). Psychological aspects of sport injury rehabilitation: Toward a biopsychosocial approach. In D. I. Mostofsky & L. D. Zaichowsky (Eds), *Medical and psychological aspects of sport and exercise* (pp. 41-54). Morgantown, WV: Fitness Information Technology.

Brewer, B., Avondoglio, J. B., Cornelius, A. E., Van Raalte, J. L., Brickner, J. C., Petitpas, A. J., et al. (2002). Construct validity and interrater agreement of the Sport Injury Rehabilitation Adherence Scale. *Journal of Sport Rehabilitation,* 11, 170-178.

Brewer, B. W., Cornelius, A. E., Van Raalte, J. L., Petitpas, A. J., Sklar, J. H., Pohlman, M. H., et al. (2000). Attributions for recovery and adherence to rehabilitation following anterior cruciate ligament reconstruction: A prospective analysis. *Psychology and Health,* 15, 283-291.

Brewer, B. W., Linder, D. E., & Phelps, C. M. (1995). Situational correlates of emotional adjustment to athletic injury. *Clinical Journal of Sport Medicine,* 5, 241-245.

Brewer, B. W., Van Raalte, J. L., & Linder, D. E. (1991). Role of the sport psychologist in treating injured athletes: A survey of sports medicine providers. *Journal of Applied Sport Psychology,* 3, 183-190.

Brown, T. J., & Stoudemire, A. G. (1983). Normal and pathological grief. Journal of the *American Medical Association,* 250, 378-382.

Cellar, D. F., Nelson, Z. C., York, C. M., & Bauer, C. (2001). The five-factor model and safety in the workplace: Investigating the relationships between personality and accident involvement. *Journal of Prevention and Intervention in the Community*, 22, 43-52.

Collinson, J. A. (2003). Running into injury time: Distance running and temporality. *Sociology of Sport Journal*, 20, 331-350.

Crombez, G., Eccleston, C., Baeyens, F., & Eelen, P. (1998). When somatic information threatens, catastrophic thinking enhances attentional interference. *Pain*, 75, 187-198.

Duda, J. L., Smart, A. E., & Tappe, M. K. (1989). Predictors of adherence in the rehabilitation of athletic injuries: An application of personal investment theory. *Journal of Sport and Psychology*, 11, 367-381.

Duhlberg, H. N. (1988). Injury: How athletes deal with hurt. *Sport Care and Fitness*, 53, 2.

Ferron, C., Narring, F., Cauderay, M., & Michaud, P. (1999). Sport activity in adolescence: Associations with health perceptions and experimental behaviors. *Health Education Research*, 14, 225-233.

Fiore, N. A. (1988). The inner healer: Imagery for coping with cancer and its therapy. *Journal of Mental Imagery*, 12, 79-82.

Fisher, A. C., Domm, M. A., & Wuest, D. A. (1988). Adherence to sports injury rehabilitation programs. *The Physician and Sports Medicine*, 16, 47-51.

Fitts, W. H. (1965). *Tennessee Self-Concept Scale*. Nashville, TN: Counselor Recording and Test.

Fletcher, D., & Hanton, S. (2003). Sources of organizational stress in elite sports performers. *The Sport Psychologist*, 17, 175-195.

Flint, F. (1999). Seeing helps believing: Modeling in injury rehabilitation. In D. Pargman (Ed.), *Psychological bases of sport injuries* (2nd ed., pp. 221-233). Morgantown, WV: Fitness Information Technology.

Gayman, A., & Crosman, J. (2003). A qualitative analysis of how the timing of the onset of sports injuries influences athlete reactions. *Journal of Sport Behavior*, 26, 255-271.

Goffman, E. (1972). *Encounters*. Harmondsworth, UK: Penguin.

Gordon, S., Milios, D., & Grove, J. R. (1991). Psychological aspects of the recovery process from sport injury: The perspective of sport physiotherapists. *Australian Journal of Science and Medicine in Sport*, 23, 53-60.

Gordon, S., & Lindgren, S. (1990). Psycho-physical rehabilitation from a serious sport injury: Case study of an elite fast bowler. *Australian Journal of Science and Medicine in Sport*, 22, 71-76.

Gould, D., Udry, E., Bridges, D., & Beck, L. (1997a). Down but not out: Athlete responses to season-ending injuries. *Journal of Sport and Exercise Psychology*, 19, 224-248.

Gould, D., Udry, E., Bridges, D., & Beck, L. (1997b). Stress sources encountered when rehabilitating from season-ending ski injuries. *The Sport Psychologist*, 11, 361-378.

Green, L. B. (1999). The use of imagery in the rehabilitation of injured athletes. In D. Pargman (Ed.), *Psychological bases of sport injuries* (2nd ed., p. 199-218). Morgantown, WV: Fitness Information Technology.

Grove, J. R., & Bianco, T. (1999). Personality correlates of psychological processes during injury rehabilitation. In D. Pargman (Ed.), *Psychological bases of sport injuries* (2nd ed., pp. 89-110). Morgantown, WV: Fitness Information Technology.

Grove, J. R., Stewart, R. M. L., & Gordon, S. (1990, October). Emotional reactions of athletes to knee rehabilitation. Paper presented at the annual meeting of the Australian Sports Medicine Federation, Alice Springs.

Hanley, G. L., & Chinn, D. (1989). Stress management: An integration of multidimensional arousal and imagery theories with case study. *Journal of Mental Imagery*, 13, 107-118.

Hardy, C. J., Burke, K. L., & Crace, R. K. (1999). Social support and injury: A framework for social support-based interventions with injured athletes. In D. Pargman (Ed.), *Psychological bases of sport injuries* (2nd ed., pp. 175-198). Morgantown, WV: Fitness Information Technology.

Hardy, C. J., Richman, J. M., & Rosenfeld, L. B. (1991). The role of social support in the life stress/injury relationship. *The Sport Psychologist*, 5, 128-139.

Harter, S. (1986). Processes underlying the construction, maintenance, and enhancement of self-concept in children. In J. Suls & A. Greenwald (Eds.), *Psychological perspective on the self* (Vol. 3, pp. 136-182). Hillsdale, NJ: Erlbaum.

Hattie, J. (1992). *Self-concept.* Hillsdale, NJ: Erlbaum.

Heil, J., & Fine, P. (1999). Pain in sport: A biopsychological perspective. In D. Pargman (Ed.), *Psychological bases of sport injuries* (2nd ed., pp. 13-28). Morgantown, WV: Fitness Information Technology.

Henderson, J. (1999). Suicide in sport: Are athletes at risk? In D. Pargman (Ed.), *Psychological bases of sport injuries* (2nd ed., pp. 287-302). Morgantown, WV: Fitness Information Technology.

Hobfoll, S. E., & Stokes, J. P. (1988). The process and mechanics of social support. In S. W. Duck (Ed.), *Handbook of personal relationships: Theory, research, and interventions* (pp. 497-517). New York: Wiley.

Ievleva, L., & Orlick, T. (1991). Mental links to enhanced healing: An exploratory study. *The Sport Psychologist*, 5, 25-40.

Kotarba, J. (1983). *Chronic pain: Its social dimensions.* Newbury Park, CA: Sage.

Kubler-Ross, E. (1969). *On death and dying.* New York: Macmillan.

Lajunen, T. (2001). Personality and accident liability: Are extraversion, neuroticism, and psychoticism related to traffic and occupational fatalities? *Personality and Individual Differences*, 31, 1365-1373.

Lamb, M. (1986). Self-concept and injury frequency among female college field hockey players. *Athletic Training*, 21, 220-224.

Leahey, T., & Harris, R. (1997). *Learning and cognition* (4th ed.). Upper Saddle River, NJ: Prentice-Hall.

Leddy, M. H., Lambert, M. J., & Ogles, B. M. (1994). Psychological consequences of athletic injury among high-level competitors. *Research Quarterly for Exercise and Sport*, 65, 347-354.

Loeser, J. (1982). A multifaceted model of the components of pain. In M. Stanton-Hicks & R. A. Boas (Eds.), *Chronic low back pain* (p. 146). New York: Raven Press.

Lynch, G. P. (1988). Athletic injuries and the practicing sport psychologist: Practical guidelines for assisting athletes. *The Sport Psychologist*, 2, 161-167.

Lysens, R. L., Weerdt, W., & Nieuwboer, A. (1991). Factors associated with injury proneness. *Sports Medicine*, 12, 281-289.

Manheimer, D., & Mellinger, G. (1967). Personality characteristics of the child accident repeater. *Child Development*, 38, 491-513.

May, J., & Johnson, H. (1973). Psychological activity to internally elicited arousal and inhibitory thoughts. *Journal of Abnormal Psychology*, 82, 239-245.

McCullagh, P., Weiss, M. R., & Ross, D. (1989). Modeling considerations in motor skill acquisition and performance: An integrated approach. In K. B. Pandolf (Ed.), *Exercise and sport sciences reviews* (Vol. 17, pp. 475-513). Baltimore: Williams and Wilkins.

McDonald, S. A., & Hardy, C. J. (1990). Affective response patterns of the injured athlete: An exploratory analysis. *The Sport Psychologist*, 4, 261-279.

McGowan, R. W. (1991, June). *Diminutive effects of athletic injury on self-esteem*. Paper presented at the annual meeting of the North American Society for the Psychology of Sport and Physical Activity, Monterey, CA.

Messner, M. A. (1992). *Power at play: Sports and the problem of masculinity*. Boston: Beach Press.

Meyers, M. C., Bourgeois, A. E., & LeUnes, A. (2001). Pain coping response of collegiate athletes involved in high contact, high injury-potential sport. *International Journal of Sport Psychology*, 32, 29-42.

Meyers, M. C., Sterling, J. C., Calvo, R. D., Marley, R., & Duhon, T. K. (1991). Mood state of athletes undergoing orthopaedic surgery and rehabilitation: A preliminary report. *Medicine and Science in Sports and Exercise*, 23, S138.

Nideffer, R. M. (1989). Psychological aspects of sports injuries: Issues in prevention and treatment. *International Journal of Sport Psychology*, 20, 241-255.

Nixon, H. L. (1992). A social network analysis of influences on athletes to play with pain and injuries. *Journal of Sport and Social Issues*, 16, 127-135.

Orchard, J. W., & Powell, J. W. (2003). Risk of knee and ankle sprains under various weather conditions in American football. *Medicine and Science in Sports and Exercise*, 35, 1118-1123.

Pargman, D. (1976). Visual disembedding and injury in college football players. *Perceptual and Motor Skills*, 42, 762.

Pargman, D., & Lunt, S. D. (1989). The relationship of self-concept and locus of control to the severity of injury in freshmen collegiate football players. *Sports Training, Medicine, and Rehabilitation*, 1, 1-6.

Pargman, D., Sachs, M., & Deshaies, P. (1976). Field-dependence-independence and injury in college football players. *American Corrective Therapy Journal*, 30, 174-176.

Parsons, R. D., Hinson, S. L., & Sardo-Brown, D. (2001). *Educational psychology: A practitioner-researcher model of teaching*. Belmont, CA: Wadsworth/Thompson Learning.

Pedersen, P. (1986). The grief response and injury: A special challenge for athletes and athletic trainers. *Athletic Training*, 21, 312-314.

Pegula, S. M. (2005). Fatal occupational injuries to members of the resident military. In U.S. Department of Labor, Bureau of Labor Statistics. *Compensation and Working Conditions Online*.

Pike, E. C., & Macguire, J. A. (2003). Injury in women's sport: Classifying key elements of "risk encounters." *Sociology of Sport Journal*, 20, 232-251.

Quinn, A. M., & Fallon, B. J. (1999). The changes in psychological characteristics and reactions of elite athletes from injury onset until full recovery. *Journal of Applied Sport Psychology*, 11, 210-229.

Ray, O. (2004). How the mind hurts and heals the body. *American Psychologist*, 59, 29-40.

Rees, T., Smith, B., & Sparkes, A. (2003). The influence of social support on the lived experiences of spinal cord injured sportsmen. *The Sport Psychologist*, 17, 135-156.

Richman, J. M., Rosenfeld, L. B., & Hardy, C. J. (1993). The social support survey: A validation study of a clinical measure of the social support process. *Research on Social Work Practice*, 3, 288-311.

Rose, J. M. C. (1991). *Running the risks of running.* Unpublished doctoral dissertation, The University of Alberta, Alberta, Canada.

Rotella, R. J. (1985). The psychological care of the injured athlete. In L. K. Bunker, R. J. Rotella, & A. S. Reilly (Eds.), *Sport psychology: Psychological considerations in maximizing sport performance* (pp. 273-287). Longmeadow, MA: Mouvement.

Rotella, R. J., & Heyman, S. R. (1993). Stress, injury, and the psychological rehabilitation of athletes. In J. M. Williams (Ed.), *Applied sport psychology: Personal growth to peak performance* (2nd ed., pp. 338-355). Palo Alto, CA: Mayfield.

Rotter, J. B. (1954). *Social learning theory and clinical psychology.* Englewood Cliffs, NJ: Prentice-Hall.

Safai, P. (2003). Healing the body in the "culture of risk": Examining the negotiation of treatment between sport medicine clinicians and injured athletes in Canadian intercollegiate sport. *Sociology of Sport Journal*, 20, 127-146.

Sarason, B. R., Sarason, I. G., & Pierce, G. R. (1990). *Social support: An interactional view.* New York: Wiley.

Scheier, M. F., & Carver, C. S. (1992). Effects of optimism on psychosocial and physical well-being: Theoretical overview and empirical update. *Cognitive Therapy and Research*, 16, 201-228.

Scheier, M. F., Weintraub, J. K., & Carver, C. S. (1986). Coping with stress: Divergent strategies of optimists and pessimists. *Journal of Personality and Social Psychology*, 51, 1257-1264.

Schwartz, B., & Reisberg, D. (1991). *Learning and memory.* New York: Norton.

Severeijns, R., Vlaeyen, J., van den Hout, M., & Picavet, H. (2004). Pain catastrophizing is associated with health indices in musculoskeletal pain: A cross-sectional study in the Dutch community. *Health Psychology*, 23, 49-57.

Silva, J. M., & Hardy, C. J. (1991). The sport psychologist: Psychological aspects of injury in sport. In F. O. Mueller & A. Ryan (Eds.), *The sports medicine team and athletic injury prevention* (pp. 114-132). Philadelphia: FA Davis.

Smith, A. M., Scott, S. G., O'Fallon, W. M., & Young, M. C. (1990). Emotional responses of athletes to injury. *Mayo Clinic Proceedings*, 65, 38-50.

Smith, R., Smoll, F., & Ptacek, J. (1990). Conjunctive moderator variables in vulnerability and resiliency: Life stress, social support and coping skills, and adolescent sport injuries. *Journal of Personality and Social Psychology*, 58, 360-370.

Sokolove, M. (2004, Jan. 18). The lab animal. *The New York Times Magazine*, pp. 28-33, 48, 54, 58.

Suinn, R. M. (1967). Psychological reactions to physical disability. *Journal of the Association for Physical and Mental Rehabilitation*, 21, 13-15.

Sullivan, M., Bishop, S., & Pivik, J. (1995). The pain catastrophizing scale: Development and validation. *Psychological Assessment*, 7, 524-532.

Theberge, N. (2000). *Higher goals: Women's ice hockey and the politics of gender*. New York: State University of New York Press.

Tracey, J. (2003). The emotional response to the injury and rehabilitation process. *Journal of Applied Sport Psychology*, 15, 279-293.

Tricker, R. (2000). Painkilling drugs in collegiate athletics: Knowledge, attitudes, and use of student athletes. *Journal of Drug Education*, 30, 313-324.

Trimpop, R., & Kirkcaldy, B. (1997). Personality predictions of driving accidents. *Personality and Individual Differences*, 23, 147-152.

Udry, E. (1996). Social support: Exploring its role in the context of athletic injuries. *Journal of Sport Rehabilitation*, 5, 151-163.

Udry, E. (1999). The paradox of injuries: Unexpected positive consequences. In D. Pargman (Ed.), *Psychological bases of sport injuries* (pp. 79-88). Morgantown, WV: Fitness Information Technology.

Udry, E., Gould, D., Bridges, D., & Beck, L. (1997). Down but not out: Athlete responses to season-ending injuries. *Journal of Sport and Exercise Psychology*, 19, 229-248.

Vollrath, M., Landolt, M. & Ribi, K. (2003). Personality of children with accident-related injuries. *European Journal of Personality*, 17, 299-307.

Wall, P. D., & Melzack, R. (Eds.). (1986). *Textbook of pain* (2nd ed.). Dallas: Churchill.

Wallston, B. S., Alagna, S. W., DeVellis, B. M., & DeVellis, R. F. (1983). Social support and health. *Health Psychology*, 2, 367-391.

Weiss, M. R., & Klint, K. A. (1987). "Show and tell" in the gymnasium: An investigation of developmental differences in modeling and verbal rehearsal of motor skills. *Research Quarterly for Exercise and Sport*, 58, 234-241.

Weiss, M. R., & Troxel, R. K. (1986). Psychology of the injured athlete. *Athletic Training*, 21, 104-109.

Wiese, D. M., Weiss, M. R., & Yukelson, D. P. (1991). Sport psychology in the training room: A survey of athletic trainers. *The Sport Psychologist*, 5, 15-24.

Wiese-Bjornstal, D., & Smith, A. M. (1999). Counseling strategies for enhanced recovery of injured athletes within a team approach. In D. Pargman (Ed.), *Psychological bases of sport injuries* (pp. 125-155). Morgantown, WV: Fitness Information Technology.

Witkin, H. A., Dyk, R. B., Fattuson, H. F., Goodenough, D. R., & Karp, S. A. (1962). *Psychological differentiation: Studies of development*. New York: Wiley.

Yaffee, M. (1978). Psychological aspects of sport injuries. *Research Papers in Physical Education*, 67, 3.

Young, K., & White, P. (1995). Sport physical danger and injury: The experience of elite women athletes. *Journal of Sport and Social Issues*, 19, 45-61.

# CHAPTER 10

# A MODERN APPROACH
# TO HIGH-PERFORMANCE TRAINING:
# THE BLOCK COMPOSITION CONCEPT

VLADIMIR B. ISSURIN

Many generations of scientists, coaches, and athletes have attempted to develop and improve a training system that can achieve optimum performance and maximal results. These efforts have been focused on three generalized areas:

- How to design a rational training plan for a sufficiently long period;
- How to realize this plan in an optimal manner;
- How to reach the most favorable combination of all athletic abilities precisely at the time of a major competition.

These issues in essence belong to the branch of sport science called *training periodization*, which can be defined as the purposeful sequencing of different training units (long-, medium- and short-term training cycles and sessions) for the attainment of the athlete's desired state and planned results. Because training periodization contains so many variables and depends on a number of influencing circumstances, the ideal model can exist only as a virtual image. Nevertheless every year we take another step in the direction of more conscious planning, rational training performance, and a more complete understanding of training as a whole. This review summarizes the most general positions of training periodization with respect to the classic approach, which has been predominant for many years, particularly with regard to the block composition design that has become widely used in high-performance athletes' preparation during the last decade. Moreover, I hope that many of the practices and reflections presented in this chapter will be implemented by sport psychologists, coaches, and specialists in sport theory.

## SCOPE OF TRAINING PERIODIZATION

Training periodization was founded initially during the 1950s in the former USSR and was established as a scientific concept by Soviet scientists Matveyev, Ozolin and others in the mid-1970s (see, for example, Matveyev, 1981; Ozolin, 1970). This theory was originally propagated in Eastern Europe and more recently in Western countries (see Bompa, 1984; Dick, 1980), and has become a compulsory part of training planning in high-performance sport. In general, the training periodization theory exploits the periodical changes of all biological systems and social activities typical to human beings. Specific to sport reality, at least four rationales should be considered as the factors determining the periodical changes in the content and character of training:

(a) **The patent of nature.** Exogenous rhythms are one of the fundamentals of organic life; the seasonal changes as well as the changes of day and night determine all biological activities. The months and weeks naturally divide social and economic life into historically and traditionally consolidated cycles, which are incorporated into general adaptation; the weekly resting rhythm, for example, is fixed and stabilized from the initial period of life. It is certain that all biological, social, and industrial activities are subordinate to exogenous rhythms of nature; it would be strange if sport were an exception to this rule.

(b) **Adaptation as a general law.** The adaptation law in general determines the athletes' sport training. According to this law athletes should avoid excessive accommodation to habitual loads. Accustomed stimuli cannot continue to be effective; in order to regenerate the adaptability of the athletes, their training program and exercise repertory must be periodically changed and renewed. In other words, an excessively stabilized and fixed training program leads the athlete to an adaptation barrier, where he/she is forced to dramatically increase the magnitude of habitual workloads in order to increase the body response. From this viewpoint, a periodical change of the training program should be a consequence of the adaptation law.

(c) **The sequencing of different training aims.** Training in any sport is characterized by complexity, diversity, and variety. General and sport-specific motor abilities, and technical and tactical skills, cannot be developed simultaneously; they should be shared in time. A specific technical skill, for example, should be based on the appropriate level of motor fitness. Basic work precedes more specific technical mastery, and the competition accomplishes this linkage. This sequence in its entirety forms several training cycles which, being repeated periodically, form another more prolonged training cycle. Hence, cyclic training design should be used in designing long-term training.

(d) **Competition schedule.** The preparation of every high-performance athlete focuses on certain competitions, which take place periodically. Bodies such as the International Olympic Committee and international, national, and domestic sport associations control the frequency and timing of competitions. Thus, the competition calendar determines the season's preparation and, consequently, any periodical changes of the training program. The quadrennial cycle of Olympic preparation provides an excellent example of periodic changes which affect the activities of selected athletes and the world athlete population.

All the above illustrates that periodical training units or so-called training cycles should form the basis for planning and analysis. An up-to-date specification of periodical training units is presented in Table 1.

It should be emphasized that the repertory of periodical training units provides a great deal of freedom for creativity in the training design. Although external factors, such as the competition calendar and seasonal changes, dictate the most strenuous phases and restrictions in training conditions, the coach selects the sequencing, content, and duration of the training cycles; he or she also defines the priorities and particularities of each training means and method.

Table 1 also presents different modes of planning which relate to appropriate training units. The aspects of long-term planning belong to the prospective area of conceptual interpretation of the training as a whole, and will be considered below.

**Table 1** Hierarchy and Duration of the Periodical Training Units

| Training units | Time duration | Mode of planning |
|---|---|---|
| Quadrennial (Olympic) cycle | Four years – period between Olympic Games | Long-term |
| Macrocycle, may be annual cycle | One year or a number of months | |
| Training period | A number of months as part of the macrocycle | Medium-term |
| Mesocycle | A number of weeks | |
| Microcycle | One week or a number of days | |
| Workout or training session | A number of hours (usually not more then three) | Short-term |
| Training exercise | A number of minutes | |

The compilation of an annual training plan has the greatest conceptual importance; this plan should concentrate on principal positions such as timing, peaking, and workload distribution. Initially, the classic approach presupposed one or two macrocycles in one year; later modification allowed the planning of three macrocycles within the annual cycle. Each macrocycle is subdivided into three essential periods, which are characterized by specific combinations of training aims, and by the workloads' particularities (see Table 2).

Training cycles of medium duration, called mesocycles, were traditionally proposed by classic theory, although there are several authors who do not mention these training units in their research (see, for example, chapter 2 in this book and Letzelter, 1978). The modes, aims, and content of mesocycles have been considered by many analysts, who have suggested from eight to ten types and sub-types with more or less convincing argumentation (e.g., Harre, 1982; Matveyev, 1981; Platonov, 1997). In fact, these classifications of the mesocycles did not always prove to be acceptable for practical purposes, and coaches of many countries used various terms according to their own understanding and preference.

The microcyles, as the small training cycles, are the most comprehensive and least disputable terms, and are mostly identified as weekly cycles. However, even the classic approach allowed freedom in time duration; shorter and longer microcycles were also used occasionally.

## WHY THE TRADITIONAL PLANNING APPROACH SHOULD BE REVISED

For many years the classic theory monopolized all practical approaches to long-, medium-, and short-term planning. Several contradictions pointed out by scientific or coaching critics were ignored or considered to be negligible. However, since the 1980's several

**Table 2** The General Characteristics of Training Periodization According to the Classic Approach (based on Matveyev, 1981 and Harre, 1982)

| Period | Stage | Aims | Workloads' particularities |
|---|---|---|---|
| Preparatory | General preparatory | Enhancing the level of general motor abilities; enlarging the potential of various motor skills | Relatively large volume and reduced intensity of main exercises; high variety of training means |
| | Special preparatory | Development of the special training level; enhancement of more specialized motor and technical abilities | The loads' volume reaches their maximum; the intensity increases selectively |
| Competitive | Competitive preparation | Enhancing event-specific motor fitness, technical and tactical skills; formation of the model of competitive performance | Stabilization and reduction of the volume; increase of intensity in event-specific exercises |
| | Immediate pre-competitive training | Accomplishing event-specific fitness and reaching readiness for main competition | Low volume, high intensity; the fullest modeling of forthcoming competition |
| Transitory | Transitory | Recovery and rehabilitation of physical, functional, and emotional spheres | Active rest; use of pleasant, attractive, and variable activities |

postulates of the traditional concept have been shaken by prominent global tendencies. These tendencies still exist and are worthy of consideration. They can be seen in the following:

• The number and level of competitions;
• The total volume of training workloads;
• The limitations of the classic approach in simultaneously developing different motor and technical abilities;
• The appearance of new concepts affecting the elucidation and design of alternative training periodizations.

## THE NUMBER AND LEVEL OF COMPETITIONS

The general trend in the number and level of competitions is displayed in Figure 1. The obvious tendency typical for high-performance athletes in every sport is a remarkable increase in competition days over the year.

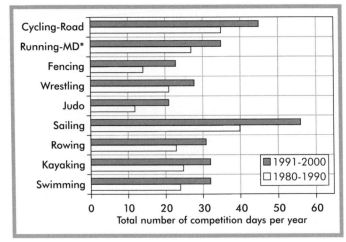

**Figure 1**
Participation in competitions of various levels of international class athletes in different sports. (The data were collected by questioning world-recognized experts in the corresponding sports.)
* MD = Middle distance

The highlighted trend in competition activity cannot be incidental. At least three universal factors have affected this marked tendency, namely:

a) **A rise in the number of competitions** in international and national tournament programs. In the last two decades, international sport federations have initiated and supported the organization of a traditional series of Grand Prix, World and Continental Cups, Memorial Trophy, various competitions, etc., which have become popular among top athletes and the sport media. Similarly, the national federations have built extensive competition schedules, with the purpose of engaging a larger population of sub-elite athletes into ambitious preparation programs.

b) **A substantial increase in the financial motivation of top athletes.** The amount of premiums that potential prizewinners can receive has apparently become a stimulus to reaching peak-performance level – more than was previously proposed by the traditional periodization chart. Consequently, athletes of the second echelon are modifying their competitive strategy according to the top-athletes' patterns.

c) **The contribution of the competitive workload** to the total balance of the training stimuli has increased dramatically; more frequent and emotionally-stressed competitive efforts break the routine and change traditional relationships between loading and recovery. At present advanced coaches exploit more frequent competitive workloads in order to intensify and rationalize the preparation process.

## THE TOTAL VOLUME OF TRAINING WORKLOADS: TREND AND ACTUAL STATE

This factor can be characterized in brief as the considerable reduction of total volume of training workloads in high-performance athletes (see Figure 2).

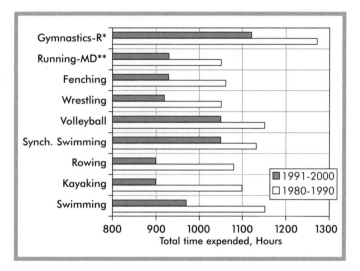

**Figure 2**
Total time expended for training over an entire year of international class athletes in different sports. (The data were collected from questioning world-recognized experts in the corresponding sports.)
* R = Rythmic
** MD = Middle distance

The tendency to reduce the total volume of training exercises has been marked in different sports and in many countries. A number of circumstances can be considered as the factors conditioning this global trend, namely:

a) **The remarkable progression of training methods and sport technologies.** The up-to-date knowledge of long-, medium-, and short-term training effects allows for the rationalization of training designs and the prevention of excessive workloads. The follow-up technologies for monitoring heart rate, blood lactate, and movement rate have been incorporated into the training routine. Now the acute and immediate training effects are much more measurable and predictable. In particular, the modern approach to training planning enables the slogan "miles make champions" to be replaced by "knowledge gives power." This factor interacts with the next one, which relates to the sharing of experience by advanced coaches.

b) **Sharing successful experience among the world-wide coaching population.** The modern sport world is more open and dynamic than ever before. International training centers host athletes from different countries for training camps and prolonged preparation. Coaches' clinics, seminars, and courses employ top international experts who don't hesitate to reveal items that were previously "top secret." Many successful coaches from countries where experience-sharing was previously regulated by sport policy have been hired all over the world. These coaches possess long-term experience in the use of extreme and sub-extreme training workloads from the time when general volumes were strictly prescribed. They know that a substantial part of these workloads was excessive, and they have begun to utilize this knowledge under new conditions.

c) **Enlargement of the competitive loads and performance numbers.** This factor, which was already mentioned as a central fact in any sport, has definitely altered the balance of workloads, where the impact of highly intensive competitive efforts increases while the impact of more extensive training loads decreases. Therefore, the excessive training loads were partially superseded by greater competitive activity.

d) **Rejection of illegal pharmacological programs.** It is no longer a secret that certain illegal pharmacological interventions used by some athletes facilitated their physiological responses (such as muscle hypertrophy, speedy recovery, etc.), and affected performance of the higher workloads. The out-of-competition doping control initiated by the International Olympic Committee in the mid 1990s has become an indispensable part of modern sport, and has made great inroads in preventing the use and sharing of these harmful technologies in high-performance sport. Consequently, the possibility of performing high-load training programs has been reduced as well.

e) **Social and political changes in the post-Communist countries.** It is well known that the highest workload volumes were performed by athletes of the former Communist countries, where athletic preparation was rigidly centralized. The integrative parameters of the training process, such as total mileage and total time expended for training, were put forth to the National teams as planning directives. Very often these directives proposed excessive training workloads as a tool to obtain more successful athletic performances. The social and political changes in these countries were followed by the democratization of top sport, with the subsequent reduction of administrative pressure and liberation of the coaches' initiative. On the other hand, economic upheavals in those countries resulted in the depletion of the top-sports' financial resources. As a consequence, top-level athletes' preparation became less centralized, the number and duration of training camps were reduced, and, as a result, the total workload volume decreased substantially. This trend induced similar changes in other countries where the tendency to reduce loads occurred as well.

## THE LIMITATIONS OF THE CLASSIC APPROACH IN THE SIMULTANEOUS DEVELOPMENT OF DIFFERENT MOTOR AND TECHNICAL ABILITIES

Certainly, the classic approach postulated reasonable changes of training aims, training means, and methods. Nevertheless, the universal methodological approach prescribed the complex development of many fitness components when a number of motor and technical abilities were trained simultaneously. This approach has been and remains valid for preliminary and early specialized athletic preparation, health-related training, and different forms of physical education. The obvious benefits of this approach are the high variety and the emotional and physical attractiveness of multilateral training. From the viewpoint of sport progression, the classic design is fruitful for low- and medium-level athletes, who receive the diversified multilateral training stimulation that enables them to improve many of their fitness components. However, the high-level athletes' preparation requires not only quantitative alterations but more importantly qualitative alterations in the training compilation; a simple increase of the training workloads without their re-structuring does not produce the desirable training effects.

The classic theory and its appropriate practical approach cause a number of contradictions which dramatically reduce the effectiveness of high-level athletes' preparation (see Table 3). For example, the training of top athletes in endurance sports, combat sports, ball games, and aesthetic sports in the preparatory period presupposes the development of general aerobic ability, muscle strength and strength endurance, improvement of general coordination and general explosive ability, basic mental and

**Table 3** The Main Contradictions of the Traditional Approach to Training Designing in High-level Athletes

| Factors | Contradictions | Sequences |
|---|---|---|
| Capacity of the energy store | Concurrent performance of the diversified workloads can not be provided by sufficient energy supply | The energy is addressed to many targets while the main target doesn't get the appropriate priority |
| Restoration of different physiological systems | Because of heterochroniety of recuperation in different physiological systems, the athletes can't get sufficient restoration | The athletes suffer from fatigue accumulation and can't concentrate their efforts on the main targets |
| Compatibility of various workloads | Exercises of various modalities often interact negatively, due to energy deficit, technical complexity and/or neuromuscular fatigue | Performance of certain loads eliminates or reduces the effect of previous or subsequent workouts |
| Mental concentration | Performance of stressed workloads demands high level of mental concentration that can't be addressed to many targets simultaneously | The mental concentration dissipates; a number of exercises are performed with reduced attention and motivation |
| Sufficiency of the training stimuli for progression | The sport-specific progression of high-level athletes demands a large amount of training stimuli that can't be obtained by concurrent training for many targets | Complex simultaneous development of many abilities doesn't provide sufficient improvement in high-level athletes |

technical preparation, accomplishment of a repertory of tactics, and treatment of previous injuries. Each of the above-mentioned targets requires specific physiological, morphological, and psychological adaptation; many of these workloads are not compatible and conflict in their responses. The problem of high-level athletes is that their progression demands a large amount of highly concentrated workloads which cannot be simultaneously directed at a number of targets.

## NEW CONCEPTS AFFECTING THE ELUCIDATION AND DESIGN OF ALTERNATIVE TRAINING PERIODIZATION

Modern understanding and explanation of athletes' preparation deals extensively with so-called training effects, which are of primary importance. The current taxonomy of training effects (Zatsiorsky, 1995) distinguishes among *acute effect*, relating to changes induced by a single exercise; *immediate effect*, relating to changes induced by one workout or training day; *cumulative effect*, the result of a series of workouts; *delayed effect*, relating to changes that occur over a given time interval after a certain program; and *residual effect*, that operates with the retention of changes induced by systematic workloads after the cessation of training beyond a certain time period. The residual training effect is the least studied characteristic of the athletes' response. Counsilman and Counsilman (1991) were the first to conceptualize the residual training effect; however, as an operative term it remains relatively new and not widely used.

The phenomenology of the residual training effect is closely connected with the process of detraining, which was previously understood as the loss of "trainedness" when training is stopped. In fact, detraining in high-performance sport may selectively occur relative to a certain ability when it does not receive sufficient training stimuli. For instance, in highly trained endurance athletes the maximum oxygen uptake decreases when the total weekly volume is reduced below a certain level (Steinacker, 1993; Steinacker, Lormes, Lehman, & Altenburg, 1998). Wilmore and Costill (1993) reported a remarkable decrease of swimming-specific strength after four weeks of reduced activity. Mujika (1999) considered the risk of detraining and loss of aerobic endurance during the reduction, despite the large volume of highly intensive exercises. One of the principal positions of the top-athletes' preparation is the consecutive but not simultaneous development of sport-specific abilities (Bondarchuk, 1981; Issurin & Kaverin, 1985). Therefore, the duration of short-term

**Table 4** The Duration and Physiological Background of the Residual Training Effect for Different Physical (Motor) Abilities (Issurin & Lustig, 2004)

| Physical (motor) ability | Residual's duration, days | Physiological background |
|---|---|---|
| Aerobic endurance | 30 ± 5 | Increased amount of aerobic enzymes, mitochondria number, muscle capillaries, hemoglobin capacity, glycogen storage, higher rate of fat metabolism |
| Maximal strength | 30 ± 5 | Improvement of neural mechanism, muscle hypertrophy mainly due to the muscle fibers' enlargement |
| Anaerobic glycolitic endurance | 18 ± 4 | Increased amount of anaerobic enzymes, buffering capacity and glycogen storage, higher possibility of lactate accumulation |
| Strength endurance | 15 ± 5 | Muscle hypertrophy mainly in slow-twitch fibers, improved aerobic/anaerobic enzymes, better local blood circulation and lactic tolerance |
| Maximal speed (alactic) | 5 ± 3 | Improved neuromuscular interactions and motor control, increased phosphocreatine storage |

residuals should definitely be taken into account in order to obtain the rational sequencing and timing of different training cycles that, for many abilities, are alternatives to simultaneous training. From this position, it is extremely important to know which factors affect the duration of training residuals, and in what manner (see Table 4).

It is known that the rate of the trainedness loss is very different in various motor abilities; some physiological systems retain the increased level of adaptation longer than others. For example, improved aerobic productivity is determined by an increase in the capillary density, glycogen storage, and, particularly, the amount of the activity of the aerobic enzymes, which increases in the order of 40-90%. This is in contrast to the much lesser local adaptations seen in athletes after sprint training: increases of phosphocreatine storage (2-5%), peak lactate accumulation (10-20%) and anaerobic enzymes (2-20%). Consequently, aerobic ability, which is supported by pronounced morphological and biochemical changes, retains a near-to-peak level for a number of weeks; anaerobic abilities, particularly maximal sprint, are conditioned by relatively weak changes and retain a near-to-peak level for a short while.

The gain of maximal strength in top-level athletes is determined by pronounced morphological, biochemical, and neural changes, such as the enlargement of the cross-sectional area of the muscle fibers, an increase in the number of fibers (hyperplasia), recruitment of previously inactive motor units and synchronization of their activity, and an increase of the discharge frequency of motoneurons (Zatsiorsky, 1995). All of these meaningful adaptations affect the relatively long training residuals of strength training.

The training residuals of strength endurance are dependent on performance duration and the degree of mobilization of anaerobic recourses. Strength endurance for long-duration performance has relatively longer residuals, thanks to pronounced aerobic adaptation.

The changes induced by training for peak speed ability are characterized by fewer gains and shorter residuals. Highly concentrated sprint training causes relatively small increases of quickly available energy sources such as ATP and phosphocreatine, as well as enzymes such as creatine kinase (Thorstensson, 1988). In addition, the peak speed ability is based on very delicate and highly precise neuro-muscular interactions, which are relatively unstable and cannot be maintained on the highest level without specially organized training stimulation.

The above-mentioned knowledge of training residuals and temporal detraining is extremely important when the planning concept turns from simultaneous to consecutive development of the sport-specific fitness components. Indeed, when we stop to develop some function or ability, we should predict how long this ability will remain at a sufficient level. Using this information, the sequencing and timing of the appropriate training cycles can then be selected.

## THE BLOCK COMPOSITION CONCEPT: GENERAL POSITIONS

Based on all the above contradictions and restrictions of the traditional approach and the world-wide tendencies of top-athletes' preparation, as well as on up-to-date findings of sport science, the general positions of an alternative training concept can be proposed.

This revised approach, coined the *Block Composition Concept* (BCC), summarizes the general principles of building up the renewed training system, and provides guidelines for alternative training periodization and short-term planning. General principles of the renewed training system reflect the essence of the BCC; unity and subordination of these principles are displayed in Figure 3.

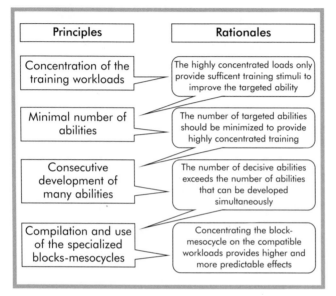

**Figure 3**
The general principles of the Block Composition Concept (BCC) and the rationales determining their unity and subordination.

Concentration of the training workloads is the most decisive and fundamental principle of the BCC. The rationale which mediates it is the long-established fact that only highly-concentrated training workloads can produce sufficient stimuli for any remarkable gains of the appropriate motor and/or technical abilities in high-level athletes.

This principle is the cornerstone which determines the following: the highly concentrated training demands minimizing the number of abilities that can be affected simultaneously (the alternative is the complex design where many abilities are developing simultaneously); consecutive development that is the only possible approach when the number of sport-specific decisive abilities is more than the number of abilities that can be trained simultaneously (the alternative complex approach has no hard limitation in this item, when one meso- and one microcycle combines the workloads for many abilities); and finally, the concept that blocks-mesocycles should be specialized and compiled in order to produce one of three different effects: *accumulation* (the athletes should accumulate basic motor and technical abilities for potential use); *transmutation* (the athletes should transmute their potential to event-specific preparedness); and *realization* (the athletes should realize their preparedness in readiness for competition and reaching the planned result). Therefore, the medium-size training cycles called blocks-mesocycles are the most prominent incarnation of the general idea of the BCC: they are much more concentrated, more specialized, and more manageable for the whole training program.

## THE ANNUAL CYCLE COMPILATION

Similar to the classic approach, the annual cycle planning starts with the determination of the target competitions, which are usually allocated by international and national sport authorities. The specific item of the revised training approach is the subdivision of the entire annual cycle into a number of training stages, where each one contains a consecutive combination of extensive work on basic abilities, more intensive work on sport-specific abilities, and the reduction that is accomplished by trial or competition. The BCC presupposes localization of these three workload types in the appropriate blocks-mesocycles, namely, accumulation, transmutation, and realization (see Table 5).

*Table 5* The Main Characteristics of the Three Types of Blocks-Mesocycles

| Main characteristics | Accumulation | Transmutation | Mesocycle type Realization |
|---|---|---|---|
| Targeted motor and technical abilities | Basic abilities: aerobic endurance, muscular strength, basic coordination | Sport-specific abilities: special endurance, strength endurance, proper technique, etc. | Integrative preparedness: modeled performance, maximal speed, event specific strategy |
| Volume-intensity | High volume, reduced intensity | Reduced volume, increased intensity | Low-medium volume, high intensity |
| Fatigue-restoration | Reasonable restoration to provide morphological adaptation | No possibility to provide full restoration, fatigue accumulated | Full restoration, athletes should be well rested |
| The tests' battery | Monitoring of the level of basic abilities | Monitoring of the level of sport-specific abilities | Monitoring of maximal speed, event-specific strategy, etc. |

The rational sequencing of the mesocycles within the training stage allows the optimal superposition of the residual training effects to be obtained, as displayed in Figure 4. This diagram shows the principal possibility of obtaining optimal interaction of the training residuals, which allows competitive performance at a high level of all motor and technical abilities. This possibility is based on the fact that training residuals of basic abilities last much longer then residuals of more specific abilities, while the residuals of maximal speed and event-specific readiness are the shortest ones (see Table 4). Following this diagram, the duration of the training stage is determined by the length of the training residuals and should be close to two months. In fact, the training stages can be shorter (near to peak season, for instance), or longer (at the season's beginning or due to specific needs). In the second case special measures can be fulfilled to prolong the residual training effects (see

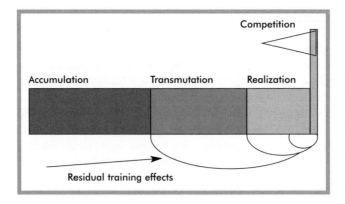

**Figure 4**
Superposition of the residual training effects induced by the sequenced blocks-mesocycles (adapted from Issurin & Shkliar, 2002)

short-term planning). It should be noted that each training stage looks like an annual cycle in miniature: it includes a training block resembling the preparatory period (accumulation), a training block resembling the competitive period (transmutation) which ends by taper (realization), and competitive performance. Based on all the above-mentioned considerations, the annual cycle design can be presented as the sequence of more or less autonomous stages, where similar aims can be obtained by means of a partially renewed and qualitatively improved training program.

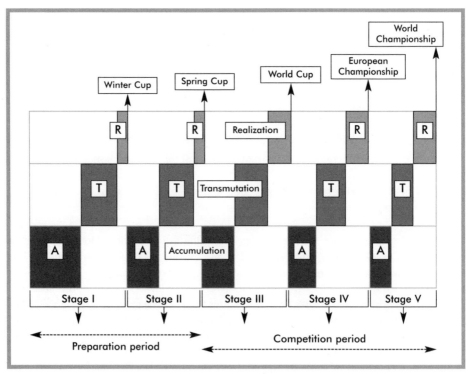

**Figure 5** Presentation of an annual cycle chart designed following the BCC (the transition period is not shown): top – main competitions; middle – blocks-mesocycles; bottom – training stages and preparation periods.

The test battery that should be reproduced in each stage, together with the competitive performance results, provide monitoring of the training process as well as feedback that can be used for current evaluation and program correction.

Finally, the number of training stages in an annual cycle depends on the particularities of the specific sport, the calendar of important competitions, etc., and usually varies from four to seven. A typical annual cycle followed by BCC is shown in Figure 5.

The practical realization of BCC provides a number of benefits as compared with the traditional model:

- Total volume of exercises; the Block Composition model allows the total mileage and time expenses for training to be reduced, without substantially changing the total number of workouts;
- Monitoring of trainedness is more purposeful and effective; a reduced number of targeted abilities requires the appropriate tests; the "dose-effect" analysis can be easily performed with respect to different training stages;
- Psychological particularities are more beneficial: the athletes should be focused on the reduced number of targets, consequently the mental concentration and motivation level can be maintained more effectively;
- Nutritional aspects can be more carefully taken into account; a high protein diet can be offered to enhance the anabolic effect of strength training; carbohydrate nutrients are particularly important in mesocycles for special and strength endurance (Wilmore & Costill, 1993).

*Table 6* Principal Differences of Training Designing Following the Classic Approach and BCC

| Characteristics of the training designing | Traditional model | Block Composition model |
|---|---|---|
| The dominant principle of the workloads' compilation | The complex use of different workloads directed to many abilities | The use of highly concentrated workloads directed to minimum targeted abilities |
| Temporal sequencing in development of different targeted abilities | Predominantly simultaneous | Predominantly consecutive |
| The main meaningful planning component | Period of preparation: preparatory, competitive and transitory | Stage of preparation that includes and combines blocks-mesocycles of three types |
| Participation in competitions | Predominantly in the competitive period | Predominantly at the end of each stage |
| General physiological mechanism | Adaptation to concurrent training stimuli affected to many different targets | Superposition of residual training effects induced by highly concentrated training stimuli |

When summarizing the above-mentioned particularities of traditional and non-traditional models, a number of prominent differences can be seen. These differences are presented in Table 6.

## BASES OF THE SHORT-TERM PLANNING

It is likely that the general positions of BCC should be made more concrete with respect to short-term planning, which deals with training designing in microcycles and several workouts. At least two basic positions of the BCC immediately affect the process and outcomes of the short-term planning, namely:
- Concentration of the training loads on the minimum abilities-targets;
- Mainly consecutive development of the different abilities-targets.

It can be proposed that short-term planning within the framework of BCC has specific features, and differs from the training routine typical of the classic approach. Moreover, even the classic positions of microcycle compilation presented in the textbooks (e.g., Bompa, 1999; Harre, 1982; Matveyev, 1981; Platonov, 1997) need to be updated and further developed. In particular, three aspects of the short-term planning draw special attention, namely:
- Load-related differentiation of workouts;
- Compatibility of different training loads in several and adjacent workouts;
- Basics of the training microcycle compilation.

*Load-related differentiation* of workouts is of high importance from the viewpoint of both physiological adaptation and mental concentration. For practical purposes, it is necessary to point out three general functions of workouts: development, retention, and restoration. The appropriate load level should be selected corresponding to these aims. In fact, each training plan is a certain combination of these types of workouts. However, from the viewpoint of practical coaching, the aim-load related workouts' classification is necessary. Table 7, based on the load-related classification of Zatsiorsky (1995), presents the classification which offers the workouts' quantification using a scale of 1 to 5 reference points.

*Table 7* Quantification of Several Workouts: Aim-Load Related Classification (based on Zatsiorsky, 1995; modification by Issurin, 2003)

| Workout's aim | Training load level | Restoration time (h) | Load assessment, reference points |
|---|---|---|---|
| Development | Extreme | > 72 | 5 |
| | Large | 48-72 | 4 |
| | Substantial | 24-48 | 3 |
| Retention | Medium | 12-24 | 2 |
| Restoration | Small | < 12 | 1 |

The load-related aspects of the offered classification need an additional clarification with regards to the time duration desirable for full restoration. The main limitation relates to workouts associated with prominent psychological and neuro-physiological efforts. The classification presented above engages time for full restoration as an objective indicator of the load level. In fact, this approach pertains to conditioning training such as strength, power, endurance, and speed exercises. The high coordination training and workouts inducing accentuated neuro-emotional stress usually require a shorter time for full restoration; however, it is not always possible to select the integrative objective markers and indicators based exclusively on the duration of restoration. Nevertheless, the practically approved approach presupposes a compilation of several workouts, which corresponds to a desirable load level according to the pedagogical and sport-specific estimation. In addition, the internationally used Borg scale of perceived exertion can be used for the load's level quantification as well (Borg, 1973).

The introduction of the term "developing workout" is particularly important for the practical implication of the ideas of BCC. The high concentration of training loads demands that exercises be selected which focus on minimum-targeted abilities, so that a more deterministic and pronounced effect can be obtained. This can be realized by means of thoroughly planned developing workouts that immediately affect these targeted abilities and stimulate the adaptation process. The most important developing workouts, which are focused on the main current training directions, are qualified, and termed "key workouts". Further explanations will clarify the key function of this workout category.

*Compatibility* of the specific training modalities within the single workout, and within the workouts series, is an extremely important factor conditioning the acute and immediate training effects. The negative interaction of several immediate training effects has been one of the major disadvantages of the classic approach to high-performance training. The BCC allows the prevention or at least reduction of this negative interaction by the use of a compatible combination for certain training modalities. This approach to the workouts' compilation can be achieved thanks to the minimized number of abilities-targets that are subjected to development.

Table 8 displays some typical compatible combinations of the dominant training modality within a specific workout.

*Basics of the training microcycle compilation* contain a number of specific positions related to up-to-date tendencies of an alternative training approach.

In light of the BCC, the workout's program should contain no more than three training modalities (usually one dominant, the second compatible with the main purpose, and the third modalities of restoration exercises). It is postulated that 65-70% of the entire training time of the developing workout should be allotted to one or two purposed training modalities; this condition is important for obtaining high workloads' concentration and for receiving sufficient stimuli for the desirable training effect.

The high frequency of workouts typical for top sport (usually 9-14 a week and even more) is conditioned on the specific demands of the adjacent session after the key workout; the basic approach to training designing is the remarkable reduction of the workload after the key workout. Another option, the planning of two adjacent key workouts, provides very high load concentration, which can be excessive. Strength workouts for muscle hypertrophy have very special demands for the planning of adjacent sessions within the restoration period: the use of high workloads during this period causes deterioration of the anabolic

**Table 8** The Typical Compatible Combinations of Different Training Modalities and Psycho-Physiological Factors Affecting the Beneficial Interaction of Different Workloads

| Compatible combinations of training modalities | Psycho-physiological factors affecting the loads' interaction |
|---|---|
| Aerobic endurance – alactic sprint ability | The brief sprint bouts break the monotony; the wide spectrum of muscle fibers is recruited and activated during subsequent aerobic workloads |
| Aerobic endurance – strength endurance | The increased oxidation can be exploited in the strength exercises; combination of conventional and resistence exercises enriches training program |
| Anaerobic (glycolitic) endurance – anaerobic strength endurance | The glycolitic capacity storage can be effectively used combining velocity-assisted, conventional and high resistance exercises; the mental factors of lactate tolerance are subjected to augmented impact |
| Alactic sprint ability – explosive strength | The explosive strength components (jumps, throws, strokes, etc.) engaged into alactic work intervals accentuate the motor output generation |
| Maximum strength – flexibility | Stretching exercises facilitate muscular and mental relaxation, which is a compulsory part of the athletes' restoration within maximum strength workout |
| Maximum strength – aerobic exercises | Low intensity aerobic exercises activate metabolic recovery and muscular and mental relaxation, which can be used for restoration within and after strength workout |

phase of muscle restoration and eliminates the hypertrophy process. Thus, to obtain the required anabolic effect, it is necessary to substantially reduce workloads for at least 20 hours and to engage in the appropriate restoration means.

It should be emphasized that minimizing the number of training modalities is particularly important and typical for high-performance training: the daily program for less experienced and particularly for junior athletes may be more diversified and multilateral, and therefore more attractive.

## CONCLUSIONS

The final remarks of this review relate to two actual tendencies of top-level training designing: standardization of the training program and renewal of the exercise content. The first tendency presupposes the use of more or less standardized workload combinations within meso- and microcycle programs. The positive aspect of this tendency is the possibility of comparing the results and responses obtained in different training cycles with the same (or similar) workload combinations. This gives good prerequisites for current training control and improvement of sport-specific training technology. The negative point is the excessive accommodation when the athletes' response to a continuing stimulus is decreased, followed by a decrease in the training effect as well.

The second tendency relates to the effect of novelty, when the unaccustomed exercises induce more pronounced athletes' response. The problem is how to increase the stimulus level when the athletes are accustomed to any kind of the sport-specific exercises. From this position, BCC, as a professional tool, can approach a solution to this problem.

## REFERENCES

Bompa, T. (1984). *Theory and methodology of training – The key to athletic performance.* Boca Raton, FL: Kendall/Hunt.

Bompa, T. (1999). *Periodization: Theory and methodology of training* (4th ed.). Champaign, IL: Human Kinetics.

Bondarchuk, A. P. (1981). *The physical preparation designing in power disciplines of track and field.* Kiev: Health Publisher (Zdorovie).

Borg, G. (1973). Perceived exertion: A note of "history" and method. *Medicine and Science in Sports*, 5, 90-93.

Counsilman, B. E., & Counsilman, J. (1991). The residual effects of training. *Journal of Swimming Research*, 7, 5-12.

Dick, F. (1980). *Sport training principles.* London: Lepus Books.

Harre, D. (Ed.). (1982). *Principles of sport training.* Berlin: Sportverlag.

Issurin, V. (2003). Aspekten der kurzfristigen Planung im Konzept der Blockstruktur des Training. *Leistungsport*, 33, 41-44.

Issurin, V., & Kaverin, V. (1985). Planning and design of annual preparation cycle in canoeing. In *Grebnoj Sport* (Rowing, Canoeing, Kayaking) (pp. 25-29). Moscow: FiS Publishers.

Issurin, V., & Lustig G. (2004). Klassification, Dauer und praktische Komponenten der Resteffekte von Training. *Leistungsport*, 34, 55-59.

Issurin, V., & Shkliar, V. (2002). Zur Konzeption der Blockstuktur im Training von hochklassifizierten Sportlern. *Leistungsport*, 6, 42-45.

Letzelter, M. (1978). *Trainingsgrundlagen, Training, Technik, Taktik.* Hamburg: Rowolt Verlag GmbH.

Matveyev, L. (1981). *Fundamentals of sport training.* Moscow: Progress Publishers.

Mujika, I. (1999). The influence of training characteristics and tapering on the adaptation in highly trained individuals: a review. *International Journal of Sports Medicine*, 19, 439-446.

Ozolin, N. G. (1970). *The modern system of sport training.* Moscow: FiS Publishers.

Platonov, V.N. (1997). *General theory of athletes' preparation in the Olympic sports.* Kiev: "Olympic Literature".

Steinacker, J. M. (1993). Physiological aspects of training in rowing. *International Journal of Sports Medicine*, 14, S3-S10.

Steinacker, J. M., Lormes, W., Lehman, M., & Altenburg, D. (1998). Training of rowers before world championships. *Medicine and Science in Sports and Exercice*, 30, 1158-1163.

Thorstensson, A. (1988). Speed and acceleration. In A. Dirix, H. G. Knuttgen, & K. Tittel (Eds.), *The Olympic book of sports medicine – Encyclopedia of sports medicine* (Vol. I., pp. 218-229). Oxford: Blackwell Scientific Publications.

Wilmore, J. H., & Costill, D. L. (1993). *Training for sport and activity – The physiological basis of the conditioning process.* Champaign, IL: Human Kinetics.

Zatsiorsky, V. M. (1995). *Science and practice of strength training.* Champaign, IL: Human Kinetics.

# ABOUT THE EDITORS

**Dr. Boris Blumenstein** is the Director of the Department of Behavioral Sciences and Methodology at the Ribstein Center for Sport Medicine Sciences and Research, Wingate Institute, Netanya, Israel. He received his Ph.D. in Sport Psychology in 1980 from the All Union Institute for Research in Sport, Department of Sport Psychology, Moscow, Russia (the former USSR). He was a sport psychology consultant and advisor to the Soviet national and Olympic teams, and since 1990 has served as head of the psychological services in the Elite Sports Unit of the Israel Olympic Committee (including the delegations to the Atlanta 1996, Sydney 2000, and Athens 2004 Olympic Games). He is the author of over 90 refereed journal articles and book chapters, and was senior editor of the book *Brain and Body in Sport and Exercise: Biofeedback Applications in Performance Enhancement*, published in 2002 by Wiley. He has also presented more than 50 scientific works at international and national conferences, and has given numerous invited lectures and workshops on sport psychology in the United States, Canada, Germany, Poland, South Korea, and China. In addition, he is Past President of the Israeli Society of Sport Psychology and Sociology.

**Dr. Ronnie Lidor** is an Associate Professor at both the Zinman College of Physical Education and Sport Sciences at the Wingate Institute and the Faculty of Education of the University of Haifa (Israel). His main areas of research are skill acquisition, talent detection, early development in sport, and learning (cognitive) strategies. Dr. Lidor has published over 90 articles, book chapters, and chapters in congress proceedings in both English and Hebrew. His has had papers published in prestigious international journals such as *The Sport Psychologist, Journal of Sports Sciences, Psychology of Sport and Exercise Journal, Physical Education and Sport Pedagogy, International Journal of Sport and Exercise Psychology*, and *Pediatric Exercise Science*. He is the senior editor of the books *Sport Psychology: Linking Theory and Practice* (1999), *The World Sport Psychology SourceBook* (3rd ed., 2001), and *The Psychology of Team Sports* (2003), all published by Fitness Information Technology (USA). He is also one of the editors of the *Handbook of Research in Applied Sport and Exercise Psychology: International Perspectives* (2005), also published by Fitness Information Technology. From 1997 to 2001 Dr. Lidor served as President of the Israeli Society of Sport Psychology and Sociology. Since 1997 he has been a member of the Managing Council of the International Society of Sport Psychology (ISSP). In 2001 he was elected Secretary General of ISSP. He has been the editor of *Movement – Journal of Physical Education and Sport Sciences* (Hebrew) since 1999.

**Dr. Gershon Tenenbaum**, Benjamin S. Bloom Professor of Educational Psychology, a graduate of Tel-Aviv University and the University of Chicago, is a Professor of Sport and Exercise Psychology in the Department of Educational Psychology and Learning Systems at Florida State University, USA. He is a former director of the Ribstein Center for Research and Sport Medicine Sciences at the Wingate Institute in Israel, and was coordinator of the graduate program in sport psychology at the University of Southern Queensland in Australia. From 1997-2001 he was the President of the International Society of Sport Psychology (ISSP), and since 1996 he has been Editor of the *International Journal of Sport and Exercise Psychology*. He has published extensively in psychology and sport psychology in the areas of expertise and decision-making, psychometrics, and coping with physical effort. Prof. Tenenbaum has received several distinguished awards for his academic and scientific achievements, and is a member of several scientific and professional forums and societies.

# ABOUT THE AUTHORS

## Contributing Authors (in alphabetical order)

**Dr. Michael Bar-Eli** is a Professor in the Department of Business Administration, and Nat Holman Chair in Physical Education, at Ben-Gurion University of the Negev, Israel. He studied psychology and sociology at universities in Israel and Germany. Bar-Eli has published over 130 international refereed journal articles and book chapters, as well as numerous publications in Hebrew, and has served as associate- and section-editor of leading sport psychology journals. He held senior psychology positions in the Israel Defense Forces and is psychological consultant to elite athletes and teams in various sports. Prof. Bar-Eli is currently senior vice president of ASPASP (Asian-South Pacific Association of Sport Psychology).

**Sarah Carson** is a doctoral student in the Department of Kinesiology at Michigan State University. While earning her master's degree in exercise and sport science at the University of North Carolina at Greensboro, Sarah worked with youth and collegiate athletes on mental skills training. In addition, she served as a facilitator of team-building sessions for an outdoor challenge program that focused on improving group functioning through experiential activities. While working closely with the Institute for the Study of Youth Sports, Sarah has continued to consult with university and community athletes, and has directed her research efforts toward important youth sport topics such as hazing in high school athletics and coach, athlete, and parent relationships.

**Dr. Daniel Gould** is the Director of the Institute for the Study of Youth Sports and Professor in the Department of Kinesiology at the Michigan State University, where he teaches courses in sport and exercise psychology and is deeply involved in graduate education. Dan has studied the stress-athletic performance relationship, sources of athletic stress, athlete motivation, youth sports issues, and sport psychological skills training use and effectiveness. His recent research focuses on talent development in Olympic athletes, the role of parents in junior tennis success, and how coaches teach life skills to young athletes. Dan has served as a performance enhancement consultant with the U.S.A. Ski Team, NASCAR pit crews and drivers, professional tennis players, and numerous Olympic athletes. He has been heavily involved in coaching education, having made over 600 clinic presentations. Dan has served on the U.S. Olympic coaching development committee for over 10 years, and co-chaired the sport science and technology committee. Currently, he serves as vice chair of the USTA Sport Science and Coaching Committee.

**Dr. Keith Henschen** is a Professor in the Department of Exercise and Sport Sciences at the University of Utah, whose area of expertise is the psychosocial aspects of sports. Dr. Henschen received a P.E.D. degree from Indiana University in 1971, and has been a member of the University of Utah Faculty for the past 32 years. His research interests include: the psychology of performance, use of psychological interventions in sports, and sport psychology for special populations. He has had over 200 articles, 25 chapters of books, and five monographs published, and has co-authored four textbooks. He has directed 40 doctoral dissertations and 20 masters' theses. Dr. Henschen is a frequent research presenter and conference speaker, with over 400 presentations to his credit.

Dr. Henschen has served as President of the American Alliance of Health, Physical Education, Recreation and Dance (AAHPERD) (1997-98) and of the International Society of Sport Psychology (ISSP) (2001-2005). He has consulted with numerous world class, professional, and elite level athletes, as well as five National Governing Boards (NGB's) for the United States Olympic Committee. He has been a sport psychology consultant for the United States Gymnastics Federation (USGF), the United States Biathlon Association (USBA), the United States Association for Track and Field (USATF), the United States Skiing Association (USSA), and the United States Speed Skating Association (USSSA). He has been the sport psychology consultant for the last 15 years for the Utah Jazz of the National Basketball Association (NBA). Dr. Henschen also works with numerous college teams in a variety of sports.

**Dr. Tudor O. Bompa,** Professor Emeritus of York University, Toronto, Ontario, Canada, is regarded worldwide as a leading specialist in the areas of training, coaching, and fitness theory, to which he has contributed several new concepts. Dr. Bompa's theories, especially those of planning-periodization, periodization of strength, power, speed and endurance, periodization of fitness, bodybuilding, psychological periodization, and periodization of nutrition, have revolutionized training in most countries of the world. Dr. Bompa has published 14 books which have been translated into 18 languages. Many of these books have been used as textbooks in universities, coaching institutions, certification programs, and continuing education courses in more than 150 countries. He has also published over one hundred research papers, while at the same time making presentations in over 35 countries on topics such as training theory, planning-periodization, training methods, strength and power training, specifics of training for team sports, and more. Tudor Bompa has also been a very prolific coach. In only eight years of international coaching, his athletes have won 11 medals (four gold) in Olympic Games and World Championships. He has also compiled training programs for professional teams, including the St. Louis Blues NHL Hockey Team and the Argentinian National Soccer Team. He has also guided individual athletes to the highest athletic achievements. In recognition of his contributions to the body of knowledge in training, fitness, and coaches' education, Dr. Bompa has received 21 prestigious honors and awards, 18 of them internationally.

**Michael Carrera** is a sought-after health and lifestyle expert. He has a Master of Science degree in Exercise Science and a Specialized Honors degree in Kinesiology and Health Science. Nationally certified as a Professional Fitness and Lifestyle Consultant (PFLC), he holds a certificate in Fitness Assessment and Exercise Counseling. Throughout his educational training he has administered fitness test protocols and trained elite athletes, including national level swimmers and professional hockey players. He has also created and administered strength test protocols for provincial and national-level athletes, in ice hockey, soccer, figure skating, and swimming. After working for the past 10 years as both a student and colleague of the internationally revered fitness expert Dr. Tudor Bompa, Michael has become a specialist in the field of periodization, a phase-based exercise philosophy. As Director of the *Tudor Bompa Training System*, Michael created international sport and fitness certification and education courses for personal trainers. Michael is also a published author who has contributed articles, chapters, and manuals in the areas of fitness, health, and sports conditioning to numerous scientific journals. He recently coauthored a book entitled *Periodization: Training for Sports* (2nd ed.). In addition to his writing accomplishments, Michael is an international presenter. He has appeared as a health expert on numerous radio and television shows across Canada. As a leading Health Consultant, Michael has created and implemented corporate wellness programs and health management strategies for large North American companies, and was an in-house health expert for a leading Canadian health care corporation before taking on the challenge of creating and implementing one of the world's largest health and fitness websites.

**Dr. Dave Collins** is Professor of Physical Education and Sport Performance at Edinburgh University, Scotland. As an academic he has over 90 peer review publications and 16 books/book chapters published. In applied terms, he is an accredited sport psychologist who has, to date, worked with 28 World or Olympic medalists. His current research interests include Talent Identification and Development (TID), coach development, sport psychophysiology, and the promotion of peak performance across different challenge environments. He has also worked with high-level dancers and musicians in performance enhancement settings, and has coached martial arts and rugby at a national level.

**Dr. Anne-Marie Elbe** is a sport psychology researcher at the University of Potsdam, Germany. She received her Ph.D. from the Free University in Berlin, Germany in 2001. She is currently working on a research project examining the personality and performance development of young elite athletes. Her publications and research interests focus on motivational and self-regulatory aspects of athletic performance, recovery, and cross-cultural comparisons. Anne-Marie is vice-president of the Berliner Sport-Club, vice-chair of the Berlin board for women in sports, and a member of the German Association for Sport Psychology. She is a licensed track and field coach and consulted the German track and field athletes preparing for the Athens Olympics in 2004.

**Dr. Vladimir B. Issurin** serves as a scientific and professional coordinator at the Elite Sport Department of the Israeli Olympic Committee. He completed his undergraduate studies on Sport Sciences and his Ph.D. dissertation on aquatic motor fitness and movement techniques of swimmers at the Leningrad Sport University (1963-1972), and his post-doctoral studies on motor/technical sportsmanship in individual water sports at Moscow Sport University (1988). He served as a scientific adviser and head of a complex scientific group of the USSR Olympic canoe/kayak team during three quadrennial cycles (1978-1991). Since 1991 Prof. Issurin has lived in Israel, and he has worked as a researcher at the Sport Science Department (1991-94), professional consultant and coordinator of Israeli Olympic teams (since 1992), lecturer at the School of Coaches at the Wingate Institute, and promoter of several Ph.D. dissertations. As a member of national Olympic delegations, he has taken part in five Olympic Games – twice as a team leader of Israeli kayak and swimming national teams (2000 and 2004). He has published over 150 scientific articles in national and international journals and edited books, and has made more than 50 international presentations (27 invited). He has authored or coauthored nine books. Dr. Issurin is a member of the International Informatization Academy associated with UNESCO, and a member of the editorial board of two international scientific journals. Currently his research is focused on the methodology of high-performance training, and the further development of original coaching concepts for elite athletes.

**Dr. Michael Kellmann** is an assistant professor of sport psychology in the faculty of sport science at the Ruhr-University of Bochum in Germany. He completed his degree at the University of Potsdam in Germany in January 2002. He is a member of the Association for the Advancement of Applied Sport Psychology and the German Psychological Association. He serves on the executive board of the German Association of Sport Psychology and the editorial board of *The Sport Psychologist*, the *German Journal of Sport Psychology*, and the *German Journal of Sport Medicine*. Michael's research has appeared in more than 50 publications. He is coauthor of *Recovery-Stress Questionnaire for Athletes: User Manual*, and he edited the book *Enhancing Recovery: Preventing Underperformance in Athletes*, both published by Human Kinetics (USA). He has consulted with and conducted research for the National Sport Centre Calgary in Canada, the Canadian national speed skating team, and the German national rowing team.

**Dr. David Pargman** is Professor in the Department of Educational Research, Florida State University, Tallahassee, Florida, where he is completing his 31st year of service. He is Program Coordinator for Educational Psychology and Coordinator of Sport Psychology. He is also an Adjunct Professor in Florida State University's School of Music. He did his undergraduate work at the City College of New York, his Masters degree at Teachers College, Columbia University, and Ph.D. at New York University. Prior to coming to Florida State University he taught at Boston University and the City College of New York. He has served as major professor to more than 40 doctoral students. Dr. Pargman has authored or co-authored more than 70 articles, book chapters, and refereed abstracts, and has delivered approximately 200 regional, national and international lectures at various professional forums. For nine years he provided a weekly commentary about various issues related to sport and exercise psychology on a local affiliate of National Public Radio. Dr. Pargman has served on the Executive Board of the Association for the Advancement of Applied Sport Psychology, was Chairman of its Health Psychology Section, and is a past Chairman of the Sport Psychology Academy of the American Alliance for Health, Physical Education, Recreation and Dance. He is a Fellow of the Association for the Advancement of Applied Sport Psychology, the Research Consortium of the American Alliance for Health, Physical Education, Recreation and Dance, and the American College of Sports Medicine. He is a member of the United States Olympic Committee Sport Psychology Registry and a Certified Consultant of the Association for the Advancement of Applied Sport Psychology. David is also a member of the International Association of Applied Psychology, the International Association of Sport Psychology, the North American Association for Sport Psychology and Physical Activity, and the North American Association for Sport Sociology.

**Alan MacPherson** is currently a postgraduate research scholar at the Moray House Institute of Education of the University of Edinburgh, Scotland. A proud Scot and frequent kilt wearer, he has completed all of his academic training "north of the border," resulting in multiple postgraduate qualifications in research design and performance psychology. His current research interests encompass social psychology, using a dynamical systems approach to enhance the dynamics of high performance teams. Alan's doctoral research focuses on the role of rhythmicity in elite performance, and involves applied work in a variety of sports with high level athletes, including a current World champion.

**Dr. Traci Ann Statler** is an assistant professor in the Department of Kinesiology at California State University - San Bernardino, with expertise in the area of applied sport and performance psychology. She received a Ph.D. in Exercise and Sport Science from the University of Utah in 2001, with an emphasis in applied sport psychology. Dr. Statler's research interests include the "art" of applied sport psychology consulting, the psychology of human performance, and the psychology of injury and rehabilitation, with numerous professional presentations in these areas. She currently serves as a performance psychology consultant to the United States Association for Track and Field (USATF), and to a variety of collegiate athletic programs, as well as conducting individual performance enhancement sessions with professional athletes, police officers, and fire fighters in southern California. Dr. Statler was elected in 2001 to the Managing Council of the International Society of Sport Psychology (ISSP).

**Dr. Thomas Schack,** received his Ph.D. in 1996 for his research on mental training. He earned his M.A. in Sport Sciences and Social Science at the University in Zwickau in 1990 and finished a second Master's degree in Psychology at the University of Leipzig in 1999. Dr. Schack was formerly a researcher and lecturer at the Technical University in Chemnitz, and has been working at the Sport University in Köln since 1996. His main research interest concerns the cognitive architecture of movement, mental movement representation, mental training, and the neurophysiological basis of complex movement. Additionally, he is interested in research topics such as mental control, anxiety, and cognitive robotics. He has published more than 190 works and presented his research at various conferences in Asia, America, and Europe. Dr. Schack was successful as an athlete in motor cross sport, biathlon, and long distance running (and ran the ultra-marathon 15 times). In addition, he is certified as a coach. As a consultant he works with the German Women's Volleyball National Team and with the Men's Volleyball Paralympic Team, winner of the gold medal in Sydney 2000. Since 2002 he has been an Assistant Professor in the field of psychology and motor control at the Sport University Cologne. Since 2004 he has been an Assistant Professor in motor control and biomechanics at the Martin-Luther-University in Halle, and since 2005 at the Friedrich-Schiller-University in Jena.